Desk Pilot

By

Harry Ernest Fitch

Table of Contents

Dedication

To Tom Dellafiora and all my cohorts at "Carefree Air Force Base" 1968-1972.

Acknowledgement

From an early age, I have loved the written word and what it creates. Over the years I came to appreciate many authors. Perhaps those who have influenced me most were: Mark Twain, Joseph Heller, Kurt Vonnegut, Sherman Alexie W. P. Kinsella, Walter M. Miller, and E.B. White.

Certainly, my journalism professors and some English instructors instilled the need to research and be accurate, even in fiction.

But most importantly, when it comes to Desk Pilot, there is the woman I met one Fall evening in 1965. We have had a loving marriage since late 1969. When I approached her with the crucial step we would need to take for this novel, she replied, "Go for it. It's your dream."

You're never too old to dream.

About the Author

A native of Newark, Ohio and graduate of Kent State University, Fitch is a retired high school English teacher living in the Atlanta suburbs with his wife and their Sheltie. He has published two novels previously: *Common Ground*, a tale of neighborhood covenants and toxic waste, and; *The Number Two Pencil Solution*, a teacher's battle against forces bent on destroying public education.

Chapter 1

I flew a desk in the Air Force during Vietnam. Stateside.

I did not have napalm, five-hundred-pound bombs, twenty-millimeter guns, or destructive weaponry of that ilk. My non-lethal armaments were a dial phone with four push-button extensions, a Remington manual typewriter, a wooden twelve-inch ruler, other typical office supplies, and the only government-issue equipment that never broke down. For whatever reason, my black ballpoint pen did not run out of ink. I used the same one for the nearly twenty months I spent piloting that work station in the public information office of Carefree Air Force Base in Arizona. And then there were the two weapons that kept me sane for most of my tour.

My cynicism and sarcasm.

Those two sustained me in acting off base while I supposedly served my country on base. They matured as I journeyed from the sidelines of student protest to the forefront of anti-war dissent, such as it was while flying my desk. I even would take pride in being more off base off the base. But I'm getting ahead of myself. So let me go back a few years to the beginning of my radicalization. I can trace it to those malignant beings who inhabit every person's childhood. The school martinets and the bullies.

I was a perfect little cherub until junior high school. But when the administration disciplined me for cheating, along with Richie Hummel, I changed my attitude toward authority. Somewhat bigger than I, Richie threatened to break every bone in my body if I didn't do his math homework. So naturally, in the interest of self-

1

preservation, I complied. I had had a bigger kid sit on me unnoticed one recess in third grade, and a fellow fourth grader scratched me when he became an overaggressive tiger in another recess. But no authorities found out, and I, being somewhat of a wimp, never complained to my teachers or the principal. But when it came to long division in our math class, and Mr. Warner put two and two together to realize that Richie and I had the same wrong answers on our homework, he referred us to the principal. He never bothered to take into account my standing as an outstanding pupil and Hummel's status as a bully. So we were paddled. And when I saw that our discipline differed from that for what I considered a more egregious offense, I stopped believing in the wisdom of authority figures and became one meekly rebellious soul. Certainly, if cheating on homework warranted paddling, then so did fighting in gym class, right? Wrong.

I wasn't the one who did the actual fighting, but my encounter with one of the combatants started my decline into cynicism. That pugilistic punk was Joey Messina. Three years old than I, Joey should have been in high school, but his piss poor attitude helped him manage to flunk school three separate times and be left with little twerps like me as classmates.

Actually, Joey was a little twerp himself. Despite our age difference, he stood no taller than my shoulders. And he had other disadvantages, most notably his freckles. They didn't have a somewhat loose pattern like most kids. His mostly came together in ugly clusters, the biggest on his right cheek, looking almost like a major attack of mosquitoes had left a permanent scar of gigantic proportions. He had other smaller clusters and then the random freckle here and there that made most of us turn away in disgust whenever we saw his face. And Joey's hair, slicked with enough grease for any semi truck that slogged through town on Route 16, made the sight of him even worse. Then there was his body odor. Apparently, baths and showers were anathemas in his household. Capping it off was his aforementioned attitude.

My first and only close encounter at school with Joey Messina came at the end of a routine day in gym class. We all, except for Joey, had taken our obligatory showers so that we would not offend the noses of the girls in our remaining classes. Guys, too, but we had started realizing that girls were not the evil creatures we boys had classified them as in our elementary grades.

I had finished dressing and strode to the lone, scratched mirror in our dressing room, fully prepared to comb my hair. I had just run the comb once through my mane when Joey rudely pushed me aside with a snarling, "I'm combing my hair now."

I stood my ground. The unwritten laws of a boys' junior high gym class dressing room were that you had to defend yourself against anyone and everyone. You could not expect any classmates to come to your aid. And none did, even though I was certain that I had several friends I could count on if necessary, whereas Joey had none. I pushed back, my two arms shoving his left arm. "You can have it when I'm done," I told him, surprising resolve in my voice. This was, after all, a more serious threat to my well-being than those made by Richie Hummel. We had actually made forcible physical contact here.

Joey clenched his fists and his teeth but decided to use neither except to snarl at me. The brown glop that encircled most of his teeth suggested that like bathing, toothbrushes, and toothpaste were alien to Joey. "I said I'm combing my hair now," he repeated, pushing at me with open palms. The episode might have escalated, except just then, we could hear our PE teacher, Mr. Abbott, coming down the stairs. Joey moved away.

"Bell's about to ring, boys," Mr. Abbott announced, peeking his head inside the doorway. "Gather up your gear." Not knowing what had just transpired and believing that we boys would dutifully heed his instructions, he turned and left.

As I finished putting my gym clothes inside my gym bag, Joey sidled up to me and scowled in a low voice. "You wanna go outside about it tonight, eh? Wanna go outside about it?" His threats always included at least one *eh*. But he did not pronounce it like a long *a* as Canadians do. His was more like a short *e*, like in the word *dead* but without the *d*'s as bookends. *Eh* was distinctively nasal and in your face. If you were short enough. That meant that most of the time, Joey's snarl was at chest or shoulder level, like when he challenged me. The little runt.

I said nothing and walked away, ready to head to my next class, music with the petite Miss Mueller. Unfortunately, Joey Messina was in that class as well, even though he couldn't sing worth shit. Such was the case in junior high class scheduling. So he decided he would take the chair right next to mine. To keep our skirmish alive.

Even though Joey parked himself beside me, intent on continuing his bullying, I figured I was safe with Miss Mueller to back me up. After all, I was a good student with a fine voice that contributed mightily to our chorus. And she was young, no more than a couple of years out of college, so I figured she understood the teenage battles between good and evil, the model citizens like me, Taylor Forsberg, and the scummy, hoody future gangsters like Joey Messina.

4

I was wrong.

Class had barely begun when Joey, noticing that Miss Mueller was elsewhere in the room, poked his left elbow into my right ribcage. "Wanna go outside about it tonight, eh, eh? Wanna go outside about it?" he challenged. I ignored the thrust. Of course, that did not stop him. Again, he attacked my rib cage, this time a little harder. As he challenged once again with his ever-consistent "Wanna go outside about it tonight, eh, eh?" I pushed back. Miss Mueller noticed the altercation this time. I believed my salvation would come immediately. But I should have known that the consistency of punishment in a school environment would remain. No right or wrong existed in teen disputes in schools. All involved parties would receive equal discipline.

"That's it, you two!" she ordered with as much authority as her gentle voice could muster. Fortunately for her, her position as a teacher proved enough to stop Joey Messina. "You!" she ordered, pointing to Joey. "Follow me." Sullenly but obediently, he did, to a chair at the end of the back row, next to a girl who hoped he would not bother her. But she still would have to contend with his body odor. Miss Mueller then went to her desk and took out two slips of paper. Detention slips. She filled them out, took one to Joey, then came and stood before me, handing me mine. "Both of you will serve this after school tonight."

So much for good versus evil.

As we left music for our next class, I felt relieved that Joey Messina would not bother me anymore that day. At least not until after detention. But he was not yet done for the moment. A sharper jab to the ribs, accompanied by "I'll see you outside about it tonight,

5

eh, eh?" reminded me that Joey planned to extract revenge once the school day and our mutual imprisonment in detention ended.

Once again, I was wrong.

Not wishing for any more trouble with school authorities, I dutifully reported to detention in the school library at the end of classes. I took my seat along with several other of the day's miscreants save one. Joey Messina had not bothered to come to serve detention. This did not relieve my anxiety about a showdown with Joey one bit. I figured his way of thinking was more like, "What the hell? I'll get in trouble some more when I punch the living shit out of Forsberg. So I'll just wait outside for him." So I sweated the half hour of detention, wondering when and where Joey would accost me. Would it be right outside the door as I left? Would he be that bold? I decided to steer clear of some of the alley shortcuts I often took home and stay on the streets. Maybe walking somewhere where the assault stood a better chance of being seen by some adult sitting on a porch would save me. But I doubted that. Joey Messina wouldn't care if any grownups saw his attack, just so long as he inflicted injury on me.

I decided to leave the school through the main front doors by the office instead of the east exit like I normally did. Joey was not that smart, but I figured even he would think I would depart through the same door we students always did. At least going out the front increased the chances that maybe our principal or some teacher would be leaving at the same time and would provide some short-term protection. True, I took the risk that the lone faculty member who would see us would be the authoritarian Mr. Evers. That vice principal would find a convenient principle to haul us both in for punishment.

But as I came to the front, no faculty member was in sight. Furtively, I gingerly crept out the door, then slowly scanned from side to side, looking for where my expected assailant lay in wait. No sign of Joey. That only increased my fears. Even though I knew that he did not know where I lived, I envisioned him stooped behind some bushes or on a nearby vacant porch watching so that he could follow me until he could pounce on me from behind. I decided to try not to look scared and just walk at a normal pace to my home.

So I crossed Main at the traffic light, then took the safe route home up Oakwood, turning down Tuscarawas to Dewey and hanging a right to my house. Only when I turned to our porch did I look around to see if Joey had followed me. I did not see him, exhaled for the first relaxed breath of my walk home, and went inside.

Joey Messina would not meet me outside any night, would not bother me again in school. But he had not finished as a troublemaker before finally being expelled. It happened a couple of weeks after he had threatened my life and limb. And again, it occurred in gym class. Apparently, Joey believed that gym class was the best place to be a prick.

"Hey, look!" someone shouted, and all eyes in the gymnasium save for four turned toward where that someone pointed. There, hopping across the gym floor, was Jim Callaway with Joey Messina in a headlock and Joey twisting his best to break free. But Jim, Joey's height but more slightly built, had a firm grasp and would not let go. We watched this struggle for what seemed like minutes until we heard Coach Abbott, who had left the gym for some reason, shout, "What's going on here?" as he stomped toward the two combatants. Reaching in like a linesman at a hockey scuffle, he finally broke the two boys apart, although Joey tried to get in a couple of swings at Callaway.

But the coach's quick moves thwarted that effort. With each hand firmly gripped on Joey's and Jim's arms, he pulled them out of the gymnasium into the office, handing them over to the principal.

Fighting in school. I felt elated that Joey Messina would get just rewards for his actions. I also knew that Jim would get the same, and I felt sorry for him. I was wrong.

"Nope," a relieved Jim Callaway, smiling in both relief and triumph, told me and others outside the next morning as we waited to be allowed into the building. We always had to stay outside for the entry bell unless inclement weather intervened on our behalf. "Mr. Sterling took me alone into his office and asked me what had happened. So I told him. Thought for sure I'd get paddled. But all he did was give me three detentions."

Three detentions? That was it? I felt betrayed. Sure, I was glad for Jim and told him so. But I told myself that something was not right. How could he fight in the school and not receive a paddling? How could I cheat on homework under threat of life and limb and get my butt walloped? How could Miss Mueller send both to detention when she knew full well what a scumbag he was and what an overall good student and citizen I was? Authority had not dispensed justice fairly, and I resented it. At that point, I decided I would not bend over backward to always toe the line. I resolved not to become a Joey Messina, but I would find my own ways to rebel in my own time.

For his latest episode, the school expelled Joey Messina. Justice had been served somewhat, in my mind, but still . . .

"Yep!" Callaway beamed. "They kicked his butt out of school." He said *butt* rather than *ass* because we all knew wrath would descend upon any curser heard by the powers on school grounds. One couldn't take chances.

Jim continued to tell us more about the scuffle, what the principal had said to him, and other aspects of his bout with Joey Messina. But we had trouble following the account because several of the school's hoods, the duck-assed, badass leather-jacketed Elvis wannabes, kept interrupting. The ones without the sappy Love Me Tender shit. They would approach our group, pat Callaway on the back, grab his shoulders affectionately, and congratulate him.

"Way to go, Jimbo!"

"Jim-mee! You sure took care of Messina!"

"Cal-la-waaay! You sure showed that asshole." Such fellows did not care if foul language added to their occasional troubles at school.

And other accolades came Jim's way. Apparently, Joey was not exactly a pal of the others of a similar ilk here.

Nonetheless, despite my joy for Jim, I remained determined to no longer be a model of decorum and acquiescence. I would not join the greased hair crowd. I doubted that they would accept me anyway. A few shoves were not as awe-inspiring as a hopping headlock, even though Jim never thought of joining the rebellious group either. But I would observe, calculate, and act as I saw accordingly when I felt someone in power had wronged me.

So far as I know, Joey never returned to continue his education, such as it would have been in any of the city schools. I never again encountered him on the east side or downtown or anywhere else in my remaining years in Newark. I figured he was an annoyance that would screw up my life only briefly and that that time had come and gone. Good riddance.

I was wrong.

Chapter 2

Granted, being somewhat of a pseudo-rebel rather than full-blown teenaged insurgent limited how, where, and when, if ever, I would overtly show my disdain for the authority figures in my life. Those people did not include my parents. Until later, when my father somehow forgot about the old cliché of love being blind.

Part of my growth into recalcitrance came from natural teenage restlessness, true, but I also became more aware of the inequities within society. Especially with many in my age group becoming whipping boys for many adults. It would develop the seeds for what, within a decade, would be called the generation gap. I would develop into a willing participant, even though the gap would exist mostly between me and another member of my age group. After all, the divide really existed between attitudes, not ages.

So at East Junior High, the actions and attitudes of the administration and some faculty, most notably Mr. Evers, the assistant principal who had wielded the paddle in that most unfortunate of disciplines, would irk me from time to time. In a couple of instances, I felt certain that Evers had it in for me, even though, in the first one, he tried to disguise his disdain by including all members of my age group. Of course, he was no different than so many adults seemed at the time. Had he been a woman, he no doubt would have flunked out of charm school. The second occasion was more covert. But I knew. And I know that he knew that I knew.

Because I continued as an overt symbol of compliance despite my newfound, though mostly latent, rebellion, I remained active in a few extracurricular activities. My next encounter with Evers came during a dance sponsored by one of the clubs of which I was a member.

Several of the club's members, including myself, had brought some of our own 45 rpm records to play at the dance. Shortly into the affair, I trudged upstairs through the balcony from the gym to the control room to see about loading one of my platters onto the turntable. In charge of the record player, Mr. Evers sat nonchalantly next to it while leafing through the local newspaper. His puffy jowls reminded me of Vice President Nixon.

"Hi, Mr. Evers," I greeted him, trying to sound polite and deferential.

His eyes glanced up, barely noticing me. "Why are you here?" he asked, returning his indifferent gaze to an article on an inside page. He continued to puff on his pipe, the sweet scent of Cherry Blend permeating the small room.

"Just want to play one of the records I brought," I somewhat meekly stated.

Without looking up, he pointed a finger toward a stack of 45s next to the turntable. Both sat on a table under the paneless window used for the movie projector at such assemblies as required it. "It's undoubtedly there," he mumbled.

I stepped over and began leafing through the mass of records. My clubmates and I had brought quite a number for the students to enjoy. After sifting through a couple of dozen, I found my record and handed it to Mr. Evers. None of us would dare to work the turntable ourselves.

"Witch Doctor," he noted, scorn coming from his mouth as he read the label, his teeth clacking on the pipe stem. "That's the song with the ting tang walla walla bing bang for, and I say the word loosely, lyrics, isn't it?" He did not wait for my reply nor look up from the label for my nod. "No wonder kids like you end up in trouble, like cheating on homework, when all you can find for enjoyment are songs like this garbage. What nonsense." He set the record down next to the turntable.

A song that my parents sang to me when I was younger came to mind, although I had told them four years ago that I had outgrown it. Certain that it had been popular with Evers at some time in his life, I wanted to argue, "I suppose mairzy doats and dozey doats and liddle lamzy divey created model citizens in your day." But I still had not gained the courage to get into war games with someone in authority. Part of being a teenager who did not slick his hair with axle grease and wear his collar up, I suppose. So I merely shrugged my shoulders, turned, and left the control room. Neither of us said a word as I left.

Evers had not finished with me yet. Late in the eighth-grade year, the administration consulted with some of our teachers to determine what students were to run for what offices in ninth grade, the big man on campus year of junior high. I still had enough of a solid reputation away from Mr. Evers that I became one of the nominees for class president. Trouble was, I would run against Clark Dennis, by a wide margin the most likable person in our class. He was affable (I wasn't). He had a spotless disciplinary record (I didn't, although that probably would not have mattered to our classmates). There also was a girl nominated as well. I don't remember who. Pretty bold, but in the late 1950s, a girl running for class president seemed no more than a token. Girls were more likely to get elected as secretary or treasurer, the offices that actually required work. So I did not mind running against

Clark. Nor did losing to him a certainty. But the pre-election assembly orchestrated by Mr. Evers did raise my anger.

With us rising ninth graders in attendance at the gym, Mr. Evers strode stiffly, almost like a general, out from the hall entrance to the microphone stand positioned in the middle of the basketball jump circle. He stood behind the mic, eyes focused on the papers before him, seemingly waiting for the already silent students to quiet down.

Finally, he did the requisite tapping of the mic to make certain it was on, cleared his throat too close to it, and immediately caused ear-piercing feedback. He stepped back, but true to form, he offered no apology for the assault on our hearing.

"Students," he boomed, with a pomposity that might herald the Second Coming. "We're here for you to meet the candidates for office for next year, the top class of East Junior High. You will also be allowed to show your support for the candidates of your choice for each of the four offices by coming and standing behind them when I read their names."

My heart sank. I muttered a cynical "thanks a lot, Evers" under my breath. I knew full well that almost all the boys and at least half the girls would swarm down upon the gym floor when he summoned Clark Dennis' supporters. I knew that Evers the martinet was doing this just to remind me that I, a documented cheater at math and fan of "ting tang walla walla bing bang," did not deserve to hold office. My worst fears and worse came when he called for Clark's backers. Even my close friends, who I thought would stand by me, joined the mob. When Evers called out the girl candidate's name, the last eight girls left seated in the balcony went down to the floor. Then Evers read my name.

I walked down alone. And stood alone briefly. Then, I became aware of someone behind me. I turned to see two of the Elvis wannabes behind me, their shirt-collars up in the rebellious style of the day.

I recognized them as being from the Joey Messina congratulatory aftermath for Jim Callaway. One had spent time at reform school in Lancaster after police caught him with Pall Malls and Boston cream pies he had pilfered from a grocery store. The other earned his reputation by beating up smaller kids around the east side, but not on school property. I did not shake hands with them, but I nodded thanks in return. They each responded with a thumbs up. Maybe word of my shoving incident with Messina had reached them after all. Evers gave a disapproving look to the three of us but nothing more.

Two days later, after the votes were counted, certified, and secured in the principal's office, Evers posted the totals on the school bulletin board. I had a pretty good idea where my two other votes, besides my own, came from. At least I probably had more than spur-of-the-moment support from the two hoods. Still, I did not seek them out to thank them.

As for Evers, it was the first time I ever called someone a motherfucker. But I did it only in my head. I did not want to take any open chance with his authority.

For whatever reason, I went through ninth grade unscathed by the animosity of Mr. Evers. No incidents occurred to put us at odds, at least in my mind. If he had any thoughts of his own as to my worthlessness, they never became overt. I'm certain that when I was named valedictorian of the class, he disapproved. But he was only an assistant principal. His advice could be ignored in such a case.

But the seeds of my disdain for the abuses of authority had begun to mature. Thanks to the real and imagined consequences of my encounters with Richie Hummel, Joey Messina, and Mr. Evers, I had determined that the world could sometimes be unjust and that such injustice could affect me negatively as well as it could the next guy. But almost all my reactions came against those that affected me personally. Living in a small city with its own newspaper and three television stations from Columbus limited my exposure to authorities, making life hell for other people elsewhere. Any notices at all were small blurbs on inside pages of the daily newspaper or brief mentions, without film, on the TV news. More in-depth and consistent coverage came in the voluminous Sunday newspaper out of Columbus. That exposure directed me to consider a career in journalism where I could explore and expose misuses of power.

Little did I know in those last years of my youth that a place called Vietnam and a thing called the Air Force would alter and yet enhance my approach. It became more personal once Uncle Sam called me to what many considered my patriotic duty. I would judge it and those in command as an annoyance. One anointed leader would become the focus of my battle. And, in a rare twist of fate, my fight would come full circle.

My three years of high school would pass rather calmly, mostly because no Mr. Evers surrogate or clone existed there to pose a daily threat to my well-being. Even though high school had more administrators, it also had more students, and those in charge seemed more occupied with the serious malcontents, the ones who posed real threats to life and limb. The Joey Messinas who had not yet dropped out or been expelled.

But there were still teachers who enjoyed wielding power, even if one so-called transgression was done in an act for the common good. Such was the one case in my three high school years that mirrored life with Mr. Evers.

Our gym teacher and coach from East Junior High had moved up to the high school the same year that I and Clark Dennis and others did. And one day in our junior year, Clark and I were among a handful of known good citizens (at least to Mr. Abbott) that he called into his office after we sweated through games of dodge ball on the gym floor.

"Someone in class is stealing wallets while you guys are trying to knock the crap out of each other with dodge ball," Mr. Abbott announced, a slight grin on his face. He always had a way of injecting sly humor into most things he said. "I haven't been able to find out who. But I know I can trust you young men to help catch the culprit."

One of the reasons I respected him was that he had a decent vocabulary to go along with his warm personality. Other coaches had our respect, but they also looked and acted like the stereotypical jocks they probably had been before they ate their stomachs over their belts.

Mr. Abbott decided that he would give each of us five one-dollar bills (a good sum of money then) to place in our wallets. However, those dollars would have ditto machine ink plastered on them so that anyone touching the money would have incriminating evidence all over his hands. The culprit would then be easy to spot, purple ink and all. Incontrovertible evidence.

"Make certain that your wallets are in plain sight in your baskets next gym class after I give you the bills," he instructed us. "They will be too tempting. He should bite at such easy pickings from at least one of you. So when you come for your next class, stop by my office first, and I'll give you the money."

Next gym class, we did as Mr. Abbott required. And it worked. The fellow was nabbed, his hands heavily stained with the unmistakable ditto ink. Even though he confessed, caught purple-handed, he refused to say where he had discarded Clark's wallet.

Because it was Clark's, he became the envy of the rest of us. Even though he was out of money, including the incriminating dollar. The compatriots that we were, fighting for justice, we all vowed we would find his wallet for him.

I did. But in doing so, I ran into the blind side of enforcing the rules, punished for committing one of the deadly sins of high school studenthood while practicing good citizenship.

I committed the heinous crime of stepping on part of the campus lawn, most certainly stomping the luscious green grass beyond recovery.

Ever vigilant, I spied a wallet lying against the wall of one of the school buildings while changing classes at our campus-style school. Certain that it belonged to Clark, I went to retrieve it. Unfortunately, I was performing a punishable offense if caught.

Unfortunately, one of the school's drill sergeant types spied me.

"What are you doing, young man?" the voice came from the walkway behind me. Because of the off-key tones, I knew immediately that my antagonist was Hugh Brophy, assistant band director.

17

Brophy may or may not have had the ability to lead marching band musicians, but his voice always sounded like he had not yet finished puberty, what with all the times it cracked. Yet, as best I could judge, he had more than forty birthdays behind him. I turned to see him standing there, dressed in his marching band uniform as he was most school days. Many of us non-hornblowers surmised that he had more than one such outfit. Either that or his wife spent many an evening washing and ironing his marching regalia. Although none of us who snickered at him knew whether or not he had a wife, we hoped for her sake that they owned an automatic washer.

We also guessed that if he did have a wife, he insisted on her being on top whenever they had sex. Our demented adolescent minds surmised that that way, he could direct her up and down rhythm with his spindly little baton. We also shared the belief that the wand replicated his cock. No doubt the couple owned a plethora of Sousa records to fuck to. I hoped they were albums. Otherwise, if the records were 45s or 78s, they would have too many pauses in their mutual pleasure. And I wouldn't wish that on anybody. Not even Brophy.

"I'm just retrieving this wallet of my friend's," I said over my shoulder as I turned back to pick up the stolen item. "I'm sure you heard about the thief in our gym class," I continued, although one never knew if Brophy possessed an awareness of anything beyond marching cadences.

"I have," he replied. His voice remained stern. "You are, however, breaking school rules by walking on the grass. Leave the wallet there and come here."

It probably did not help that I shrugged my shoulders in an exasperated, slightly petulant way. But by the time I strode the twenty or so feet to the uniform-bedecked disciplinarian, Brophy had pen and detention slip pad out, scribbling away, noting my nefarious infraction.

"Your name?" he demanded in a crisp cadence, rather than asking.

"Taylor Forsberg," I sighed.

"Be careful of your tone, young man," Brophy warned. "I can mete out more punishment here."

"I'm sure you can, pineapple head," I said inside my mind. Brophy's head was somewhat of an exaggerated oval, like a cartoonist's rendition of that fruit. Years later, I would think that he had served as the model for Bert on Sesame Street, head-wise anyway.

Done with his paperwork, Brophy handed the detention slip to me. I took it and noted that I would be serving it the next afternoon with Coach Abbott in charge. I also saw that Brophy had misspelled my name as Tyler Fortburgh. I thought about skipping detention with the pretense that I was not the student identified on the paper, but I decided to show up. Why press my luck.

"Go on your way to class now," Brophy ordered. "I'll get the wallet and turn it in."

He about-faced from me and marched over to the wallet. In my mind, I could hear the drums beating time for him. He was that precise.

I heard later that day from a band student that Brophy had had a terrible time trying to wash away the ditto ink that covered his hands from when he fetched the wallet. And next afternoon, when I told

Coach Abbott the whole story of why I had received detention, he smiled and suggested, "Go ahead and get out of here. But steer clear of the band room. Tyler Fortburgh or whoever you are."

I took his advice.

I endured, such as it was, only one more incident during high school, which added more cement to my hardening cynicism. Well, technically, I had finished high school. It happened at our football field right after graduation. Of course, it involved dear Hugh Brophy.

Clark Dennis, Jim Callaway, and I had joined one another after the ceremonies had concluded. Because we belonged to National Honor Society, we wore gold cords around our necks, complementing our crimson robes and mortarboards. As we lingered after the ceremony, Callaway suggested that we tie the cords around our waists to look like pious monks. Most people would find such a stunt after graduation humorous or clever. Hugh Brophy, true to form, would not.

Because he conducted the band in playing the obligatory ceremonial music at graduation, Brophy wore his uniform. So, having spotted us committing such sacrilege at such a solemn occasion, he marched over to us. As I saw him striding in perfect cadence, I could not help but wonder if he had made love to his wife to get in the mood for graduation. I also pondered why that thought had not occurred to me before.

Frowning with the best scowl he could muster, he sneered at us, "I suppose you fellows think it's funny to make fun of such a dignified ceremony as this. I should take you by those gold ropes of yours and string you up from the gym rafters."

20

Clark, who had been class vice president and always displayed the decorum to go with that lofty position, laughed. "Well, Hughie," he replied, a broad grin crossing his face. "You can't. Because we're graduates now! You can't play prison guard to us anymore. So why don't you go blow off steam by marching around the track a few laps."

Speechless, Brophy stormed away, "hut, two, three, four," echoing in my mind as he did.

Speechless, Jim Callaway and I stared in wonderment at Clark. Did we know this guy?

As we laughed, Mr. Abbott approached, a wry grin on his face. "So you three have decided to take vows of silence and poverty, have you?" He chuckled. "Perhaps you should have already started so that . . ."

I interrupted him. "Mr. Abbott, with all due respect . . ."

It was his turn to cut in. "Relax, boys. I wouldn't chastise you. Besides, had Mr. Brophy hanged you from my rafters, I would have cut you all down. I would have saved your lives."

"Time would have been of the essence," Clark rejoined. "You might not have been quick enough to save all of us." He paused, then asked the coach, "Who would you have cut down first?"

Mr. Abbott did not hesitate. "Why Callaway, of course," he chuckled. "After all, he helped get Joey Messina expelled at East with his bouncing headlock in my gym." We laughed together at that response. Then he shook each of our hands and patted each on the shoulder. "Good luck, boys. I've enjoyed having you as students." Then he walked away.

"Hughie?" Jim turned to Clark.

"Brophy earned it. I always felt he thought he deserved blind respect. But he is a prick."

It was our last laugh together.

Less than seven years later, on January 1, 1970, First Lieutenant Clark Dennis took a Viet Cong bullet in a firefight in Kon Tum Province and died. Thus began what would become a climactic year in my cynicism. And a nemesis from my youth would play a key role.

Chapter 3

My college years did little to enhance my cynicism and sarcasm, at least insofar as my formal education was concerned. However, they did grow because of my relationship with my parents, particularly my father. Not that unusual, considering our ages, and at a time of the burgeoning generation gap.

At least my father had wisely waited for my finishing high school before finding new employment that he believed was more challenging and more rewarding financially. So that summer, we moved to Canton, where he began working in the offices of the main Republic Steel plant there. Erik Forsberg, of Swedish Lutheran descent, believed in working hard in order to provide his sons with a college education. My older brother, Erik Jr., had disappointed him by marrying his high school sweetheart two weeks after she had graduated high school. I was Dad's last hope. So, too, for my mother, Jessica Taylor Forsberg, her surname becoming my given name. Dad left it to Mom and her Scottish Presbyterian background to see to it that my brother and I received a solid religious education. He would obligingly go with us to church but usually fell asleep within fifteen minutes into the service. At least he never snored. Perhaps because Mom would elbow him whenever she thought he would begin.

Mom's Presbyterian faith did not work with my brother, who would become a father six months after his marriage. Nor did it work with me. The belief in predestination helped me to start considering rebellion, reasoning that if an afterlife of fortune or doom was in my eternity, what did it matter what I did while I lived. I had no intention of becoming a Richard Speck or Clyde Barrow, but the mathematics-induced paddling in junior high began my life of cynicism and unholiness. Add the hypocrisies and prejudices I noticed more and more within religion throughout my high school years. I primed more each day to become the Taylor Forsberg I would become by 1968 and now am.

The main catalyst within the family came with the 1960 Presidential elections. Dad had voted Democratic for as long as I could remember, even going against the Eisenhower tides of 1952 and 1956. Which was as long as I could remember and 1952 only vaguely. But he was also fervently anti-Catholic. After all, as he often reminded us whenever he found it convenient, "Luther started standing up to the Pope. It's my obligation to continue." He bragged this, even though he had not set foot in a Lutheran church in years, and Luther had no Swedish blood so far as anyone knew. So once John Kennedy became the Democratic nominee for 1960, Dad announced he would be voting for Richard Nixon.

"Why?" I asked him one night at dinner when the election came up in conversation.

"I think Nixon has more experience," he replied. He may have been right, technically speaking, but I knew his reason was he did not want a Catholic in the White House. He believed that if Kennedy became President, then we all would be eating fish on Fridays and speaking Latin whenever we had occasion to act holy.

His intolerance showed itself again shortly after our move to Canton. Suggesting that I commute to one of the local colleges to help the family with expenses, he instructed me not to visit the one affiliated with the Catholic church. "I'm not going to have my son receive a mackerel snapper education. If you can call what they teach education, which is nothing more than fealty to the Pope."

Reluctantly, I said I would check out the Quaker school. All I knew about Quakers was that they once wore odd clothing and made oat cereal. Gabby Hayes had informed me on television years ago that they shot it from guns. And I knew they had something to do with the founding of Pennsylvania. And, oh yeah, Nixon was a Quaker. So as I drove to their campus, I had no desire for any religious indoctrination, no matter how overt or subtle. I had become too worldly and had every intention of staying that way... As far as I was concerned, I could see life clearly, contrary to those suffering from blind religious beliefs. Or prejudice, like my father's.

So as I drove my 54 Dodge into the main parking lot of the Quaker institution, I already was conniving to reject attending that institution. The first sight helped convince me.

At the far end, on a slight rise, stood the college chapel, looming like a menacing carnivorous beast from the Old Testament. Its double doors stood wide open, waiting to swallow me whole into its dark, gorging interior of certain hellfire and damnation. I had fallen so far from religion that I feared that Monstro lurked for me, Gipetto, rather than the whale waiting to devour Jonah. I turned the car around and did not look back as I pulled away from the evil beast. I drove a few blocks until I spied a McDonald's beckoning me for a cheap burger and Coke. I pulled in, went to the window for my order, then returned to the Dodge to conceive my plan as I munched my inexpensive snack, one more of over one million served. Or so said the golden arch sign at the burger joint's entrance.

I presented my scheme to my father that evening after dinner and shortly before The Red Skelton Show was about to air. I figured he would battle my decision, if he fought it at all, quite briefly rather than miss one of his favorite programs.

"What do you mean you can't go there?" Dad asked, somewhat confused, when I told him the Quaker college had no appeal for me. "What's wrong?" His tone was soft, so I believed I could reason with him. I was right. Skelton and Clem Kadiddlehopper loomed just minutes away.

"Well, you know, Dad, I want to become a newsman, a newspaperman," I said, although I had not expressed that desire forcefully until now. "And they don't have a journalism program there." Maybe they did. I hadn't looked into it. And he wouldn't know.

"I also checked the two-year campus here of Kent State, and they have none of the school's journalism courses," I lied. I had not set foot on the Stark campus. For all I knew, they may have offered a whole slew of early news writing courses. But I did know that Dad would not bother to investigate to see for himself. "I really need to start up at Kent this fall." The Kent main campus was about an hour away, close enough that Mom would feel assured that I had not wandered into the wilderness forever, never to be seen again. And it was a state school, so tuition would be cheap.

Dad did not hesitate. "Okay," he agreed. Thank you, Red Skelton.

And that is how I met Angela.

I did not meet her right away. In fact, we did not connect until my junior year. Angela would be a fledgling, new to the world away from the sheltering arms of parents, entering college the Fall of 1965, when

26

even formerly innocent young ladies were discovering spheres their parents never imagined. Our relationship almost never happened.

I had grown somewhat discouraged during my first two years at Kent. Neither I nor any of my fellow journalism students had cars on campus, forbidden by the administration for most students. So we could not venture into nearby cities like Akron, Youngstown, or Cleveland in search of hard news to sharpen our reportorial skills. What off-campus reporting we did end up doing was of Kent city council meetings, where we furiously took notes about such mundane items as plans for an extension of the town's water system. One of the hard facts of learning journalism was that we had to learn how to make such earth-shattering stories readable to the public. In my sophomore year, I decided to expand my writing expertise by making an attempt at a humor column in the student newspaper. It met with little fanfare, perhaps because of overall student apathy. However, it did create a stir within the administration when I wrote satirically about the plethora of tickets for a campus visit by Robert Goulet that were readily available for university and local bigwigs. But tickets for students were scarce. The powers that be expressed their displeasure with me and the newspaper for my audacity in suggesting favoritism. It was the only time in those two years that my sarcasm seemed to strongly irk those who had become targets of my cynicism. Otherwise, my wit would have a little effect...

But considering the times, I wondered why any students would even want tickets for Robert Goulet in the first place. He was not big in the flourishing youth culture.

I did, however, make enemies among some of those who abhorred apathy and, at the same time, attempted to lead campus youth into what they considered a worldly lifestyle. About thirty students had

27

formed Societe de la Renaissance to share among themselves and with the rest of campus, if it so desired, their love of various forms of art and poetry and individualism. Their meetings came with the requisite bongo drums, a relic from the beatnik days of the Fifties now on life support. Curious about them, I attended a meeting where I had some difficulty hearing some of the conversations because I sat too close to the bongo player. I then wrote a satirical column for the student newspaper in which I emphasized how difficult it was for me to find paragons of individualism in a group where I was the only attendee not wearing a light blue denim long-sleeved shirt and stone-washed jeans.

That afternoon, as I waited in the hallway for my class in Great Contemporary Issues to begin, a co-ed in a light blue denim long-sleeved shirt and stone-washed jeans approached me. Her huffing and puffing alerted me before I turned to her and her confrontational attitude. I was taken aback because as she glared up into my eyes, I thought Joey Messina had resurfaced in my life. Only this time, he was in drag.

"You fuckin' don't know a fuckin' thing about what the fuck we're doing, do you, you fucker?" she growled. Even her voice suggested the long-departed Joey Messina, except a couple of forms of *fuck* supplanted the *eh ehs*. "We're fuckin' trying to bring some fuckin' culture to this fuckin' wasteland!" And then she stormed away. I hoped it was toa class that she felt was a total waste of time.

I could only reply, shouting after her, "Judging from your fuckin' limited vocabulary, I'm guessing you're not one of the fuckin' poets in the Societe." Several surrounding students broke into laughter at my retort. If only briefly, I felt as if I had reached an audience. But none of them bothered to ask me if I wrote the column in the Stater.

Maybe none of them read the paper, apathetic as most students at Kent seemed to be.

Similar disappointment to the lack of journalistic opportunities occurred in my attempts to date women and hopefully begin a romance. I never knew so many young ladies preferred to wash their hair or study on Friday or Saturday nights rather than go on a date with an erudite and humorous young man who could charm them if given the chance. Or how many had family emergencies pop up just as the weekend was to begin. And what few ladies I did date prior to the autumn of 1965 had too little in common with me, as we usually found out about an hour into our date. I seem to recall one female who I had three dates with who suddenly started to need to wash her hair on weekends. I can't be sure because all my failures had begun to blur together.

But all that changed when Angela and I met, at her instigation, on the third floor of the campus library on an unseasonably warm night in November.

I had a term paper assignment in American Government that drew me to the library that evening. The professor had given the class leeway on topics, so I decided to see if I could document enough evidence to counter the Supreme Court decision in Brown vs. Board of Education. I hoped to impress the man, even though the class was in neither my major nor minor, by taking a contrary position on something somewhat fresh in our nation, the verdict being little more than a decade old.

I had had little luck with microfiche but managed to find two books and three magazine articles that dealt with the landmark ruling. But as I sifted through my sources, looking for anything that could help focus my approach, my frustrations grew. I did not pay much attention to a co-ed at the table across from me, but I did notice that she had brunette hair cut at her chin line, and she seemed to smile indirectly in my direction occasionally. She seemed like she found me slightly amusing. My first thoughts were that she was attractive. Maybe she noticed my expressions of exasperation as I grew increasingly frustrated with my research.

I had my head buried in a passage that showed promise when I became aware that a hand had just set a folded sheet of paper slightly beyond my grasp but obviously meant for me. By the time I reached for it and turned to see who had left it, she was disappearing between shelves, headed for the elevator. Of course, my curiosity rose, so I opened the letter. It read:

> You looked so sad each time I looked at you that I thought you should know that patience works in the end. Of course, we don't know each other, but I want you to realize that someone watching your struggles hopes you will succeed if you persevere.

Well, so much for research that evening. Maybe my frustration with women would come to an end. I had to catch up to her, to ask her why she had taken the time to be so forward with a stranger. Plus, judging by her note, she seemed to have an excellent vocabulary. I could not pass on the opportunity to actually make headway with a pretty co-ed, especially since it seemed she had made an intentional first move.

I did not see her until I had left the library. She was about fifty yards ahead of me, so I picked up my pace to overtake her. In the fading light, I noticed that she had nice legs stretching down from her cutoff shorts. Promising! When I had reached about ten feet behind her, I called out, "Hey!"

She stopped abruptly, then turned slowly to face me. "What took you so long?" she asked, her eyes dancing like an upbeat Jackie Wilson song. Not a spine-wrenching ditty like The Twist. Or a spasmodic Jerk. Immediately, I thought that she was either crazy or wanted to be friends. After all, she had written that note. And now she had asked a loaded question. I had never had a woman make the first move on me. Such a welcome change in my dating fortunes seemed providential despite my lack of belief in such matters.

"Flirtatious, forward woman," I thought. "I like that."

"I had to close my books after reading your letter," I grinned. Then I decided to put her on the defensive if, indeed, we were playing a game at all. "Why didn't you wait at the elevator?"

"I didn't know which you would find more important. Your schoolwork or the girl who made a pass at you."

"I'm standing here with your answer, aren't I?" I made certain she saw my humor working. I need not worry. She did. So I joined her, continuing our walk across campus toward her dorm.

She told me her name, Angela deAngelis, and that she came from Austintown, a suburb of Youngstown. And she was a freshman.

As we neared her dormitory, I finally worked up the courage to ask her for a date. Spurred by my awareness of her apparently educated vocabulary, I wanted to impress her, to make her think she had met her equal in intellectualism. So I asked, "Look, I have an assignment in my speech class to see Oedipus Rex Thursday. Would you like to come with me?"

31

She feigned disbelief at such a magnificent invitation. "Oedipus? Such a light, romantic comedy! Did the theater department get Rock Hudson and Doris Day to star in it?" She rolled her eyes. "How can I refuse? Yes, that would be nice."

I knew I could show humor with her. "You won't decide at the last minute to decline because you have to wash your hair, will you?"

"Huh?"

I explained to her about the standard rejections I had heard too many times over the past couple of years. She smiled, her brown eyes dancing with that Jackie Wilson song friskiness that had immediately captured me and would enchant me long afterwards. "Remember who wrote who a letter a few minutes ago. Even if I need to wash my hair, I'll hold off. I wouldn't want to miss the light charm of Oedipus Rex," Angela assured me.

I picked her up at her dorm the evening of the play, dressed in my white Levis and a madras shirt. I felt relieved when she came to the lobby in a burgundy and white striped skirt and burgundy sweater, and flats. I had feared she would appear more formally in a dress and heels. I guessed that she had already adapted a good bit to the college lifestyle in the six weeks or so since she arrived. No need for her to put on airs. Certainly not for me.

We sat in the balcony, engaging in small talk before the play began. For the rest of the time, I hardly turned toward her except to speak briefly during intermission. I wanted to appear engrossed in the play, and to a degree, I was. But my primary reason for my absorption was my hope that she would think of me as a bona fide academic. It nearly backfired.

We had gone only a few steps outside the Music and Speech building when she spoke, her eyes, void of dancing, looking straight ahead. "Did my perfume fail me?"

I looked at her, but she did not return my gaze. "Huh?" My response hardly sounded like that of an intellectual. She sensed my confusion, turned toward me, and smiled.

"You hardly said a word the whole evening," she frowned playfully. "I thought maybe I had b.o., and you hoped the night would end quickly."

I stopped and grabbed hold of her arm. I knew she was trying to make light of my ignorance of her presence as my date. "I'm sorry," I assured her. "I guess trying to make you think that I was some kind of cerebral student of ancient Greek tragedy nearly boomeranged. Actually, I was bored somewhat."

"So you don't like psychological drama? With so much pathos and tragedy?" She still smiled coyly.

Trying to still appear of a higher learner, I answered, "Well, I liked Becket much more." Becket had been on movie screens the year before, starring Richard Burton and Peter O'Toole.

She frowned. No sign of playfulness this time. "You like movies about religious conflict?"

"I did like how Burton and O'Toole made the slight disagreement between Becket and Henry interesting," I joked. A dispute between two men that ended with the assassination of one of them hardly could qualify as minor.

"Oh. Well, many arguments involving religion escalate. I should know."

I did not respond immediately. I could not decide how to. Finally, the simplest of questions came to me. "Why?"

Angela stared at me, a seriousness to her gaze. "I'm Catholic. Didn't you think that? With my name obviously Italian? I encounter some prejudices from time to time. Have heard others call me words like guppy gulper behind my back."

"You won't have that problem with me. I'll say it to your face," I smiled.

"Good," she laughed, seemingly assured. Still, she decided to press things further. "I don't know that I can handle a Wasp," she joked.

"The only part of Wasp I'm certain of is white," I retorted with a smile. "I don't think my mother's Scottish ancestors were Anglo-Saxon, and I'm no religion now. So that eliminates Protestant for me. Also Jew, Hindu, Buddhist, you name it."

We would not have religious problems with each other. Our parents, however, would manage to cause many on their own. Neither side surprised either of us.

Inklings of resistance from mine came within a few weeks. While home for Thanksgiving, I said nothing about Angela and our enjoyment of each other's company. Instead, I spoke glowingly of my classes, other than my political science one, in which I had received a poor grade for my paper on Brown vs. Board of Education. Some things, even with the best of intentions, never work out. I would probably earn a C in that class and a B in speech, but my journalism grades were solid. After all, I had chosen that path.

But when my parents brought me back to campus after three days of turkey feasting, Angela was in my dorm lounge waiting for me. Without hesitation, she walked up to the three of us, hugged me, and kissed my cheek. "Welcome back!" she smiled.

I had no choice, turning to my parents while gently separating from Angela's embrace. "Mom. Dad. This is Angela deAngelis." I did not know whether my next words would hurt Angela or not. "We've become close friends," I announced somewhat weakly. Angela noticed. I wondered how I would handle this faux pas once we were alone.

The four of us chatted for a few minutes, then Angela indifferently said she had to return to her dorm and left. No hug or cheek kiss this time.

"She seems nice," my mother smiled, that expression that said I really don't know what I can say, so I'll just stay the standard words that most parents say when they unexpectedly meet their child's possible romantic friend for the first time. So Mom did not disappoint me. I expected that.

Dad did not fail in what I expected of him either. He said nothing about Angela during the rest of our visit. That would come during Christmas, the time of good will toward men.

Our story-and-a-half house in Canton provided me with a great deal of privacy during college breaks, as I had the whole upstairs to myself. With a cheap Philco stereo turntable and our original seventeen-inch Sylvania television, I usually had my own private domain in which to relax. An old recliner gave me a comfortable place to sit. However, my room did not serve as a sanctuary if Dad had something on his mind. Such was the case a few days into the quarter break. I had just settled back in my chair to drool over Mary Ann in Gilligan's Island when he strode in, smoking his pipe, and stood next to the television. At least, he did not block my view. So my eyes kept moving back and forth between him and Mary Ann as our conversation went on.

"I'm guessing from her name that Angela is Catholic," he puffed as he spoke. "Does she have you eating fish on Fridays?" Dad usually made his point in such not-so-subtle ways.

Angela and I were not even serious yet, but I liked her well enough to defend her. My folks and I had had fish sticks and tartar sauce for dinner that evening, so I decided on my comeback.

"As a matter of fact, she had me eating fish sticks and tartar sauce last Friday," I chirped straight-faced. I did not want Dad to fully catch my sarcasm. I also did not give him a chance to make the next comment. "And she's helping me brush up on my ninth and tenth grade Latin. Veni, vidi, vici," I added calmly. I did not come to see and conquer. I was already in my chair. But he might have had subjugation in mind.

Dad stood there for a moment, obviously at a loss for words. Finally, he spoke, "I guess you'll be swearing allegiance to the Pope before long." He turned and walked away, the stench of his pipe smoke lingering. I did not have any air freshener at hand, and near--zero temperatures outside prevented me from opening my window. Besides, I would have had to rise from my chair.

I did not retort. I could now fantasize about Mary Ann again, unimpeded. Watching her parade around that tropical island on a Hollywood set blew the pipe smoke stench away from my senses.

Angela had endured a similar "discussion" with her father during the break. Hers, however, was heavily one-sided.

"It was so close-minded of him," Angela lamented as we lunched on Big Chefs, fries, and Cokes at the Burger Chef near the campus library the evening we had returned to campus. "Asked why, after they had raised me as a good Catholic, I had to run from my faith, my upbringing, to some Protestant boy. Said I'd be lucky if I even got a chance to spend time in Purgatory for cleansing. I'd probably go straight to Hell. Then he threatened to pull me out of Kent and send me to a Catholic school. But he didn't sound earnest."

"Get thee to a nunnery? What'd you say to him? You know you could have made it worse by telling him I have no religion whatsoever," I quipped.

"What you should have told your father. That we're not serious yet."

"Maybe I am," I countered.

She seemed mildly surprised. "Oh."

I had to press her teasingly. "You did say not yet."

Angela laughed, took a sip from her Coke, then grinned. "We'll see." The girl could be downright coy when she wanted to be.

Over the next few months, we did become serious within the limitations we faced. We graduated into heavy petting during that time. But various obstacles prevented us from going any further.

Certainly, we could not engage in intercourse when visiting in each other's dorms. The school had a rule that the room door had to remain open at least eight inches, and at least three feet of our combined four had to remain touching the floor. Certainly, some creative souls may have tried to have sex in positions that met that criteria, but Angela and I did not. Our most daring violation of these rules may have been the size of the door opening. We never bothered to measure.

Even after I moved off campus, we somehow remained chaste. For one thing, my room was upstairs in a house owned by a droll Philosophy professor who lived downstairs. My lease stated clearly that I would face eviction if I brought any coed to my room "for immoral purposes." It did allow me to have female guests, of whom Angela was the only one, and I did not have to keep the door ajar a few inches. But we did not want to test the professor's hospitality. Plus, any activity on my bed would probably echo all the way downstairs.

Even though my parents were paying for most of my education, I had to foot some of the bills, so even renting a motel room to end our virginity stayed out of the question.

And then there was my 54 Dodge. A Royal sport coupe, two-tone coral and white, it undoubtedly had been a sexy car when new. But now, little more than a decade later, it showed the ravages of time with faded paint and a broken rear passenger window. Still, it served me well, and the school had allowed me to bring it to campus beginning that winter quarter after my "veni, vidi, vici" talk with my father. But the back seat upholstery had jagged rips in it, and the front had so many obstacles, such as the steering wheel and window knobs sticking out at all angles that Angela and I decided even trying to engage in sex would be uncomfortable and ruin the mood no matter how great our passion. Our day would come.

In those remaining twenty-four months of my campus life, I managed to irk a few more people, but their efforts to silence or punish me were lame and met with no results. Other than that, I continued to write my column.

One of my targets was the town's paragon of purity, respected by her peers but not the vast majority of students. Priscilla Barnhill had grown more adamant over the last few years about the sinful permissiveness (her words) not only on the Kent campus but nationwide. A self-appointed guardian of youthful purity, she campaigned against 3.2 percent beer, men's and women's dorms sharing common dining and recreation space, campus dances, go-go girls, miniskirts, sunbathing in skimpy bikinis, and other instruments of sexually depraved living.

So I wrote a column saying that I had heard she had made plans to build a factory that would make chastity belts for her to donate to the school administration to pass out free of charge to all female students.

The day after publication, our advisor pulled me aside. "Taylor, some of the main movers in town expressed to me their displeasure at your attack on Miss Barnhill. I tried explaining to them that satire is not really an attack but merely a humorous approach to a topic of interest. Especially to its readers. You know how persons of importance, as they like to think, are sensitive when one of them gets shone in an unflattering light. Try to be kind to our older folks, okay?" He patted me on the shoulder and walked away. Encouraged by his backing, I thought about looking for another local off-campus target but decided against it. I could think of none other than Priscilla Barnhill, who was rattling a large number of the student body and deserved sardonic scorn.

In fact, my remaining time as a columnist passed with few instances of expressed dissatisfaction from others with my writing. I took a page from my Robert Goulet column and said that the reverse had happened when comedians Pat Paulsen and Bob Einstein of the Smothers Brothers Hour came to campus. I noted it was strange that plenty of students could get tickets, but town and school officials could not. Several students pointed out that the bigwigs did not give a shit about those two entertainers because of their apparent left-wing leanings. I said that that was precisely my point. Whatever brouhaha might have been never came about.

I also did a satire on The Undraftables, a group of students opposed to the draft and the Vietnam War. Largely made up of males who went to great lengths establishing personas that they hoped would make them 4-Fs once they left school, they tried to hold rallies by the Victory Bell on the school's commons below the journalism building. The group had a few females, already ineligible for the draft because of their gender but who wanted to vocalize their disdain for the establishment in every way they could. I say the group tried to hold rallies, but hardly anyone other than members showed up. I pointed that out in my column.

Eric Holmes, their nominal leader, accosted me in the Student Union the next day. "Why did you trash us, man?"

"All I did was point out that no one comes to your rallies," I generalized in my defense. "That should come as no surprise to you. After all, this school isn't called Apathy State for nothing." Generally speaking, Kent's student body had no political views whatsoever at the time, changing classes as passively as sloths eat.

Holmes paused, then nodded in agreement. "Damn, students here don't give a fuck about their brothers shipping out to die in Vietnam. What the fuck," he shrugged, turned, and walked away. For the remainder of my time at Kent, whenever I would pass one of their rallies, I would give Holmes a hearty wave. He would respond by flipping me his middle finger.

But with a smile.

And the number of students attending the rallies slowly increased as more and more men our age returned home from Vietnam in body bags. Or with missing limbs. Or emotional scars.

During my remaining Kent years, Angela and I had enough problems with our parents but not with each other. Love and the generation gap bloomed. Separately, of course.

Once, when the distance between Dad and I had grown even more, I could not resist crowing about an incident some four centuries in the making. "Must really piss you off that the Pope and the Archbishop of Canterbury got together. And in Rome, of all places," I jabbed at him. It was the first time those holding such holy titles had met in the aforementioned time. "How long before you think the Pope will have the Episcopalians eating fish in surrender?" I asked. Dad did not reply. He had long since given up on convincing me of the virtues of religious prejudice.

And Angela had dared, as they became more fashionable, to buy a miniskirt and raise the hemlines on most of her other skirts and dresses. "You're going straight to hell," her father blared at her when she greeted her parents on a rare visit of theirs to campus. "What the hell kind of slut are you becoming?" Obviously, the schism between her and her parents was widening. A couple of girls in the standard Societe garb of denim shirts and stone-washed jeans started to come to Angela's defense, but she politely waived them away.

My parents expressed their disapproval a little more kindly. Actually, Dad said nothing, but I thought I caught him leering at her when they first saw a lot more bare legs than they ever had previously. "I wish girls today would be more modest," Mom confided to me later. She had the decency not to comment in Angela's presence or mention her by name, but I knew who she meant.

And, oh yeah, I had no problem with Angela's new shorter hemlines at all. They helped me focus on her becoming more of my life and also forget about Mary Ann on Gilligan's Island.

For Angela, the big hubbub about prejudice came with the Supreme Court's 9-0 decision on interracial marriage in the Loving v. Virginia case.

"God, Taylor!" she fumed almost before I had put the Dodge in gear to head for a movie when I visited her that last summer of college. "My dad went ballistic on the Warren Court and everybody else who might remotely be involved in the case. He says the mongrelization of humanity is coming. Everyone will want to marry someone of another color just for spite. I half expected George Wallace to enter the room. I'm glad you came tonight to my rescue," she concluded, leaning over, kissing me on the cheek, and giving a slight squeeze of my crotch.

We petted heavily that night at the drive-in. I can't remember what movies were on the screen. Couples like us didn't go to the drive-in to see the movies anyway.

But all too soon, my days at Kent would end with my earning my degree. That happened in December 1967. It probably did not matter, but the Tet Offensive began a little more than a month later. I say it probably did not matter because I am certain that the fine, upstanding members of my draft board in Licking County already were salivating over every list of newly eligible young males to send off to the God-forsaken jungles of Southeast Asia... I now became one of them.

And those upstanding citizens worked with all deliberate speed to get me in uniform. Most men on the board had served during World War II. In fact, one had survived the Bataan Death March. So I tried to understand their thoughts on what they considered my duty and that of other males my age. But it bothered me that they seemed to not understand our view that Ho Chi Minh was neither Hitler nor Tojo. He had no dreams of world conquest. But, yes, he was Communist, and it did not matter to the board that the leaders of "free" South Vietnam were corrupt to the core. They still believed that any healthy male like me had the duty to serve in the country's military. I begged to differ, and I hoped that childhood illnesses would lead to me being deemed unfit for soldierly duty.

Once again, I would be wrong.

In the meantime, I had the greatest difficulty finding employment in my chosen field. Newspapers in the nearby major cities expressed their reluctance to hire me so long as I had a five-ton Selective Service 1-A classification chain around my neck. I finally landed a job at a small town daily, the Garrettsville Bulletin, about a thirty-minute

43

drive from Kent and Angela. Although they did hire me, neither my start nor my short tenure there proved fruitful. Except for fodder for my disdain for those in positions of authority.

"At least you're not a draft dodger like so many coming out of college," the editor, an ancient man not far from retirement or the grave, grunted.

I attempted a joke. "Not that I haven't tried." He didn't smile.

Even when I ventured at writing interesting news, things backfired. One day about a month into my time at the Bulletin, I came across a sheriff's report that a farmer out on Eagle Creek Road west of town had reported a strange aircraft in a field on his property. I figured any story about a UFO would make for fascinating reading, especially in a small-town newspaper. So I drove my Dodge out to visit the man.

He told me that on the evening of the incident, he had heard a commotion among some of his animals and went out to investigate. That was when he saw the object "bigger'n my house" sitting in a field about fifty yards away. It remained there for about two minutes, then "zipped straight up inta the air and gone in no more'n three seconds." He also said the craft had flattened the grass out where it had been and took me out to show it to me. Sure looked like something unusual had visited his property.

The story did not impress the ancient editor. "It isn't our business to hold our readers up to ridicule just because they think they saw something strange."

"But he showed me the flattened grass where the UFO sat," I pleaded.

"I don't care if he showed you a picture of little green men," he countered, tearing up the story. "Stick to the stories that matter here.," he ordered. "Besides, that old goat is known to be a little bit off his rocker."

So I did stick to stories that "matter," spending most of the rest of my time writing about such newsworthy stories as the planned repaving of Water Street between Center Street and Maple Avenue. And that the Portage Pentecostal Church of Garrettsville was planning an early summer revival at a farm out on Eagle Creek Road just a stone's throw from the UFO landing site. I thought about trying in some way to encourage attendees to venture over to the farmer's flattened field. I figured at least some of them believed the Second Coming would be via spaceship. But I decided against it. Why press my luck with my grouchy editor?

Then came the time in May when Vice President Hubert Humphrey visited Kent State to speak. Although neither of us cared for Humphrey—Eugene McCarthy and Bobby Kennedy appealed to our politics—Angela and I wanted to hear him. Even though it was a weekday, I had the day off, so I drove to Kent. Angela and I sat high up in the bleachers on the home side of the gym.

Humphrey's speech did hold our attention, although neither we nor most of the crowd applauded anything he said. Then suddenly, a group of about ten black students rose from their seats and walked out in protest. I recognized them as members of Kent United Black Students, or KUBS, and turned to Angela, "Let's go. I've got to track them down for a story." I assumed I would come up with a good interview story for the Bulletin. After all, I was a staff reporter at the event. First-person news for a small town daily.

We tracked them down not far from the gym's main entrance. I recognized Rufus Hill, a light-skinned black with shorter hair than most blacks wore at the time. He and I were identical in height. I found it advantageous to stand eye-to-eye with him. I introduced myself to him and showed him my credentials as a member of the press.

"I graduated from here a couple of months ago," I explained. "So I know a good bit about KUBS. Why did you walk out on the vice president?" I asked, my demeanor suggesting I was every bit the serious reporter.

Hill smiled back warmly. In a moment, he told me why. "Yeah, man, I recognize your name. Liked some of your columns, especially the one about Ali." He had a good memory. I had written a satirical piece the previous year about Muhammad Ali's woes, thanks to his refusal to serve in the military. "We want our rights!" he emphasized, raising the requisite closed fist of black activists of the time.

I waited an uncomfortable pause for him to elaborate. Finally, I asked, "What rights are those?"

"We want our rights!" he reiterated. "We're tired of oppression."

Certainly, much had occurred in the civil rights movement over the past few years. He had much to present, but try as I might, I could not get him to give specifics. I tried changing the tone of the interview, anything to get a worthwhile story. I noticed that no black women were in the group.

"So, where are all the sisters?" I asked. Hill noted that I accompanied my question with a wry grin. He did not take offense.

Instead, he joked, "They all too busy primpin' their 'Fros," he cracked. In kind, I referred back to my early problems with girls "washing their hair" when I hoped for a date. "We sure have our problems with women and their hair, don't we?"

He gazed at Angela. "Looks like she don't want to do her hair."

Angela smiled, "I'm slowly becoming a hippie. Preened hair's not high on my list." We all, including the brothers with Rufus, had a good laugh over that. We visited a little more and then departed. It had been only a month since the Martin Luther King assassination, so I thought Rufus would have had much more to say. He had disappointed me.

As it was, I still felt that I had the makings of a good story for the Bulletin. We rushed over to the school newspaper offices, where I borrowed a typewriter and pounded out a first-person story. After saying goodbye to Angela, I drove back to Garrettsville to hand in the article. I should have known better.

"We don't give voice to this Black Power nigger shit," my editor scowled.

Damn, but I wondered if real journalism ever existed at the Bulletin. Or any small-town newspaper mired in its provincial ways. I still pleaded, "But this was basically in our back yard. And it involved the vice president. It's news."

"Our back yards have green grass and maybe a flower bed or two," he retorted. "Maybe even a small garden. For all I care, Humphrey could have made his speech back in Minnesota. Kent State isn't in our back yard. And we ain't, I repeat, ain't givin' any coverage to niggers moanin' about their rights." Once again, another

47

journalistic masterpiece of real news written by me ended up in his trash basket. I was getting good practice at rejection for my later role in Air Force public relations, although I had no way of knowing it at the time.

The mundane routine and narrow-mindedness of this small-town newspaper had become so tedious that when Bobby Kennedy was shot a month later, my time at the Garrettsville Bulletin ended abruptly. Of course, the editor's attitude had something to do with it.

"Good! Another of them damn Kennedys is out of the way," the editor croaked to the few of us in what amounted to the newsroom the morning RFK died.

"And fuck you!" I shouted back without hesitation. "You're supposed to be a newspaper, open-minded, but you're just a provincial asshole. I quit!" I walked out, not even caring if the bastard sent me a final paycheck.

In the meantime, when I received my letter with President Johnson's signature stamped on it, ordering me to report to Fort Hayes in Columbus for my pre-induction physical, I felt optimistic. Certainly, my poor health during my childhood would reap the rewards. I neglected to realize that since Tet, just a few months before, this country had started inducting every eligible male who could crawl, breathe or show any semblance of a heartbeat.

So I kept my appointment with Uncle Sam's corps of doctors at Fort Hayes.

Along with perhaps a hundred or so other hapless souls who arrived for Army testing, I went through the requisite bending over, coughing, and other rituals of the pre-induction physical. I thought I might have a chance for disqualification when I never could tell when I would hear the beep in the hearing test, but the doctor waived me on.

Then came mounds of paperwork. I paused for a few moments when I reached a multi-page form from the House UnAmerican Activities Committee. It listed, I guessed, several hundred organizations that it believed at one time or another were subversive and intent on undermining or overthrowing the United States government. It wanted to know if I had ever belonged to any of them. I started going down the list, curious about what groups had become perceived threats. Then a thought came to me. What if I picked one or two and said that I had held membership? That might disqualify me.

The first one I decided on I had heard of before, The Loftus-McKenzie Defense Fund. It seems that men by those names had tried to unionize toilet paper manufacturing in the Midwest shortly after World War II. The other? The Mason-Dixon Realignment Council. I figured that any group that apparently wanted to redraw the Pennsylvania-Maryland border had to be subversive as hell. But then I guessed that someone seeing my checkmarks would refer me to someone in intelligence who knew all those organizations inside and out, and I would flunk the interrogation. So I passed on it.

I decided to rest my hopes on my childhood asthma.

Having honestly filled out the questionnaire on my history of illnesses, injuries, surgeries, and anything else in my life that had needed medical attention, I answered all the questions posed to me by the doctor holding the papers.

"And your asthma. What can you tell me about it?" he asked. His scowl suggested that any potential draftee who checked any illness or injury on the form wanted to avoid combat. Why would I be any different?

I recited the memories I had of it and how my doctor, certainly a man respected for his adherence to all medical codes of ethics, treated me within all those rules. When I finished, the Army doctor brightened my hopes of deferment.

"Get a letter from this Doctor Garshaw detailing the history of your asthma and bring it back here. We'll look into it," he said, expressionless. I tried my best to also be unreadable without changing my bearing, not wishing to expose my elation at the possibility of not meeting up with the Viet Cong at some later date. So I did as he instructed and two weeks later sat before him again. The scowl had not left his face.

"It looks like you'll be okay for military service," he smiled villainously after perusing the letter. I must admit I believe he actually read the letter. I tried to hide my disappointment as he continued. "You seem to have not had any issues since you were twelve. You've apparently outgrown your childhood illness. Your classification will be 1-A. Happy soldiering!"

I hated his smugness. I wanted to bash in his teeth. Instead, crestfallen, I mumbled, "Thanks," and left for my Dodge in the parking lot. As I drove the nearly two-hour journey back to Canton, I pondered what to do. As appealing as Canada was to many men my age, I feared that Angela would not come with me or would not join me after she graduated. We had grown serious enough in our relationship that I did not want to risk it by migrating north to that land heavily populated by geese and moose. I had no desire to go underground, sneaking from one leftist cell to another throughout the country, constantly looking over my shoulder for federal agents eager to arrest me for draft evasion. No doubt, I had but one option. I would enlist. The Air Force seemed like a good choice. Why enlist in the Army or Marines, just like being drafted? And the Navy? I cringed at the possibility of serving most of my time aboard a ship with little to see but undulating water all around me. Hopefully, with the Air Force, I would have enough time to take the test for Officers Candidate School and subsequently join up before my draft notice arrived. Hopefully, those wheels would turn more slowly than I planned on mine doing. Yes, I would have to work within the system to cooperate with the powers that be, but optimistically at least somewhat on my terms.

Certain that I had little time to waste, I drove the next day to the Air Force recruiting office situated on the third floor of a downtown office building in Canton. Sparsely furnished with just a desk and a few chairs, it was decorated with various posters extolling the benefits of flying high and slipping the surly bonds of the earth with the Air Force. And the recruiter, Tech Sergeant Monroe Washington, did all he could to encourage me that I had found my calling. I simply wanted to lessen my chances of being a target for the VC.

We went through all the formalities necessary to forge a contract. I must say he treated me affably, but after all, he had a monthly quota to reach, and my signature could help him do that. He then enrolled me in the tests necessary to have officer's school consideration. They would occur in a room down the hall from his station two days later.

I took the battery on that day. As I did so, I came to what I determined a startling conclusion. One section included a series of single photographs taken from a certain altitude, for example, 20.000 feet straight down. Then from four choices shot from totally different angles and heights, I had to determine which showed the same landscape as the targeted one. I had no clue.

"No wonder we hit hospitals and schools and houses instead of military marks," I reflected. "How the hell can anybody know which choice is correct?" But I tried diligently to figure out the correct response. And I gave my best effort on the other questions.

I passed, but it did not matter.

"You passed," Sergeant Washington smiled when I visited the next week. "But it doesn't matter. We're only taking men for flight training now. And your eyesight negates that." He need not have pointed to my glasses, but he did.

Not that I wanted to drop bombs on people anyway or have anti-aircraft guns firing away at me. And with "Death of the Ball Turret Gunner" still fresh in my mind from a literature class, I had no desire to have that happen to me. Anyway, my height negated such a gunner's fate even if the Air Force still had such men on bomber crews. So I resigned myself to waiting for word from him as to when I would take a bus to the Federal building in Cleveland, take the oath of enlistment, and fly away to humid, sultry Lackland Air Force Base outside San Antonio.

"Babe," Sergeant Washington addressed me when I answered the phone a few days later. He apparently liked to call all recruits, or at least white ones, "babe." But his voice sounded grave. "We can't take you."

Stunned, I sat momentarily speechless, gaping at the mouthpiece. Finally, I uttered, "What? Why?"

He then informed me of the idiosyncrasies of the bureaucratic nonsense that came with joining the military during times of war, at least during Vietnam. "You had asthma as a child."

"I know. But the doctor at Fort Hayes cleared me," I moaned. "He said I had outgrown it. I'm a picture of health now."

"You may now have perfect well-being," Washington continued. "But criteria for enlistment are tighter than for conscription. They can draft you, but we can't sign you up. That's just the way it is, Babe. Sorry."

"But. . ."But I was already speaking into a dead telephone. The dial tone told me so. I decided not to give up. I would find a way to get into the Air Force and lessen my chances of facing death in the jungles of Southeast Asia.

I found myself in a predicament. Over the last decade or so, I had taken pride in the little battles I had waged against the Everses, Brophys, and Barnhills of the world. People who abused their authority and position or tried to become tyrants. I had to devise a plan in which I would need someone of influence to help me. Sometimes we can make the strangest of compromising decisions when they involve our own self-interest.

I decided I needed to contact two people, an Ohio senator noted for his anti-war stance and the Secretary of Defense. So I composed a letter that I sent a copy to each, stretching the truth a bit by saying I had no problem serving my country, but I should have the right to do it in the military branch of my choosing. Of course, I would rather not have had had to choose any, but that now was out of the question. In the letter, I also lamented that regulations had forced me to make this request just because of differences in how my childhood asthma affected my eligibility. My biggest hopes for help rested on my letter to my anti-war senator. Knowing how much Clark Clifford had on his mind and daily agenda, the letter to him was more a desperate stab into the murky darkness of bureaucracy.

I was wrong on both counts.

My first reply came from the senator's office, probably shuffled to some underling who either did not read my letter or comprehend my purpose in writing. Instead of offering a solution, it seemed to merely state in lengthy legalese some aspects of the Selective Service Act, which I was trying to circumvent. My hopes were fading. But, no, I was not reconsidering a long-term commitment to Canadian residency.

But the next letter offered me surprising hope. Written from the office of some undersecretary far down on the department's ladder, in charge of something like ingrown toenails and toe fungus. That is right. It was the Department of Defense, not HEW. This kind, caring, benevolent soul suggested that I go back to my recruiter and ask him to seek a medical waiver for me.

Smiling, I marched into Sergeant Washington's office the next day, official letter in hand. I waved it above my head as he looked up from some paperwork. "Taylor, babe, what brings you here?" he queried.

Handing him the letter, I beamed. "This letter from the Department of Defense suggests I ask for a medical waiver so that I can become an airman." I wanted him to sense that I indeed desired to serve, maybe not by dancing in the skies but at least by occupying a desk... Frankly, I preferred staying a civilian, but the Army doctor had seen that I would not, at least for a time.

Sergeant Washington took the letter, examining it closely. I knew that since he was a career serviceman, he did not want to circumvent regulations. So he carefully looked it over a second time. Then he leaned back in his chair, folding his palms behind his head, and thought. For longer than I would like, but he probably took less than a minute. Then he reached for his phone and dialed a number.

His conversation was brief, merely detailing to whoever was on the other end about who had signed the letter and what the undersecretary had suggested. He listened to his contact for a few seconds after he himself had finished, then thanked the person and hung up. Then he leaned back as before and smiled broadly at me.

"Babe!" he said. This seemed promising. He had just called me Babe, not using my first name. "Take this letter this coming Thursday up to the Federal building in Cleveland and go to the induction center there. I believe it's on the fourth floor, but there will be a directory in the lobby, or someone can direct you. Ask for Tech Sergeant Downing. He'll see what he can do." Washington paused. "But make sure you have that letter. It's official." Then he rose from his chair, extended his hand, and shook mine warmly.

"Glad I could help you meet your quota," I laughed.

"Don't get ahead of things," he warned. "You're not enlisted yet. But I'm confident Downing will work things out for you."

We shook hands again. Then I floated almost like Nureyev all the way to my Dodge parked on a side street. I drove home within the speed limit, although I was flying one hundred miles an hour, listening at average decibels to songs by the Doors, Stones, Rascals, and others interspersed between the endless commercials on the AM radio. Maybe a ticket for speeding or blaring loud music could hurt my chances for enlistment but not for conscription. So I abided by the traffic laws.

The next Thursday, a receptionist at the induction center directed me through the maze of pale green cubicles and dull grey furnishings to Sergeant Gerald Downing. I did not know it then, but I would become quite accustomed to such uninspiring décor within a few months.

Downing looked every bit the man proud of his work. Close-cropped black hair, close-shaven, immaculate in his starched tan 1505 uniform, he could have been the poster boy for Air Force recruitment posters. Because of that, I feared he might not help me, that he would follow regulations to the letter.

But apparently, strange things can happen in the world of recruitment. I handed him the letter, which he eyed carefully, like a technician checking a finely-tuned instrument. "Impressive. From the Department of Defense, no less," he observed, not looking up from the paper. Then he cracked, "They certainly have enough layers of bureaucracy, don't they," obviously alluding to the lower rung undersecretary who had signed the letter. He then brought his bemused gaze up from the letter.

"Go to that window over there," he instructed me, pointing to one about twenty feet to my right. "Ask for your physical papers."

I obliged and returned to Sergeant Downing, handing him the manila folder I had received at the window. He took it from me and pulled out the stapled four pages or so of my physical results. He quickly glanced over it until he came to the page that listed previous medical conditions. He started questioning me about the ones I had marked 'yes' until he arrived at the box for asthma.

"So this is the troublesome one, I understand," he noted, looking up from the forms. "Your asthma."

I made certain I was polite. "Yes, sir," I responded.

He replied with a line I would hear many times during my Air Force tenure, whether directed toward me or someone nearby. "Don't call me sir," he said with some authority. "I'm not an officer. I work for a living. Call me sergeant."

Taking no chances, I dutifully answered, "Yes, sergeant."

"What's the story?"

I quickly related my asthma history. Then, that my physician's letter had not dissuaded the Army doctor at Fort Hayes that he believed me fit for the draft.

"And that asthma keeps you from your nation's calling in the Air Force, does it?

"Yes, Sergeant Downing." I was growing even more polite. I needed his help. It came swiftly.

He put the papers back in the folder and stared me in the eye. Accustomed to giving orders, he gave mine clearly. "Here's what you're going to do. You're going to come here next Wednesday. And you're going to take another physical. And when you get to this page asking about prior medical conditions, you're going to check *no* on everyone. You've never had any of them. You've been the healthiest creature ever to walk this planet.

"And if anyone asks you if you've ever set foot in this building before, you tell them 'no', he finished authoritatively. With that, he lifted my pre-induction physical folder over his shoulder and dropped it into the waste basket behind him.

I knew instantly that he had saved me from the draft. This time, I had no problems whatsoever with the powers that be. "I will do that, Sergeant Downing," I complied, trying not to look overly grateful. One can never be too sure. "Thank you."

Certain that I had avoided the draft and would serve in the Air Force, however reluctantly, I drove home in the same manner as my last visit with Sergeant Washington. I stayed within the speed limit and kept the radio at a somewhat quiet amplitude. No need to attract the attention of a law enforcement officer with a ticket quota. No need to potentially sabotage my enlistment.

The next week, I returned to Cleveland and did exactly as Sergeant Downing had instructed. No hitches. Within a few weeks, I would head by commercial air with several other enlistees from Northeast Ohio to the stifling August humidity of Lackland Air Force Base, Texas.

Now, I would have to convince Angela that my enlistment would work well for us in the long run. In a few weeks, she would surprise me with plans of her own.

But first, I had to endure six weeks in the Hell, otherwise known as a south Texas summer, where daytime high temperatures often reached the mid-nineties and the humidity indexes blew off the charts.

Fortunately for us trainees, the Air Force took pity when the temperature hit ninety-five or higher and marched us into air-conditioned rooms to attend boring lectures on everything the service had to offer.

The first roughly four weeks dragged on with marching, physical training, marching, lectures, marching, testing, and marching for the most part. And constant reminders to address our instructors as 'sergeant'. They were not officers. They worked for a living. But I did have a few opportunities to work on my skills for combating authority without endangering my well- being too much. Cases in point:

1. I had let my hair grow well over my shoulders prior to induction.

"We're going to shear off all that fur, hippie," a master sergeant growled as I stood in line for our first regulation, basic training haircut.

"I decided to wait so that my taxes would pay for it, sir," I replied, eyes forward.

"Don't call me sir, airman! I work for a living."

2. I developed a numbness in one foot, so my training instructor, Technical Sergeant Ben Smothers, sent me off to the base hospital where the doctor instructed me, "Keep it warm."

"What did they tell you at the hospital, airman?" Smothers asked upon my return to my unit.

"He told me to keep it warm, sir."

"Don't call me sir, airman. I work for a living."

3. Sergeant Smothers found my razor, the one that I actually used to shave, hidden deep within my foot locker and tossed it across the barracks. "Don't try to slack off, Airman Forsberg!" he roared in concert with his hurl.

"Just trying to keep my foot locker neat, sir."

"Don't call me sir, airman. I work for a living."

And so it went.

But sometime early in our fifth week, I received a shock. Sergeant Smothers had ordered us to stand at attention by our bunks. Then he called in another instructor from his office. Something about the man looked strangely familiar. Then Smothers introduced him.

"Airmen," he announced. "This man is in training to become a full-time training instructor. He'll be working with me for the last two weeks of your basic. Meet Staff Sergeant Joe Messina."

"Oh shit!" I muttered silently. My jaw dropped figuratively. I did not let it do so literally. No wonder the man looked strangely familiar. My old junior high school nemesis had reentered my life in the most unlikely of places. Joey Messina, the young hoodlum from East Junior High, was in the Air Force? As a lifer? As a training instructor? Would he push me aside while uttering his infamous "eh"?

As he marched purposefully by, I eyed him closely without appearing to do so. Under his wide-brimmed TI's hat, his hair was now in a crew cut rather than his old greasy blob. And Air Force dentistry had done wonders for his teeth. He actually looked civilized.

I could only hope that he would not recognize me. Now, he had every advantage. He gave us the usual spiel about how the military had turned him from an aimless punk into a real man and how it could do the same for each of us. All I could think of was that he now had power he could use, within limits, without facing punishment. If he wanted to push some recruit out of the way in order to handle his own personal hygiene, he could get away with it. I did not want him to remember me and use me as his whipping boy, even if for only my remaining two weeks of basic. I almost blew it.

Sometime later, a few of us in my training flight were standing around talking in one of the few free moments of relaxation we had. Talking about how things had gone in basic in general, I opined, "Ol' Smothers has been pretty fair to us."

Next thing I knew, Joey Messina was in my face as best he could. With his training instructor's hat pulled low over his eyes, he brought his chest up close to my stomach and peered up at me. "That's Sergeant Smothers, scum bag. Eh, eh? You refer to him by his rank. You understand?"

I took no chances with my usual 'sir' so that he could remind me of his rank and that he worked for a living. "Yes, Sergeant. Sorry, Sergeant," I replied, looking straight ahead. I feared if I looked down, he would somehow recognize me. He did not. He merely turned and walked away to seek some other trainee to admonish for whatever infraction he could find.

Nothing of consequence happened in the final days. Two days before we finished, we received our orders. Mine had me going to Carefree Air Force Base, Arizona, where I would work in the public information office of the combat training wing. There, a chance, I thought, to make good use of my journalism degree. We basic trainees had heard and talked of the capricious nature of the computers used to assign trainees to work fields. I feared my number would have designated me as a cook or sky cop. Or worse. I could have received orders for a tech school to learn to become a jet aircraft mechanic. I had placed third from the bottom, ahead of two girls, in testing during high school for mechanical aptitude. Had I gone to train as a jet mechanic, I hoped I would wash out before a jet I worked on crashed. But somehow, the computer assigned me relative to my skills.

I could hardly wait to tell Angela when I returned home on leave. If I had to spend time in the service, Arizona certainly seemed like a good place with its wide open spaces and abundant sunshine. I had not been farther west than Louisville, Kentucky, before I became an airman. And I would work in journalism, or something akin to it, I thought.

If I had news for Angela, she had even more for me.

Perhaps because of my troubles with the draft, she had become more anti-military and anti-war as the days passed during that struggle. The assassination of Robert Kennedy in June had also turned her more against the establishment in general. But she had gone even farther while I sweated away in south Texas. The Republican nomination of Nixon and Agnew added to her moving more to the left. I became aware of their selection by seeing a headline in a newspaper during my early days of basic training, but the imposed isolation from civilization and reality prevented me from knowing more. She would express her disgust about that later, much to my delight. I had always disliked Nixon, perhaps because he looked like he had crabapples in his cheeks. And because my father had voted for him in Sixty.

And I would not have known about the Democratic disaster in Chicago if Angela had not included a newspaper clipping in one of her letters to me. She let me know her feelings when I called her from my parents' home shortly after arriving there on leave between basic and my Carefree assignment. She unloaded almost immediately.

"Those motherfuckers," she seethed through the connection. "Mother" had now been added to "fuckers" so I knew she had really turned against the establishment. "They fucking clubbed everyone they saw, journalists, demonstrators, passers-by. You name it. They all got beaten.

"And to make matters worse, I couldn't even talk with my parents about it. When my dad said those beaten in Chicago got what they deserved, I knew we couldn't connect anymore. That's when I knew I would go with you to Arizona now. I just had to wait for you to come and get me. I'm ready, Taylor. I'm ready."

Obviously, she had changed. She made it most noticeable when she referred to "my dad", not the more personal "Dad." I said nothing over the phone. I felt much the same way. She had dropped her father from her heart. The chasm between them had deepened.

So when I arrived at Kent and she came down to her dorm lobby, I hardly recognized her. She had become more entrenched even in her appearance. She had continued to grow her hair longer and now looked the poster child for hippiedom, replete with granny glasses and granny dress. And when she pressed herself against me as we embraced, I noticed a different feel to her body. Her usually restrained breasts moved freely.

"I'm not wearing any underwear," she whispered in my ear after a long kiss. "It's too restricting."

63

"I have barely enough money so that we can do something about that," I smiled, fully aware of her insinuation.

Then she reminded me. "Oh, don't worry about that, sweetheart," she said coyly. "I'm going to Arizona with you."

I stepped back but still held her arms. "What?" I had not taken her seriously when she had told me over the phone. Now, I did not know whether to be elated or shocked. Or maybe a mixture of the two.

"I want to be with you. I've missed you. I don't give a shit about getting my degree," she insisted. Who was I to argue? "I'm taking a lot of my clothes home this weekend. Tell my parents I don't need that many. Have a huge fucking fight with them over me becoming part of the counterculture. Discarding my Catholicism. But I don't give a fuck." Fuck had become an increasingly important part of her vocabulary over the past few months. That convinced me she had become an integral part of the counterculture. "You are my life now, Taylor. We knew this would come eventually. Well, eventually is now. You know we could never have a Catholic wedding anyway. And I won't turn Presbyterian, even if by chance you would ask. Who needs marriage? Who needs religion?"

She went on to tell me that she had had many arguments with her parents, primarily for her changing appearance and attitudes. She had joined the campus chapter of Students for a Democratic Society, which had supplanted the Undraftables at Kent.

"Well, okay," I stammered when she finished. I certainly liked the idea of her going to Arizona with me. "But maybe, just maybe, we'll get married after we've been in Arizona for awhile. We can use the marriage supplement courtesy of the Air Force." That meant an extra one hundred dollars monthly, a gigantic sum for a lowly airman and his wife who had foregone her college degree.

I would be wrong about that.

Chapter 4

"Don't worry," Angela smiled as she entered her dormitory lobby, suitcase in hand. "I withdrew most of the money I had in my bank account. We have an extra two hundred dollars to get us to Arizona." With what little I had of my meager airman's pay, I felt like we had hit the mother lode. Who was I to argue?

As soon as we pulled onto the interstate just south of Kent, Angela surprised me again. She pulled out a package of Kent cigarettes, lit one, and offered it to me.

"You know I don't smoke," I reminded her. "And when did you start?" I thought it was a fair question to ask of the young woman I had been dating for nearly three years.

"While you were in basic." She laughed, the kind one does when he or she has pulled something over on someone. "Another way to get back at my parents. The rebel child. More freedom to be me. And also a way to stay loyal to our alma mater," she noted, stretching to an impossible connection between nicotine and college.

"And don't worry. I don't smoke pot. I tried it at an early SDS meeting and it did nothing for me."

"Are you getting back at me?" I frowned, keeping my eyes on the road. "I don't smoke. And I wish you wouldn't either." I said nothing about her attempted link between her cigarette and our school. Sometimes I would just let things pass.

She noted my glare, so after a couple more puffs, she put out her cigarette in the ash tray. But farther down the highway, as our conversation died and I concentrated on driving, she lit another and puffed away as she looked out her window at the scenery and billboards passing by. Unfortunately, my Dodge's radio had died months back, so she took to singing often during our drive. For What It's Worth, Eve of Destruction, Blowin' in the Wind, the same three protest songs over and over. Trouble was, she didn't know all the lyrics to any of them, so her singing, as on-key as it was, became more monotonous and redundant as time passed. Damn! I wished I had gotten that radio fixed. Fortunately, Angela sounded more like Mary Travers than Bob Dylan. Otherwise, I might have insisted that she stop warbling. Twenty-two hundred miles cooped up in the Dodge with nasality would have severely tested my eardrums. And my patience. Our trip would remain that way as we headed southwestward toward Arizona. When our talking stopped, or she finished her a capella performances, she would light another Kent and gaze out her window. I don't think she noticed the scenery. She always seemed deep in thought.

However, each night's layover cemented our relationship and erased my irritation at her singing and smoking for that day. At least our attachment returned to my mind. Her connection to me remained murky. However, we made love every night we stopped on our trip to Carefree. Fortunately, she brushed her teeth before we did, clearing her breath of the cigarette odor. Angela even threw in a blowjob on a long, lonely stretch of straightaway in New Mexico. After she had finished, she beamed a satisfied smile, "Now that's what I call sexual liberation."

I had no argument with that.

Our last morning, we left our motel in Holbrook, hoping to reach Carefree Air Force Base by sometime in the afternoon. As with the other days of our trip, we loaded up on a large breakfast to carry us through. We would get cheap drive-in hamburgers the rest of each day when we felt hungry. This day would be no different.

The road from Flagstaff to the Phoenix area was four-lane, part of the interstate system but uncrowded, to say the least. Arizona was still a lightly populated state in early October 1968, although the yearly influx of snowbirds would begin any day.

As we travelled south after crossing the Mogollon Rim, we sensed the road gradually descending toward the supposedly aptly-named Valley of the Sun. But we began to notice a pall over the landscape in the distance.

"Is that fog?" Angela asked as she puffed on another Kent. I had not convinced her to stop smoking, but at least she had her window down and would exhale and flick her ashes out it. "I didn't think that there was enough humidity out here to create fog." I had no idea from where she received any training in weather phenomena. I doubt that she had any, but was merely guessing.

"No," I answered. I had brushed up somewhat on the Phoenix metro climate. "That's smog. Phoenix sits in a valley and sometimes the weather traps the pollution from all the car exhausts. Looks like that's what they have now."

"This far out? Shit!" she frowned. "That can't be good. How can people breathe that shit?" she added as she took a drag on her cigarette, pulling all those chemicals deep into her lungs. I merely shook my head, keeping my eyes on the highway as she put out her cigarette. Angela sat silently for a few minutes, staring ahead as we continued down the highway. Then she reached into her purse, took out her journal book and pen, and began writing on a blank page. I thought nothing of it at the time, but she had turned all the way to the last page, far from her most recent entry.

"I'm hungry," she muttered as she continued to scribble. "Can we get something to eat?"

I looked over at her, but she did not lift her eyes from her writing. "We'll try, but we're not exactly in a densely populated area. Let's hope." Why was she writing so feverishly?

Shortly, we came to the exit for Black Canyon City, so we pulled off to the intersecting road and drove no more than fifty yards before coming to a single Conoco gas station with two pumps and a dirt-stained eatery with a gravel parking lot. The sign said "Mogollon Grill. Good Eats." We were a little ways from the Mogollon Rim, so I was curious about the name. Our waitress informed us that it was part of a two-unit chain. The other was in Show Low. I wondered if they had any expansion plans, considering the poor condition of the exterior, but I did not ask. At least the inside was clean, with five booths and a six-stool counter. I also wondered how much business they actually had daily. We were the only ones there, and the light traffic on the nearby roads suggested we might stay the only customers for awhile.

We ordered our standard cheeseburgers, fries, and Cokes, and ate slowly. I certainly had no desire to rush to report for duty at Carefree, and Angie seemed preoccupied. Our conversation was practically nil.

As soon as our meals came, Angie, who had been looking out the window during one of our silences, turned to me and asked, "Could I have the keys? I need to get something out of my suitcase."

I thought nothing of it, so I fished the keychain from my pocket and handed it over to her. I munched a couple of fries and took two bites out of my burger before she returned. She had a paperback that she had been reading on our trip, sat back across from me, and bit into her sandwich. She tossed the keychain back to me. "Thanks, honey," she said, dipping a French fry into the glob of catsup she had squirted onto her plate.

As we continued, just about the only thing we said was that we thought the burgers and fries tasted good, reflective of the restaurant's interior more so than the outside. I almost always hit the head after a meal, so I told Angie I had to go to the bathroom. Looking back later, I felt certain that she had hoped such would be the case this time. I took longer than usual to shit.

When I went back to our booth, Angie was not there. I assumed she, too, had needed to use the bathroom, so I sat down and picked up my Coke for another sip. Then I noticed the page from her journal under my plate. I pulled it out and turned it over. Angela was saying goodbye, what she had written shortly before we stopped to eat. It read:

> Dearest Taylor.
>
> Please know that I love you. But after seeing that smog down around where we are headed, I just can't breathe that shit into my lungs. It wouldn't be fair to us with me being unhappy, and, yes, I know, you'll probably think I'm stupid since I smoke, but I will try to quit. But I can't go to Carefree. Please don't think badly of me. It was a hard decision to make.
>
> All my love, Angie.

That sure was rash of her, I thought. She had made a decision in an instant, written it down without even discussing it with me, then bolted at the first chance. She did not say how much the last three years, and especially the last few nights, had meant to her. Did I mean anything at all? But maybe she had her period and did not think rationally. And she did not have much time. If she had not said she wanted to eat and we had not stopped at the Mogollon Grill, she may have gone all the way to the base and stayed with me. Suddenly, I knew I had to collect myself. Whoa, where is she going? I must stop her, get her back, and talk our way through this.

I looked out the window and finally spied her, already going up the northbound ramp of the interstate. Her in her granny dress and granny glasses, stumbling along like she had a broomstick up her panties-less ass, lugging her one suitcase clutched in both hands. For some reason, I thought, "I guess that's why they call it luggage." Strange thoughts would sometimes come to me out of the blue.

I scooted out of the booth, reached into my wallet, pulled out a ten-dollar bill, and tossed it on the table. "My payment is on the table," I called to the stunned waitress as I rushed past her. "Keep the change."

My Dodge balked at starting, something it had been doing off and on throughout our trip, so I lost more time. As I neared the northbound ramp, I pulled over onto the berm. No sign of Angie. Someone apparently had already picked her up.

"Fu--," I started to curse her but then stopped. I could not wish ill upon her. I sat there, hands on the steering wheel, looking up the empty ramp and hoped, almost prayed, that she had gotten a ride from a good person, that it would not be someone who would end up raping her or murdering her. Or both. For several minutes I sat staring straight ahead, hands clutching the steering wheel tighter, trying to figure out how all the time we had grown closer suddenly disappeared at the sight of dirty air. But then, Angie had changed even more over the months of my uncertainty with the draft and my enlistment than I had.

I now would have to face Carefree Air Force Base alone. Oddly, Angie's desertion caused me to determine right then that I would carry on my subtle war against authority figures, Air Force be damned. At least, I would not need to worry about the effect my actions would have on her. Something I had considered often during our silent moments heading southwest.

When I pulled up to the main gate at Carefree, a staff sergeant signaled for me to stop. His name tag told me his name was Kaminski. He asked me my purpose, so I replied cordially, "Well, Sergeant Kaminski, I report officially tomorrow. I wanted to stop in briefly and get my bearings."

"Welcome to Carefree Air Force Base," he greeted me. He sounded like a recording, probably had been taught to say it in just that way, and probably did tens of times a day while on gate duty. "Where are you headed?" He did not ask to see a copy of my orders.

"I'm to report to the 5001st Combat Crew Training Wing as an information specialist."

"Not sure where that is, but if you go around the flag roundabout to the second right, then pull into the parking lot just through the next right, the building right down from it," he paused, went inside his hut, and came back with a base map, "building 138, houses the wing information office. If that's not where you're supposed to report, maybe they can steer you to the right place."

"Thanks, Sergeant Kaminski," I replied.

"You can call me Ski," he answered. He was getting quite friendly with someone he did not know. For all he knew, I might be an anti-war protester coming to scout out the base. But my short haircut probably caused him to sense that I was who I said I was. And he was my first exposure to a habit indigenous to so many making the military a career. Somehow they would take on a moniker that came from their last names. Ski Kaminski, Will Wilson, Sonny Thompson, and Jack Jackson were just a few I would encounter, even if their first names were something entirely divorced from their surnames.

"I will need to see a copy of your orders," Ski Kaminski suggested.

I left the driver's seat and opened the trunk, retrieving a manila folder with my orders from my suitcase, then handed the orders to him. "Here you are, Ski," I said. I hoped he would not notice that I was a lowly airman straight from basic. After all, he had treated me cordially thus far, and I did not want him pulling rank. He quickly checked the form and stepped back. He eyed my coral and cream Dodge back and forth, up and down, then smiled. Ski Kaminski either liked to smile a lot or had been trained to do so. After all, he was the first person many entering Carefree would meet. The Air Force liked first impressions, especially good ones.

"I like your car. Nice color combo. Do you call it the Creamsicle?"

He did not see me roll my eyes. After all, I had stopped counting the times people would ask me that obvious question. Not replying to his, I asked one of my own.

"Ever get tired of this? Greeting people, checking their reasons for coming on base?"

"Won't do it much longer," he answered. "Got orders for 'Nam. Gonna be patrolling the perimeter of an air base there soon. Have some chances to shoot some VC."

He seemed happy about it, so much so that I half expected him to grab his holster in anticipation of some action right then and there. But he did not, so I thanked him and got back behind the wheel, wondering if he had given any thought that the Viet Cong might shoot him first. Or fatally. After the Dodge sputtered to a start again, I reached the parking lot he had directed me to, got out of my Creamsicle, and crossed the street, heading for building 138, where I would fly my desk for the next several months.

Oh, the thrill of seeing my future work environment for the first time. Pale, baby-puke green walls and partitions, drab grey desks, and swivel chairs. Completing the haute culture was an Air Force- blue-rimmed wall clock dangling precariously over the water cooler. It would never get a spread in Architectural Digest. At least the chairs were cushioned both on the seat and back. An Airman First Class rose from his chair and came to greet me. He stood about two inches shorter than me, had wavy black hair, and a mustache that stopped at the boundary between his upper and lower lips. Regulation style. Ruining his whole appearance were clear-plastic-rimmed eyeglasses. Again, government drab. I took him for a future lifer.

Apparently, he took me for what I was, fresh out of basic. My hair, which I still could not part, gave me away. "May I help you?" he asked, a bemused smile on his face. "I'm taking a chance in not calling you sir like we're supposed to with guests." He reached out as if to touch my scalp. "But I think you are not far removed from Lackland. Am I right?"

"You'd make a good detective," I laughed back. "From your actions, I'd say my hair was a dead giveaway. Yes, I just left that garden spot of Texas two weeks ago." I reached for a copy of my orders inside the manila envelope. "I think I'll be working here. Due to report tomorrow."

He extended his right hand. "I'm Mike Van Lautenschlaeger."

As we shook hands, I noticed his name strip across the left pocket of his tan 1505 uniform. It read "Schlaeger." He saw my bewilderment and looked around the room before speaking.

"The Air Force deemed my real name too long for a name tag, so I'm just Schlaeger here. Even my dog tags just have Schlaeger on them. If I were to go to Nam and get killed, I'd come home in a body bag with Schlaeger on it. Who knows whose parents would get my remains? Certainly not mine."

He raised a finger in a warning gesture. "But you'd better call me by my full name. Or Mike."

"Mike it is," I nodded. Eventually, I would call him Schlaeger and not suffer any consequences. "Don't want to speak five syllables when one will work." I shook his hand. "Taylor Forsberg."

He raised his head slightly in a knowing gesture. "Ah yes. A true American name. Great Britain and Scandinavia?"

I started to reply, but he held up a hand. "Even though you say you don't have to report here until tomorrow if you want to meet the officer in charge, I'll take you back." He handed back my orders. "You are indeed going to be one of us."

He turned to head down a walkway between some of the office cubicles toward a door that separated the airmen's work area from the apparent inner sanctum of the person or persons in charge. Before I could tell him I most certainly could wait another day, he stopped. "Won't have to. Here comes the major."

Striding toward us from the officers' den came a man about six inches shorter than me. At least partially the picture of a career man, he had close-cropped brown hair parted on the left in a comb over, no sideburns to speak of, and a starched tan uniform with the gold oak leaves on each collar. But he was definitely not of pilot stock, his ample belly pressing out against his shirt, the buttons laboring to restrain it. No way he could fit into the cockpit of any of the fighter jets on base. And first impression also told me he would have trouble pushing his chair in to the maximum when working at his desk. He eyed me suspiciously, my short hair still struggling to help me look human, a giveaway that I most likely did not come from the civilian ranks.

"Is Schlaeger helping you, young man?" he asked, his chubby face showing no emotion.

I decided to play it safe and act respectfully. After all, I would be under his command come the next day. "Yes sir, he is. I report here tomorrow."

He did not extend his hand, but he did introduce himself. "I'm Major Bob Otto. When you say here, do you mean this office? Are you Airman—" he paused, searching in the depths of his mind for my name, "—Forsberg?"

I wanted to make some kind of light joke about the double palindrome of his name but decided against it. Too early to start making waves. And he had those gold oak leaves that far outranked my one lone airman's stripe. "Yes, sir," I said politely.

"Then why aren't you in uniform?" It sounded like a threat. Or maybe at the least a show of contempt for my apparent lack of military bearing.

I thought quickly, hoping to deflect any continued harshness from this man who displayed full awareness of our rank differences. "Sir, I've just spent the last few days driving here from Ohio. I did not want to wrinkle my uniform on such a long trek." Actually, I did not give a shit whether I would have wrinkled it or not. But I had every intention of wearing that uniform only when on duty.

"Well, then, I expect you will look like a poster boy for recruitment when you do report tomorrow," he answered, his expression making it clear he would eye me up and down the next day. He turned to head back to his office, barely spinning his head back over his right shoulder to issue what sounded like a warning. "See you tomorrow, Airman Forsberg." Some men could pull rank just by mentioning it. First impressions told me Major Otto was one of them.

I would be wrong more often than right on that one, as Schlaeger was about to tell me.

Mike smiled. "I won't say you're off on the wrong foot, but you're not off on the right one. But you may eventually find the major somewhat open-minded. For a lifer."

"Thanks. I'll remember that," I replied with a slight grin. "Guess I'd better get out of here and find someplace to prepare for my grand entrance. Don't want to disappoint the major."

I could tell Van Lautenschlaeger found my attitude at least slightly amusing by his expression. But he said nothing about it, instead tipping me about accommodations. "You go out the main gain and turn right, and about half a mile down the highway on the left is a motel. Complete with pool and all ranks of Carefree personnel in cheap trysts. Try to get some sleep.

"And they have irons in the rooms so you can look sparklingly military tomorrow," he laughed.

"And how do you know so much about this motel?" I returned. "You make use of it?"

"As they say in real journalism, I have sources," he chuckled, raising his eyebrows. Made me wonder if he were his own primary source. I could tell he and I would probably form a bond at Carefree rather quickly.

"See you tomorrow," I said, turning toward the door, grinning. "I'll do my best to look my best."

But sometimes best doesn't work out for the best.

When I arrived at the Oasis Motel a few minutes later, only five cars were parked outside. Granted, it was midafternoon, so one should expect a minimum of trysts that time of day. But I also knew military personnel had all kinds of duty hours, so who knew when the facilities there got the most usage?

My room was clean enough but small. I could almost literally open my door, leap over the double bed, and land in the bathroom. Still, it had a dresser where I set my duffle bag and suitcase. It also had a closet with a few wire hangers plus an iron that worked, fortunately, and an ironing board. There was barely enough room between the bed and the dresser to set up the board, and I had to be some kind of contortionist to iron a set of 1505s for the next day. But I managed.

I walked to a nearby eatery, where I had my usual burger and fries. Several personnel from Carefree were there in uniform, but none of them said anything to me, even though my haircut should have been a dead giveaway that I was one of them. A couple of apparent locals ate in one booth behind me, and three Mexicans sat together at the far end of the restaurant, away from all the other patrons. When I finished, I left, speaking to no one except the cashier. "Thanks, that was a fine meal," I smiled and meant it. The food had tasted good.

Back at the Oasis, I tried watching television on the black and white set, but the picture kept wavering in and out even though the place was not that far from Phoenix. Adjusting the rabbit ears antenna would work for a couple of minutes then the picture would begin undulating again like waves on the ocean. Finally, I gave up and went to bed.

When I awoke the next morning, I felt no rush. I wanted to get to the office soon enough so that Major Otto hopefully would have no reason to treat me immediately like the lowly one-striper that I was. But I had no idea when the office opened. Eight a.m. seemed like a good guess.

My car, however, had other plans. It had sputtered and clanked its way from Ohio to Carefree, and apparently, it decided it had had enough. Try as I could, it would not start. So I went to the office. The clerk kindly recommended an auto shop just down the road, so a mechanic came within a few minutes. No luck with him either.

"We'll have to tow it," he told me.

"Fine. Call your truck," I relented. What choice did I have? I could see myself running short on cash in a hurry. Towing expense. Repairs. Living in poverty on an E-2's salary. Hallelujah! The tow truck came almost immediately. I paid for the towing then, and the mechanic gave me his card with his phone number so I could check with him later.

But now, how to get to my work? Even though it was October, so the temperature that morning did not bake everything under it, I did not want to risk a walk to Carefree, making my uniform fodder for Major Otto's disdain. Thanks to a dime, a pay phone, and a telephone book, I called the base, and the operator put me through to the information office. Fortunately, Mike answered the phone.

"Sure, I can come get you," he offered. Without hesitating, he asked, "You are spiffy Air Force clean, I hope?" I assured him that was the case.

My uniform may have been properly starched and "spiffy," but Major Otto found other ways to remind me of our difference in rank. "You decided to report whenever you liked?" he insinuated once I had arrived.

I had suspected he would make some disdainful comments about my not arriving promptly at 7:30 that morning, so I reminded him. "Well, sir, technically, I should report to squadron headquarters first so that they can properly process me. I know they would send me here as soon as they finished. And I assumed, wrongly of course, that the office opened at eight. Plus, I know it probably means nothing to you, but my car decided to die overnight. But fortunately, Mike came to my rescue and brought me here," I nodded toward Van Lautenschlaeger.

Major Otto gave him a disapproving look. Then he glared back at me. "Cars always seem to die at the most inopportune times." He left little doubt that he did not believe me.

I started to reach into my shirt pocket for the mechanic's business card. "You can call this man if you wish, sir," I responded with icy politeness. "He has my Dodge. He can vouch that it's dead."

"I don't have time to check whether you're lying or not. We'll find out soon enough what kind of airman you are." Again he directed his attention to Mike. "Schlaeger, since you've decided to become Forsberg's wet nurse, I suggest you take him to squadron headquarters so that they can process him. Then both of you can come back here and maybe become useful."

"Yessir," Mike agreed with sharp military bearing. "I'll see to it right away."

Major Otto grunted, then turned and headed back to his office. As we started toward the door, I had to tease Mike. "My, didn't we use proper Air Force deportment."

"Sometimes it pays to toe the line," he replied with a serious look. "Besides, the major always acts this way for newcomers. You'll see his loose side soon," he assured me. "Come on. Let's get you to headquarters."

, Processing there took little time, the NCOIC and an underling working with precision to officially bring me on board. The final act was to give me a key and directions to my barracks room. When Mike and I arrived there and unlocked the door, we received a shock. Papers and clothing were strewn all over the room, and one bed was unmade. Hardly a picture of military neatness.

"Oh, God!" Mike exclaimed with a bemused smile. "They've put you in with George Long."

"Who's that?"

"You remember, or have you seen, a cubicle in our office that was untidy as hell? Well, that's where George Long works. I'll let him tell you his story if he's here for your first night in the barracks. If not, I'll tell you myself tomorrow."

I had not noticed the unkempt cubicle. My curiosity rose, but Mike persisted in not telling me about George Long. That evening, I would learn from Long himself that he was the shortest man in the Air Force.

Chapter 5

George Long surprised me, so to speak, as I sat on my made bunk in our barracks room shortly after I had returned there that evening from a typically bland mess hall meal. He expressed more shock at my presence than I did as he stood three feet from me, hair over his collar, buttons missing from his tan uniform shirt complete with frayed pockets and chevrons designating his rank of staff sergeant. His belt buckle edge did not align with his fly, and his shoes suffered from a major amount of scuffing. Despite all these distractions, the most noticeable thing about him was the large indentation in his forehead between his scalp and right eye.

"I'm the shortest man in the Air Force," he explained to me after we exchanged pleasantries. I had tried not to stare at his forehead dent, but he had noticed. "And it's because of this." He raised his right index finger, touched the cavity, then proceeded with his story.

"Just minding my own business that morning this past winter when a VC shell exploded near me, launching a chunk of concrete at my skull. Sure messed the fuck out of me, but fortunately, the doctors say it didn't screw up my brain.

"But because of this," he kept tapping the indentation. The concrete may not have damaged his brain, but his continual tapping sure unsettled me. "Because of this, I'm supposed to get a medical discharge." He paused, whether for effect or to gather his thoughts I could not guess. I just sat and listened, still struggling not to stare at his forehead.

"But I've been waiting for that discharge for months. So I and everything concerning me are in Air Force limbo. So I'm a short-timer. Technically, I have one minute left in the service. Those papers come through," he waved his left arm in a sweeping motion toward the door, "and I'm gone. Faster than shit."

He went on to tell me that he had quickly learned that nearly everyone in authority at Carefree avoided him because no one had any clue as to when his discharge would come through. Word had spread faster than a wildfire that he could be here one minute, gone the next. Assigned to PIO, he received no assignments from Major Otto or Lieutenant Hesse because his separation orders could come through at any time, and Long would become a civilian instantly. Why give him something to do that might have to be handed over to someone else just like that? As his uniform became more and more frayed, he realized no one would discipline him for the same reason. Why set up a guy for punishment if he might be gone before numerous disciplinary forms could even be filled out? So Long allowed his workstation to remain unclean, ignored maintenance of his barracks room, and received no discipline. Not even any warnings.

"Here today, gone tomorrow, as the saying goes," he laughed. I guessed from his demeanor in telling his tale that, indeed, the wound had not damaged his brain. "I hope you won't turn on me like the careerists and do your best to ignore me. It's nice to have company."

"Don't take it personally," I grinned, "but I'm working with Mike Van Lautenschlaeger to sneakily move off base and share his apartment. This might work out well for me. If I promise to come by and visit occasionally, would you agree not to fink on me and tell them I'm not living here?" Then I added what I hoped would be the coup de grace. "I'll even keep my closet, desk, and bunk untidy. And

I'm only here for the four-year obligation, and then adios, muchachos."

Long laughed for a good half minute, then extended his right hand. I took it and shook it warmly. "It's a deal," he said. "Just make sure you do because once I'm gone, you'll need to know. No one except whoever gives me that order will care. But once I head back home, they'll be checking this barracks room. Don't want you to get written up."

"Don't worry, George. If I do, it won't be a big deal. I have no plans to become a model airman. Just bide my time. If I leave the Air Force in August of 72 still with only one stripe, I'll consider my time of service a success."

Long reflected, "I wish I'd had your attitude when I enlisted. Then I felt like I was doing something for America. But now that bureaucracy has kept me here for too long because I'm deemed unfit for service, and lifers treat me like I'm carrying some fatal virus, I don't give a shit."

Perhaps Long would end up leaving sooner than he now expected. And I, of course, had no idea then that my own exit would come some two years earlier and not under conditions that I wished or even anticipated.

Long had mentioned Lieutenant Hesse in our conversation, but I did not press him about Hesse even though I had not encountered him yet at the PIO. That would change the next morning.

"Oh, he's here all right," Mike informed me when I asked him about the lieutenant the next morning. "In fact, he's returned from a temporary duty assignment. He's in the back with Major Otto right now."

Then Mike gave me a cautionary look. "Taylor, one thing about the military. Usually, an office has a non-commissioned officer in charge to handle discipline and other matters. You know, a lifer with at least four stripes. But we don't have one as of now, even though George," he referred to my roommate, "technically is. But you know his story. Old Otto is probably filling Hesse in on his first impressions of you now. Be ready."

My moment of reckoning arrived about fifteen minutes later. The lieutenant came to my desk and towered over me, his silver bars reflecting the morning light coming through a nearby window. He may have had a German surname, but he was not the stereotypical blond-haired, blue-eyed male. Rather, he sported an ebony crew cut and chestnut brown eyes. Then I remembered that Hitler had dark hair and eyes. So much for prejudging. The lieutenant was a good six inches shorter than I but standing over me sitting at my desk made him look six feet taller. I think that's the way he wanted it. His lips crooked to the left, like he was planning to spit out watermelon seeds one at a time. Or maybe some loose tobacco from the Camel he was smoking. Or maybe he was trying to demonstrate his own sarcasm. Who could tell? He did not bother to introduce himself or even welcome me to Carefree's information office.

"Some say you're flip," he uttered authoritatively. Although we were about the same age, he outranked me by nine pay grades. He knew it and wanted me to know it.

"Flip?" I replied with a cold stare. No need to get on his good side, not after that greeting.

"Yes. Flippant," he clarified, apparently not mindful that I, too, had a four-year degree. Mine was in journalism with a minor in English, so I knew my vocabulary pretty well. I wasn't sure what his degree was in, but I guessed it wasn't in literary pursuits. He just seemed too proud of himself for using a word like flippant. Like he had discovered it while thumbing through a thesaurus to find the right word to use against me. I decided to press the issue.

"Who? Who says so? I have a right to know," I challenged.

"Not in the Air Force, you don't."

"Oh." I wanted to use as few words as possible. Editing classes had taught me to be succinct and to the point, So much for keeping the argument alive.

Hesse remained luking over me for a couple of minutes. Neither of us spoke. Just our passionless eyes mirroring each other's like two poker players trying to bluff the other. He took an ashtray from a nearby desk, set it on mine and put out his cigarette, leaving the stub and the ashes there to attack my nostrils. Then, quickly, his lips relaxed to normalcy, he did an about face and marched back down the hall to the office he shared with the major, the superior who had sent him to inform me of my disrespectful attitude.

"Thanks for the welcome," I muttered to myself.

I had to admit he put me in a quandary. How was I supposed to react now? Just go on being glib? Change my attitude to one of submissiveness to avoid trouble? I didn't like that I now was most likely on the defensive. Maybe if I had taken up chess, I would have planned my next move well in advance... But I always felt that I learned best by flying some other way common to the Air Force.

By the seat of my pants.

Schlaeger told me that Lieutenant Hesse had earned a bachelor's degree in business administration but had also been an ROTC student with an after-grad commitment to the Air Force. He couldn't remember from what college, as if that would matter. So the lieutenant's journalism education had come from the Defense Information School in Indiana, where attendees were taught to make such military actions as bombing a children's hospital look like an act of mercy. Or charity.

We would remain at odds for all my time at Carefree. They would come to a head swiftly when they did, but not soon enough. And yet too soon.

By the end of the day, I had met the other enlisted men in the office, five in all besides the omnipresent, omniabsent, and never utilized George Long. They represented the very flower of Sixties American youth. All of them, like me, had joined the Air Force rather than be drafted. Each of them had at least a bit of healthy, youthful humor and cynicism. I almost felt like they had rehearsed their introductions to me.

"I'm Chuck Mitchell," welcomed the only three-striper among the regular office personnel, a ruddy complexioned, strawberry blond about an inch or two shorter than I. "I'm a graduate of the University of Dad's Farm, five miles south of Dyersville, Iowa," he continued with a sly grin. I could picture him back there, clad in Bibb overalls, a strand of wheat straw dangling from his lips. His trusty mutt loping by his side as they herded the cows home from the pasture. True Americana. "I can tell you everything you want to know about cultivating corn."

Mitchell's academic background, such as it was, became obvious when the others introduced themselves.

"From Florissant, Missouri. Name's Mark Petersen" greeted a fair-complexioned blond about an inch taller than I. He did not like to talk in conventional sentences, usually leaving it to the listener to figure out the subject that went with the verb. And he tapped his pen slowly, like a dirge. I would soon learn that he did this with whatever writing utensil he had available whenever he spoke in the office. At least he never banged out his requiems on the typewriter.

"Graduated from Missouri. Degree in History. Can tell you probably everything you don't yet know about how we got stuck in Vietnam." He paused, except for his dirge. He apparently expected a question. "That is, if you ever want to know." His expression suggested that he already knew that I would not.

The last of this group could have passed for Frankie Avalon, with dark hair and immaculately perfect skin. Of course, there was an immaculate aspect to him. He was Catholic.

"I'm Joe Gianelli," he said, extending his right hand. I swore he was about to burst into singing Venus. "I did a little migration from my home in Trenton, New Jersey, to St. Francis in Philadelphia. I received my degree in Biology. I can tell you everything you need to know about the gestation period of groundhogs, even Punxsutawney Phil." He held up a finger, signaling I should not interrupt. "Yeah, I know Phil's a male, but..." Gianelli left it dangling.

"You all sound like you're reading from a prepared script, with only slight variations," I observed. I pointed at each of them as I guessed, "Let me see. Mitch? Pete? And Gio?"

"You're quick," Gianelli replied. "We decided just a few days ago that since everything else in our military lives is uniform, we would come up with a consistent way of introducing ourselves to new staffers. It's another way of succumbing to the military mindset," he continued, with the others laughing. "And we see you're already familiar with standard military nicknames."

"Well, who am I to deviate from the established norm?" I smiled. I then gave them my background, closing with a statement that would cement our relationship as brothers in arms. Or at least in typewriters. "I can tell you everything you need to know about real journalism," intimating that I knew what the office did was public relations and not "real" journalism.

"I'll take you to meet Tweedle Dum and Tweedle Dee," Mike grinned, motioning for me to follow him to a room just before the officers' inner sanctum. Inside its door sat a lot of radio equipment and vinyl records on shelves. And two sergeants.

"I'm Alan Cline from Augusta, Maine," the first one said with a firm handshake.

"I'm Allen Klein from Augusta, Georgia," greeted the second with an equally firm handshake.

I looked perplexed at Mike.

"That's why we call them Tweedle Dum and Tweedle Dee," he laughed. They joined in, as did I. Then they spelled their names for me. Despite their nicknames from Alice in Wonderland, I thought I would have no trouble remembering who was who. One was only about five feet seven and stocky. The other stood as tall as I and of slight build. I would not be able to recognize them by their regional accents. Those had been swallowed by radiospeak, and they sounded nearly identical. Still, I made a mental note to write down their differences in case I ever had to refer to either or both of them in a news release if neither was around for confirmation.

They told me that they had come to their Carefree assignments in somewhat muted states of shock. Cline had come from a stint in Thule, Greenland, six months ago; Klein from Elmendorf, Alaska, in July.

"I sometimes think that the Air Force assignment computer has a sense of humor," Cline observed as Klein nodded in agreement. "How else could the two of us, so similar in names and hometowns, well sort of, come to the desert Southwest from the frozen Arctic?"

The four of us just shrugged.

Mike and I returned to the main part of the office, where I took a seat at my desk next to the drab green partition that separated it from the entryway to the major section of what I learned was the base headquarters building. The base commander, a full bird colonel, and his staff occupied the area just beyond that door. I looked around and noticed the only luxuries in our spartan work area were a water fountain and a Coke machine. I had not expected even that much opulence.

For whatever reason, neither Major Otto nor Lieutenant Hesse came to our area to bother me the rest of the day. The others remained somewhat busy with assigned tasks. But Mike took time to show me the supply cabinet, from which I extracted at least some of the items I felt I would need; a ream of typing paper, a ruler, some Scotch tape, a couple of black ink pens, and a couple of highlighters. Occasionally, some or all of us broke into bits of chatter, but I spent most of my time perusing copies of the base guide and the base newspaper. The base guide obviously was oriented toward careerists and all the amenities available to them, things like base housing and the Officers and NCO Clubs. I suppressed gagging while leafing through the newspaper, the Combat Crew Courier. It overflowed with all the boring articles one would expect to find in what amounted to a house organ. Already, I hungered to see some real journalism, some real reporting. Feel-good back patting held no appeal to me, else I would have majored in public relations. Of course, now I realized that was what I would be stuck doing for the most part.

Mike came to me late in the day with some good news. "Say," he said, looking around to make certain neither of the officers lurked nearby. "Come Monday, we'll get you moved in with me. With you sharing a barracks room with George," he referred to Long, "you're probably safe from any inspections," he reassured me. "But you should at least get a couple of nights of barracks life before you move out. And George will let us know when he leaves, so by then, you'll either have permission to live off base, or we'll figure out some way to make it look like you're using your barracks room."

"How can I refuse such an offer? I had enough of barracks during basic," I grinned, knowing that the less military life I had to live, the better I would feel. "Maybe at least for the first few weeks, I ought to stop by the room to make certain it looks Georgeified."

"You're a cautious man, Taylor," Mike laughed. He paused, then added, "Say! Let's go into Phoenix Saturday. You'll not only get to see the city, but you'll get the joy of transportation via an official Carefree Air Force bus. I'm too poor to use my own gas, so you'll get the thrill of Air Force transportation."

"I'm game."

"I need to warn you, though," he continued. "The bus drops us off at the downtown YMCA, and it's right on the edge of a Mexican section. So our fair skin and short hair will kind of give us away as intruders to at least some of the locals. And we also will be close to one of the hippie havens of this Southwestern jewel."

"Should I borrow a weapon from an MP?" I half-joked. I couldn't tell if he were prejudiced or not against Mexicans.

"Rest easy," Mike tried to assure me. "I don't think it's that dangerous. I've never heard of any major problems for Carefree people down there."

He had not totally succeeded. "What about minor problems?" I asked.

"We'll leave it at that." And so we did.

When Mike came to join me that Saturday morning, he noticed that I had made my bed. He chuckled. "George'll tell you," he indicated the lump under the blanket in George Long's bunk, "that you don't need to be spotless."

I disagreed. "It would be just like them to check on my belongings and remind me that I am not George Long and that I'd better shape up and present the proper military image."

Mike thought for a moment, then nodded. "You might have a point." As we headed out the door, he added, "See you later, George." George or not, whatever lay under the blanket grunted a farewell.

We trooped down to the motor pool, where an Air Force blue bus sat parked outside, its door open. A sergeant sat at the wheel.

"Youguysgointophoenix?" he asked, barely acknowledging our presence. Mike nodded. "Getonboard," the sergeant added. We did. The only ones on board, we took seats in the middle. As he closed the door, the sergeant arched his head back and asked, "dropyouoffattheY?"

"Yep," Mike replied.

We knew from his indifference that the sergeant would not engage in conversation. I assumed this sullen three-striper was pissed that his sole purpose in life at this point was to ferry fellow airmen into Phoenix to get drunk or laid. Or to catch a flight home on leave. I could imagine him grousing, "Ifuckinvolunteeredforthis?" Had to admit that I felt a little pity for him. Had I worn his shoes, I probably would have gone AWOL long ago. Punishment of picking up litter in base beautification would certainly appeal more than bussing other airmen.

Our ride into Phoenix passed quickly. I gazed at the desert, really noticing it for the first time in my life, but it quickly became monotonous. Sand and sparse vegetation can hold one's attention only so long. Mike caught a little more sleep. Our driver said nothing until he stopped the bus in front of the YMCA.

"Hereyouare," he muttered, opening the door. I jostled Mike awake, and we clambered off the bus. He barely got in a friendly "see ya" to the sergeant before the door closed and the bus pulled away.

Both of us reacted with slight starts as we exited the bus. Even Mike, who had come here before. Maybe he did it to create a bond with me, the newcomer.

We may have been deposited outside the YMCA on Central Avenue, but the buildings we saw on the side street at our intersection suggested that we were not in the better part of town. I guess Carefree believed the best place to drop off airmen who had no other transportation was at the Y. After all, it had to be a safe place for young men. Plus, if we strayed into questionable surroundings, we could fend for ourselves. We were military, right? Or maybe those given the responsibility of bussing us back and forth had no clue as to what surrounded the Y.

"Bring any weapons with you?" I asked Mike, laughing nervously.

"Just you," he smirked.

"Thanks a lot."

Mike gave a slight gesture with a nod, suggesting I look to our left. There, approaching us from about twenty yards away, strode a man slightly shorter than me, flowing black hair greased like a hoodlum's, frayed cowboy shirt with studs for buttons, dirty jeans, and badly scuffed boots.

"Great," Mike muttered under his breath. "A fuckin' panhandler. Nice way to introduce you to Phoenix, the jewel of the desert."

The man stopped a few feet from us and smiled. Despite his otherwise shabby appearance, his teeth seemed in good shape. "How would you fellas like to contribute to the delinquency of a drunken Indian?"

His smile was so warm and sincere that he threw us off guard. Mike and I looked at each other, each knowing that the other believed that this guy proved no threat. His tone had totally disarmed us.

94

"I guess there's no harm in that," Mike replied with a slight chuckle. He started to reach into his pocket for his wallet. So did I.

The Indian raised his hand, signaling us to stop. "Hold on, fellas. If you're going to, I want you to join me. It's more enjoyable getting drunk when you have conversation."

Mike and I looked at each other, our eyes uncertain. Who knew what this stranger had planned for us? The man extended his hand. I hesitated, then reached out and shook it. It was a mild handshake, hardly any grasp to it.

"It's how we greet people," he explained. "We don't feel we have to show you how powerful we are or that we want to dominate you. It's our greeting among equals. I'm Navajo.

"And don't you dare call me Tonto," he continued, grinning. "My name's Ed. Ed Begay. With my people Begay is like Smith or Jones for you white eyes. We Begays are everywhere on what you call the reservation. But we call it the Navajo Nation."

"In breeding?" I asked, risking a joke. It must have worked. He took no offense. "Glad to see you have a sense of humor. By the way, Ed, I wouldn't call you Tonto. I know a little more about Indians than just Jay Silverheels. If I wanted to, I'd call you Geronimo or Cochise."

Begay scowled, but it was a light one. "You don't know enough about Indians," he informed us, his eyes moving back and forth between Mike and me to make certain we both were catching what he had to say. "I ain't no fuckin' Apache," he hissed. "I'm Navajo."

Mike and I looked at each other, bewildered, frightened a little, and concerned.

"Sorry," Mike apologized before I could. "We don't know any Navajo names."

Ed laughed, unable to keep a straight face. "Yes, you do, dickheads," he snorted. "Ed Begay," he added, jabbing a finger into his own chest.

"Now, are you guys gonna contribute to my delinquency, or are we gonna just stand here discussing whatever worthless shit comes to mind? You may have noticed we ain't standing in no shade. And it's getting warmer by the minute."

"We will on one condition," I replied. "You stop calling us white eyes, dickheads, and other derogatory names."

"You leave me no choice, paleface," he shot back with a smile. "Unless you tell me your names." So we did. He then turned to head down the side street and motioned for us to follow. "We'll go to Cesar's down this block." He grinned slyly. "They see you with me and they'll let you stay for awhile." He paused, then said cryptically, "Maybe."

Mike and I looked with renewed uncertainty at each other. Then he shrugged, "What the hell." So we picked up the pace and followed our new acquaintance.

Shortly, we entered Cesar's with Ed Begay. Even in the dim, smoky light, we could tell that we were the only white men in the place. A few customers sat at the bar, a couple of threesomes at tables. Every one of the patrons appeared to be Mexican.

"At least I don't see any las furcias," Mike muttered in relief.

"Any what?" I asked.

"Whores. Spanish for whores," Ed interjected.

"Looks like you two might give me a rush education," I noted. Both gave a light laugh.

"This a Mexican bar. No need for ladies of the night," Ed explained. He pointed to a series of booths by the far wall. "We'll take a booth over there. We sit at the bar, and they might not let you two stay long enough to savor your drinks. We sit there, they might think we're talking business."

"What kind of business?" Mike asked. His voice quaked slightly.

Ed laughed. "Nothing illegal. Don't worry. Or if they think it's illegal, they might offer what they think you want."

"Like what?" I asked nervously.

"Weed," Ed snorted. "Or maybe something stronger. Like peyote."

Nevertheless, we hesitated before we finally followed him slowly to a booth at the end of the row of five.

We sat there for several minutes, occasionally getting a look in our direction from patrons and employees. Finally, a man approached us. I assumed he was a waiter, judging from the towel draped over one arm and a pad in his hand. Short and bald, he had a droopy salt-and-pepper mustache that would be the envy of Yosemite Sam. Or the Frito Bandito, take your pick. But I knew better than to bring up my comparison to the Bandito. No need to press our luck with Cesar's inhabitants. Besides, the only other so-called Mexicans I knew of were that hapless Jose Jimenez or the Cisco Kid, who rode around the Old West dressed like he was in a mariachi band.

The Bandito eyed Mike and me without expression, then turned to Ed with a slight smile. "What's your order?" he asked.

Ed nodded to us, indicating we should go ahead. Mike ordered a Coors; I, a rum and Coke. Ed followed up by requesting two shots of Jack Daniels.

After the server left, Mike smiled at Ed and joked, "Jesus, Ed. I thought you wanted us to contribute to your delinquency. Not break our miserable airmen's banks." I could only guess as to the cost of the whiskey.

Ed replied, laughing heartily. "Relax, boys. The next one's on me." He paused. "If they allow you to stay that long."

He picked up what little conversation we had had to that point, turning to a more serious tone. "I sensed from what I had told you thus far that you have some empathy with me," he told us. "You understand what it's like dealing with authorities who don't really respect you.

"I'm betting you both are in the Air Force because you didn't want to risk being drafted to go tramping around in Vietnam, targets for leeches, snakes, scorpions..." He paused. "And the Cong."

"You don't know the half of it," I replied, nodding my head. I did not want to tell the story of my odyssey of real and fake physical papers to anyone else yet. "But that will be for another time."

"You're right. In my case, at least." Mike noted, "Me, too. I don't know what Taylor means by another time, but I enlisted rather than wait to be drafted. They were breathing down my neck."

Ed did not pursue the avenue of our joining the Air Force. Instead, he shifted the focus. He sat there, hands clasped on the table as a wise shaman would do. But I thought it smart not to ask if the Navajos had any. We had already sort of agreed to disregard stereotypes. "Yeah, we see it at all levels, people like you and me. Take those two Johns, for example."

Mike and I stared at each other, perplexed. The only johns we thought he could be talking about were customers of prostitutes. We never thought of them as people in power. Quite the opposite.

Ed sensed our puzzlement. "I'm talking about Ford and Wayne. Those Johns. Those bastards. You know how many times they came to the Navajo Nation and screwed things up?" He paused. "Maybe I'm being a bit harsh on them. After all, they usually came just to Monument Valley and that area, and I lived outside Tuba City. They're about eighty miles apart. I did hear that they paid my fellow Navajos, who worked on their films somewhat. But I don't think they made any of them rich.

"And the way they screwed up with stereotypes and everything. Take that movie, *The Searchers*. The Indians in the film were supposed to be Comanche. And there they were, living in the middle of the desert in teepees. Hell, there's probably never been a fuckin' teepee within five hundred miles of Monument Valley until those Hollywood bastards brought them in for motion pictures."

I interrupted. "At least they didn't put in totem poles. That would have been, what? Fifteen hundred miles or so?" Ed appreciated my input with a nod but then went straight back to his own diatribe.

"Authenticity went out the window. Hell, the chief of the Comanches, Scar I think was his name, was played by a white man.

And he at least looked something in his dress like a Plains Indian. But the rest of the Indians in the film? All Navajo brothers and sisters dressed in traditional Navajo garb. Fuckin' Comanches probably never ever saw a Navajo unless one of them got lost and wandered too far west."

Our drinks came. Mike's Coors was warm. I couldn't tell if there was any rum in mine. Ed quickly downed his first shot, then continued.

"I don't know if they had any of us riding horses in the battle scenes or if they used cowboys wearing wigs. We Navajos aren't good horsemen, best I know. Most of us ride sidesaddle or backwards if we even get on a damned horse."

He changed to a new topic. "Sad to say, but we Navajo can screw other people as well. We have some authority," he smiled. "We got those damned Hopi surrounded inside our nation. Fuckin' snake dancers can't leave their reservation without our okay to pass through our land."

He took his second shot, downed it in one gulp, then slammed the glass to the table top. Mike and I were still slowly nursing our tepid drinks. I began to wonder about the wisdom of joining Ed Begay and the Mexican clientele of Cesar's. Mike did not look too certain either.

I tried getting back on subject. "Snake dancers?"

Ed chuckled. "Yep. Every other year, Hopi men dance around with live rattlesnakes in their mouths, beseeching the gods to provide rain. Hell, it's so dry up there they should dance every fuckin' week until the gods wake up. Or the rattlers kill them all."

Mike pushed his warm beer away from himself. "So, you don't like authority figures pushing at you, but it's okay for you to do that to the Hopi? Show your disdain for them?"

"Come on, youngsters," Ed laughed, his eyes moving back and forth between Mike and me. He turned to me. "Surely you've had some time in your short life when you were lord over someone else. And you took pleasure in it. Am I right?"

I pondered his question, slowly turning my drink glass around on the table. I had no desire to swallow any more of the rumless Coke. I wanted to concentrate on his question. For whatever reason, I deemed it necessary to find something that I had done before that would verify his belief. He was challenging us to realize that we, too, each had been someone who abused some authoritative role we held, if only briefly.

"You know, Ed, you're right," I admitted. "Back in my senior year in high school, a friend and I worked as referees for youth basketball games. There was this game at a small junior high out in the eastern part of our county. We reffed two games. In the eighth-grade game, one guard on one of the teams played tight defense. Kept trying to steal the ball. I decided to foul him out of the game. Merely because I had the authority. I did it, too. Oddly, his coach didn't complain. Maybe he thought I had just cause."

"You say you decided to do it. You knew you had the authority. Did you ever feel remorse for abusing it like you see people in power doing every day?"

I actually felt some shame, even though my abuse of power had occurred more than five years earlier. "Not until now."

"Don't get me wrong, Taylor," Ed added as he unsuccessfully tried to get our server's attention. "We're human. But I've seen enough to know it's wrong, even if I think the Hopi are nothing but shit. Besides, they live about fifty miles from where I did, so I never picked on them." He paused, then grinned. "So you're contributing to my delinquency, and I'm contributing to your real-world education."

I raised my tepid drink. "I'll drink to that," I smiled, taking the smallest of sips.

"So would I," Ed replied. "If I could get another drink." He beckoned toward the bar and bellowed out an *ahem* that caught the bartender's attention. It did not seem to work, so Ed turned his attention back to Mike and me. "Keep fighting authority in subtle ways, irksome but so that those over you won't perceive your acts as threatening. Just annoying as hell. Like me here. I come in for drinks all the time. Every now and then I bring in some white guys like you just to irk the Mexicans. But they like my money. And my color almost makes me one of them. My amigos eventually will tell you to leave. But I beat them."

Mike nodded. "I hope they never figure you out."

By then, the Frito Bandito had reached our table. He smiled at Ed. "Another two shots?" He scowled at Mike and me. "It's time for you two to leave."

Ed did not argue. Nor did we. Too many menacing faces were staring our way from the bar. I just hoped none of them followed us outside. We shook hands with Ed, his grip soft, hardly noticeable. We each took out enough money to cover our first and only round of drinks. Had to contribute to Ed's delinquency like we promised.

"Remember how we Navajo shake hands," Ed reminded us. "No desire to dominate here." Yet he had admitted a difference in attitude when it concerned the Hopi.

"Stay a reprobate," Mike suggested with a smile, provoking a hearty laugh that followed us out the door. We went straight to the Y to await the bus to take us back to Carefree. The same sullen sergeant drove us back. "Youguysgetlaid?" he asked as we boarded. We did not bother to answer. Our trip back to Carefree oozed silence.

Three weeks later, I sat down at the base library after lunch to read that day's Arizona Republic. On an inside page, I came across an article that said a Navajo man named Ed Begay had been struck and killed by a hit-and-run driver outside the downtown Phoenix YMCA. Witnesses said he had staggered off the sidewalk into oncoming traffic. My heart sank. I knew it was our Ed. I wondered if the driver was associated with Cesar's in any way, finally getting back at Ed. As soon as I returned to the office, I told Mike. We both became teary-eyed. Ed Begay had educated us somewhat, and he deserved a better fate.

The Monday after our Phoenix foray, I sold my Dodge for a pittance. But Mike had picked up his 62 Plymouth Valiant and now had the transportation to make living in his apartment possible. One of a complex of three, about two miles north of the base, it sat in a space surrounded by sand and sparse desert greenery. Still, it was home for him, and he had been kind enough to allow me to move in at a reduced rent, so who was I to complain? I did not even joke with him about his Valiant, which seemed to me a far-removed vehicle in quality from my older Dodge, even though my Creamsicle had become a parts warehouse for the buyer.

The apartment was sparse, highlighted by a small living room. Partially separated from it by a wall were the kitchen and an eating area just big enough to allow four chairs and a table. Three steps down from the eating area sat the bathroom, complete with commode and shower/bath combo. To the right of the bathroom entrance stood the bedroom, rather roomy for an otherwise small apartment. It had more than enough space for two single beds, a somewhat large dresser, and a spacious enough closet for both our military and civilian clothes. Behind the apartments was an extended shaded carport. I noted happily that unless the other tenants had a few million cars each, I would have plenty of space to park my car once I bought one.

"You ever cook anything?" Mike asked once we had finished moving in.

"Never."

"Guess we'll be hitting the cheap eateries then." He, too, lacked kitchen smarts.

I had no problem with that but suggested, "Let's at least buy some sausage to cook for breakfast. No way we can screw that up."

"Wanna bet?" Mike grinned.

Somehow we, or I, did the first time, burning our patties while I relieved myself longer than expected. But the next day and subsequent ones, we managed to succeed.

I had been at the office for about a week, mostly shuffling papers, stapling forms, answering phones, and other such challenging work before Lieutenant Hesse finally came to me with a somewhat important assignment. I finally had a chance to do an official press release. I could hardly withhold my joy. Hesse handed me an older release to use as a guide. Then, in a move that paid dividends for me and my sarcasm, he tried to inject some humor.

"Looks like four coyotes and a roadrunner became victims when a Nicaraguan jet crashed this morning down on the gunnery range," he said offhandedly. After telling me to take notes, he dictated information about the accident for me to use. He left, and I perused both my notes and the standard press story that he had given me. I quickly determined that no one would publish my release if I followed form, writing a dry, dull, unimaginative piece that had nothing more than the barest of facts and the requisite last sentence. That sentence would read, "A board of officers will investigate to determine the cause of the accident."

I decided to make use of Hesse's humor, such as it was, and write the story as a comical piece that hopefully would entertain readers. Certainly, the lieutenant would not begrudge my homage to his wit.

I was wrong.

Like any trained newsman, I gave the casualties their rightful spot in the lead, but also decided to make light of the survival of the two Nicaraguan airmen. My masterpiece on base letterhead read:

> For Immediate Release—At least four coyotes and perhaps a roadrunner were killed when a Nicaraguan Air Force jet crashed on a routine training mission over the Cowlic Gunnery Range in southwestern Arizona early this morning.
>
> The crash in the desert occurred approximately seventeen miles west of the small village of Ajo.

Investigators on the scene could not be certain about the demise of the roadrunner as evidence suggested that the coyotes had been feasting on its remains when they met their fate.

The crew of the jet ejected safely, and only one experienced minor injuries. Second Lieutenant Jose Guzman suffered a few puncture wounds to his hands when he tried to extricate his instructor, Major Armando Sanchez, from a saguaro. Sanchez had parachuted onto the cactus after his successful release from the doomed aircraft. Guzman was treated at the Cowlic Range infirmary and released.

Remains of the deceased predators and their possible meal were tossed unceremoniously onto a nearby burning piece of wreckage and incinerated.

A board of officers will investigate to determine the cause of the accident.

Pleased with my effort, I rolled the release off my Remington carriage and strode down the hall, depositing it, appropriately enough, in the in-box on the officers' secretary's desk. Not allowed in the main office itself unless invited or ordered, I exchanged a few pleasantries with Lydia Pearl, the secretary, before returning to my workstation.

Barely five minutes passed before Hesse summoned me into the sacred haven.

"Forsbie, get your ass down here!" the lieutenant's voice echoed down the hall. Maybe he didn't like my plagiarism of his humor after all. So I calmly walked to his office, smiling at a perplexed Lydia as I passed her.

The lieutenant was standing behind his desk, scratching his head in apparent bewilderment at my roguishness, dragging on his Camel. Hesse and I faced each other. Major Otto was nowhere to be seen, to no surprise of mine. I had learned quickly in my first days that the major never seemed to occupy his space in the office unless he had called a staff meeting. His absence reminded me of Major Major in Catch-22, which I had recently started reading. Chuck Mitchell had informed me that if I wanted to understand Air Force lunacy better, then Catch-22 served a biblical purpose for the office enlisted staff.

"What the hell is this, Airman?" the lieutenant demanded as he thrust my news release toward me. He caught me off guard. I had half expected him to call me Forsbie again, to which I would have stood silently, refusing to acknowledge my military nickname. I took the sheet of paper and glanced at it, knowing full well what it was.

"It's my story on the plane crash this morning, Sir," I allowed.

"I know that, Airman!" Hesse's anger was causing his watermelon seed grimace to appear. "Were you trying to be funny?"

I knew full well what I had done, but I still tried to deflect some of the blame onto him even though I also knew he would not allow it. "Well, Sir, those comments you made when you handed the information to me. You know, about coyotes and the roadrunner? I thought maybe we would get more coverage by treating it in a humorous way."

He didn't bite. "We . . . Well, the Nicaraguans lost an aircraft. There's nothing funny about that. Or the way you addressed the one man's injuries. We're not here to make fools of people for others to ridicule." I immediately had a flashback to the Garrettsville UFO fiasco. Damn! Didn't anyone with authority over me believe in journalistic license?

"With all respect, Lieutenant," I replied, "I was trying to make the story more readable. Something that people might get a slight chuckle from. Your comments about the coyotes and roadrunner..." Hesse would not let me finish.

"We're not in the business of being comedians. We're not Bob Hopes."

I thought to myself, "I would hope not." I didn't dare verbalize my play on words. Besides, Bob Hope had lost most of my generation with his support for the war. He had been funny before.

"When it comes to crashes, we put out the facts and nothing but. So take this piece of shit back to your desk, use the release I gave you as a guide, and put out one that looks like the Air Force knows what it's doing. Do you understand, Airman?"

His question left little doubt in my mind. Still, I could not resist doing my best, Joe Friday from Dragnet. I hoped he would not recognize it. "Just the facts. Yessir," I answered indifferently. I would compose a piece consistent with the vapidity of most military news releases. But I had made up my mind to share my original piece of work with my cohorts. Somewhere off base, away from the eyes and ears of Lieutenant Hesse. Returning to my desk, I punched out the boring official Air Force version of the Nicaraguan plane crash in two minutes. Keeping with the military atmosphere, I marched back to Lydia's desk and deposited the fresh paper in the appropriate box. I heard nothing more from Hesse on the matter.

But my sharing of the original with my cohorts, plus my observations on the absences of Major Otto, started other wheels turning. Now began the actions of other co-conspirators in my subtle subversions.

"We need to work in miniscule ways to irk that sour Kraut," Chuck suggested, referring to Hesse as we dined onsubstandard fare in the enlisted men's mess hall. "Let's invite the others to meet up for pizza and beer after we get off work." He suggested Salvino's, an Italian eatery across the street from the garage where I had sold my dead Dodge.

We discretely mentioned Mitchell's suggestion to the others when we returned to the office. All of them, enlistees only in order to avoid the draft, agreed to begin our guerilla war against the nitpicking disciplinarianism of our masters, personified mostly by Lieutenant Hesse.

All but Klein, who said he had other obligations, would attend. "But you can fill me in on how to irk that martinet. But," he cautioned with a smirk, "I won't partake in any fragging." That action was becoming more popular with disgruntled troops in Vietnam. No way it could work as well stateside even if we had wanted it to.

"Don't worry," I assured him. "We're not the murderous types. We just want to keep Hesse in a piss-poor mood as much as possible."

After we ordered our pizza and first pitcher of beer at Salvino's, I had to pose the question. "Cline, you know Allen better than any of us. He's the only one not here. Do we have to worry about him as a mole?"

Alan laughed so hard that we all were glad he had not yet taken a drink of beer. He would have either sprayed us all, or we would have been trying to stop him from choking. "Not on your life!" he roared. "He's as much a dissident as the rest of us."

We sat there trying to decide what to do as our first course of combined action. Finally, Chuck came up with the idea that ended up suiting us.

"Taylor, you brought up your thoughts about Major Otto being like Major Major," he noted. "Maybe we could do something tied into Catch-22 in some way."

Immediately, Gianelli broke in. "What's that?"

The rest of us then related to him what we knew about Heller's novel, evoking laughter from all of us as we recounted some of our favorite episodes from the book. But once done, we all sat munching and musing, trying to come up with some action. Once again, Mitchell came through.

"Why don't we add the name of one of the characters to our sign out board?" he suggested. Situated adjacent to Petersen's desk, it logged in erasable marker wherever we went when we left the office, when we departed, and when we returned. To the precise minute. "We could put it somewhere in the middle so that it would be less noticeable," he added. "But who do we use?" he asked, rubbing his chin in conspiratorial thought.

Yossarian's name came up first, but we quickly dismissed it as one the lieutenant would notice too quickly because of its ethnicity. Gianelli feigned hurt feelings at our dismissal on such grounds. But he rebounded when Petersen, tapping his pen, suggested Lieutenant

Scheisskopf. "Uh!" Joe interrupted almost before Mark had finished. "Scheisskopf? Hesse? Germanic surnames." He thrust a playful scowl at Mark. "Dumbkopf! The lieutenant will see that and think of all the right. . ." He paused. "or wrong reasons for that selection. Besides, he probably knows that it means shithead in German." We all quickly concurred.

Our first one with possibility was Minderbender, but Mike squelched that when he reminded us, "Hell, even my name isn't on there because of its length. Another place where I've been reduced to Schlaeger. It's too long. Hesse would see it before the ink dried."

Then Chuck came up with the solution. "Nately!" he nearly shouted, raising a finger in triumph. Nately constantly tried to keep Yossarian out of trouble in the novel. Our Nately would serve as the opposite, a troublemaker in his own right. And our imaginations. "It fits in so many ways. Do I need to tell you how many?" he asked.

We all shook our heads. Of course. Nately. Short. Unobtrusive. Probably Anglo-Saxon in origin, Then we all formalized it in a unanimous vote with no objections. Nately it would be.

And Nately it was. His name appeared on our signout board about midway through the next morning. Over the next four work days, we would sign him in and out randomly to some place on base that would not arouse suspicion, like the photo lab or the security police office. Lieutenant Hesse would actually have to pay attention to our noted comings and goings in order to discover our ghostly comrade. Apparently, sometime after hours that fourth day Hesse detected Nately, still signed out to the base bowling alley. Less than half an hour into the fifth day, the lieutenant came into our work area and loomed over me while I was seated at Petersen's desk. The incriminating evidence was at my side. Nately had not returned from the bowling alley, staying there overnight, according to the log.

With his trademark watermelon seed scowl in place, Hesse looked directly at me but addressed everyone. He took a puff from his cigarette, blowing the smoke toward me. "Whoever added Nately to our signout board better remove it pronto," he suggested. Without waiting for any reply or movement from the rest of us, he did a crisp military about-face and returned to his office. When he did, I reflexively placed my left thumb between my upper and lower teeth and bit it. We waited until certain that he was out of earshot, then chuckled softly in unison.

"Well, which conspirator will remove our friend from the board?" Gianelli queried.

Mark did not hesitate. Tap. Tap. Tap. "Forsberg has to. No question. We all saw who Hesse most directly gave the order to."

I raised my hands above my head, palms out, in mock innocence. "I just happened to be sitting by the evidence," I protested. Without hesitating, I then swung in my chair, picked up the eraser, and brought Nately's term in the office to a swift end. "Nately who?" I mocked, leaving empty the spaces his name and actions had only recently inhabited.

"I'm glad Nately's gone," Chuck laughed. "He was bad for our pure image, keeping that whore of his." That reference to Heller's masterpiece evoked sniggers from us.

"Who's next?" Petersen asked, his pencil striking his desktop.

"Nobody," Chuck quickly replied. "At least not for awhile. Hesse will no doubt check the board closely every time he comes down here. We'll keep names in storage until we determine the right time."

We never did decide on such a time again. Nately was the only imagined compadre to ever grace our board, stuck for eternity at the base bowling center. We all, including both our radio pals, drank a few toasts to our exiled friend that night while gorging on pizza at Salvino's. Several of us had hangovers the next morning.

One reason that Nately ended up in his unique status was an incident that occurred a couple of weeks after his erasure from our signout board. It sobered all of us enlisted men, at least temporarily, causing us to pause in our disdain for our forced service. But like much of life, the cause of that sobriety disappeared in time, and I, and the others, reverted to our former selves.

Major Otto had called Lieutenant Hesse back to the office from somewhere else on base to introduce him to a visitor. Seated facing the lieutenant's desk was a petite woman with neck-length blond hair, wearing a plain light blue dress. The major introduced her to Hesse, and the three exchanged pleasantries for a few minutes before Otto asked her to step outside and wait by Lydia's desk. He closed the door behind him after escorting her to a seat where she and Lydia began engaging in small talk.

"I want you to assign Forsberg to do the story on her," the major informed Hesse.

The lieutenant objected. "But Major. You know his attitude. He will probably end up writing something thoughtless and irresponsible that would embarrass this office.."

"Hardly," Major Otto rebutted. "Even Forsberg isn't so callous and stupid as to do something like that. If by the slightest chance he did, we'd be on his ass so hard he would never recover. You, me, the wing commander. We'd be justified in busting him below airman basic pay grade. He may be a sarcastic little shit, but he knows the right boundaries. He won't cross this one. Plus, he has a journalism degree, so although he hasn't shown it the way we would like, I think he damned sure knows how to write. So you will assign Forsberg to do the story."

Reluctantly, Hesse relented and escorted the woman down to where we enlisted men were performing some of our monotonous functions. They stopped in front of my desk, where I was editing another dull piece for the base newspaper. This one concerned a baking contest planned by the NCO Wives Club.

"Forsberg, this is Kate Paige," Hesse introduced her. I rose from my desk and extended my hand for a cordial greeting. Her eyes looked somewhat apart from us, like those of an animal trapped in a snare. "She's the president of the base POW-MIA Wives. They don't call themselves a club because they feel that suggests people having fun. They don't." His tone suggested that he believed I did not understand or care about her situation. "Major Otto wants you to do a story on her," he added, again his demeanor indicating that he believed I could care less.

I ignored looking at Hesse, instead focusing my eyes on Mrs. Paige. "I'll do my best for you, ma'am. Although you may find it difficult, feel free to open up to me about you and the other wives' situations," I assured her. I turned back to the lieutenant. "After Mrs. Paige and I have talked, we'll also discuss some way for an appropriate photo op," I noted. "I'm sure you would agree," as I put in a dig at Hesse that he would not dare rebut in front of our guest, "that a photograph accompanying the article will add to its publishability."

"I'm sure you'll do your best," he replied indifferently. Any other time, I would have taken offense and tried to respond in kind, but I ignored his remark. As he turned away, I once again bit my thumb. Then I turned to the woman.

Mrs. Paige and I talked at length, covering some of the personal and difficult aspects of her and other wives in the group. In her case, the anguish was particularly painful because her husband was listed as missing in action. But she also spoke at length about those wives who knew that their husbands were prisoners of war and what torture and ordeals those men were going through, especially those held by the Viet Cong in the South.

Despite my empathy for her, I still used her in a display of disdain for Lieutenant Hesse. After we finished, I escorted her back to the main office. Surprisingly, Major Otto was there, both he and Hesse at their desks.

"Sirs," I addressed them, my eyes focused on the major and ignoring the lieutenant, "Mrs. Paige and I have concluded. I'll begin her story shortly." I paused, then continued, "When I finish, I'm sure you'll want to run it by her for her approval."

The major did not hesitate. "Why, of course," he agreed. Turning to Mrs. Paige, he added, "I'm sure you'll be pleased with Airman Forsberg's work." He nodded in assent toward me. Hesse stood there stoically.

I ended up writing a superb article on Mrs. Paige and the other POW-MIA wives in general "Damn good story," Lieutenant Hesse told me upon reviewing it. I never could figure out, though, if his remark had a long enough pause between *damn* and *good* to indicate his actual attitude. But I guess Hesse had it in for me, nevertheless, because he gave it to Edward Trowbridge, the Phoenix Gazette military affairs writer. Trowbridge used it word for word, but with his own byline. The Associated Press subsequently put it on the wire, with many other newspapers picking it up. Two Phoenix television stations followed up with interviews with Mrs. Paige. I did not mind the lieutenant's obvious snub for a while. The POW-MIA story held more importance than my ego. But the war with Lieutenant Hesse and his embodiment of military crap would resume after this brief ceasefire.

Chapter 6

Major Otto's newfound appreciation for my journalistic abilities, manifested in the Paige article, would cause the next Hesse-Forsberg friction. It was only a matter of time.

Even in the Valley of the Sun, some winter days can be cold, relatively speaking. Highs might reach only into the low to mid forties, with nighttime temperatures maybe dipping into the mid to high twenties. Such was the case nearly a month after my non-credited story on Mrs. Paige and the POW-MIA wives. Major Otto had summoned me into the officers' lair on a blustery day in mid-January.

"Forsberg, we're sending you on a special assignment. Your journalism skills showed through on the Paige story," he complimented me. "Now, we have another duty for you to use them," he smiled as Hesse sat expressionless at his desk.

"Of course, it's a duty. It's the military," I thought but said nothing.

"An F-111 out of Alamo in Nevada has gone missing. A crew from our Air Force reserve squadron will be joining the search. You're going with them. You may be staying overnight at Alamo. So gather enough gear. Come back here and we'll have your orders cut for you."

I thanked him for the honor, noting a chagrined look on Hesse's face. But I also faced a quandary. All my toiletries and other needs were at the apartment I shared with Mike. Fortunately, I had a godsend. George Long had decided to come to the office that day.

"Sure, I'll help, roomie," Long laughed. So far as I knew, it was the first conversation he had had with anyone at the office since I had arrived three months ago. "But unless you can pick up a toothbrush at the BX, you'll have to brush your teeth with a finger," he chuckled. "I have my personal hygiene to consider." This from a man with shaggy hair drooping over his collar and dressed in a slowly disintegrating uniform.

Good old George. He continued to carry a sense of humor with him despite his status as a pariah. I bowed to him in supplication. Then we went together to gather my necessities from the barracks room we shared in name only. We received a few quizzical looks along the way. Who knew how long it had been since anyone had been seen anywhere on base with the shortest man in the Air Force? It felt good to break a rule, even an unwritten one.

When we returned to the office, and Long went to his own personal cell, I hastened to the officers' room and received my temporary duty orders from the major. Hesse was not around, probably sulking somewhere out of Otto's sight. I called for a base taxi to take me to the reserve squadron and convinced my driver to make a stop at the BX so that I could pick up a toothbrush. Like George Long, I had hygiene to worry about, too.

The reserve squadron had its facilities at the lower end of the flight line, almost on the south boundary of the base. It sat in an older building, in need of fresh paint, somewhat neglected, almost like the proverbial poor side of town. Probably a result of the vast majority of the military budget going toward the war effort. After all, these were only part-time warriors, warriors being in the loosest sense. And how much search and rescue pops up stateside? I noted the identifying sign tacked alongside the doorway as I exited my taxi, thanking the airman driver.

"One hundred ninety-ninth Air and Sea Rescue Squadron, Air Force Reserve," I read silently. "It figures," I mused. "A sea rescue group stationed in the desert five hundred miles from the nearest ocean. That's the military way," I scoffed.

My ridicule did not carry over inside. Five men sat together at a table over cups of coffee, the insignia on their flight suits indicating their ranks from tech sergeant up to major. The major spotted me first, rose from his chair, and extended his hand. "No need to salute, Airman," he smiled, introducing himself. "Dom Dellafiora. We're terribly informal here. No need to worry about rank. We're just a social club gathered to skirt snow-capped mountaintops and dangerous ravines looking for a lost plane and crew. You must be the guy from the information office who gets to fly around with us in our jalopy."

"Yes, Major," I nodded, accepting the handshake. I felt comfortable enough and yet still cynical enough that I replied, "You do know the superstition about an albatross, don't you, sir?" referring to the nickname of the aircraft, an HU-16B, the squadron used.

The major and the others laughed. "I repeat. We don't worry about rank here," he smiled. "Even though you have only one stripe."

He continued, "This isn't some centuries-old ship burdened with a centuries-old superstition, Airman. This is a modern, twenty-year-old flying machine. And we know how to fly this bird. And I'll stop calling you 'airman' if you tell me your first name." He paused, then asked, "Want a cup of coffee? We'll lift off in about a half hour."

119

I told him my name Taylor, explaining it was my mother's maiden name. Wanting to show my appreciation for their including me in their select group, if only for a short time, I added, "So what do I call you?" making certain not to add *sir* to my question. He told me they were all on a first-name basis.

Not having a taste for coffee, I declined the offer but sat at the table with them as they each introduced themselves, reinforcing the first-name-only camaraderie. I found them friendly, unassuming, and personable, unlike the majority of the fighter jocks I had encountered thus far at Carefree, who overflowed with egotism. Their warmth made me regret that I had not considered trying to join the Reserves rather than active military. But that time had passed.

When we boarded the plane, I immediately noticed the spartan accommodations. Except for the cockpit and a couple of work areas, the interior consisted of nothing but a row of coarsely-strapped seating areas stretching the length of the plane on either side of the aisle.

"No stewardesses here to offer me a snack," I kidded myself as I sat on the left side of the cabin between two windows. The crew needed those lookouts to search for the missing plane. "But," one of the tech sergeants assured me, "we'll invite you to have a look from time to time. Don't want you to get bored."

I nodded my thanks.

Shortly after takeoff, the same tech sergeant informed me, "We've been given an area in southwestern Utah for our search. Should see some fabulous red rock country. Ever see it before?" he asked.

"Only in pictures," I replied, as I started to shiver slightly, unnoticeably. We were not at a high altitude, but the Albatross was not equipped like the only passenger planes I had flown on. Even though we would be skirting mountaintops, this was one of those January days in the desert southwest when temperatures reminded one that it was indeed winter. I rued that I had not thought this flight would be like one on an airliner and wished I had worn warmer clothes than my tan summer uniform. For an office worker, the Air Force permitted such a uniform year around at Carefree. But in an unheated search plane, one that would scour the landscape for hours, those beautiful olive drab fatigues with a field jacket would have made more sense. Now, too late, I knew that Dellafiora and his crew would not have chastised me for not yet having my single airman's stripe sewn on my fatigue sleeves. After basic, I foolishly hoped I would never need them again.

So I shivered.

Try as I might, and I did not try too hard, I could not enjoy the sometimes up-close scenery of the red rock country below me as the Albatross droned on and on over Utah. Skirting the tops of ponderosa pines, patches of snow, and scattered cattle periodically failed to enchant me or give me any appreciation of the picturesque landscape below us.

And I shivered.

I had never acquired a taste for coffee, but I gladly accepted a cup from one of the crew a couple of hours into our search. Three or four sips of the brew reinforced for me why coffee had not become a favorite beverage of mine. I hoped it might warm me, but...

I continued to shiver.

After my longest flight ever, both literally and figuratively, we finally made our way to Alamo Air Force Base, home of the missing plane and crew and the headquarters for our search operations. Alamo sat, both literally and figuratively, in the middle of nowhere more than two hours by car north of Las Vegas. We taxied to a spot near the headquarters for Alamo's search and rescue unit, where we deplaned and entered the toasty warmth of the building. Our stay was short.

"Bad news, guys," Dellafiora frowned when he returned from a meeting of the search leaders. "Billeting here is full, so they'll be busing us to Vegas and putting us up at a motel. That means a late night and early morning. They'll feed us first, though."

Our Alamo hosts may have intended to cater to us, but my ordeal had caused me to lose my appetite, so I barely touched my plate. Dellafiora tried to encourage me, but I politely declined, saying that I merely looked forward to a good night's rest at the motel. That would not come as my trauma continued on the trip to Las Vegas. Granted, the Air Force bus did have heat, but it was inadequate for the size of the vehicle.

So I shivered some more.

I wasted no time heading for my room once we checked in. "Take a hot shower, Taylor," Dellafiora suggested. "That may help. And," he added, resting his palm on my shoulder, "you call me if you need anything. Hopefully, all you need is a good night's sleep."

I did not get that rest. After my shower, I climbed into bed. Did not even feel like brushing my teeth despite the extra effort I had made at Carefree to obtain a brush. I awoke a few times during the night, sometimes feeling flushed, sometimes shaking, but I did not call Dellafiora. I did not want to do anything to hamper the search, and I knew that he needed a solid rest. I did not even join the crew for breakfast the next morning, waiting until the last minute to drag myself from my room for the return to Alamo. All the men said that I looked better as we boarded the bus for the air base and resumption of our search.

I may have looked better, but like on the ride down, I shivered.

Dellafiora and his crew received their orders for the day while I slumped in an uncomfortable chair in the day room. Fortunately, no one admonished me for being a slouch in uniform. Perhaps that was because the Air Reservists passing through were more intent on their mission than on chastising a sick airman for his unmilitary bearing.

When departure time arrived, I crawled into the Albatross ahead of the crew as they decided to follow me in case I needed a push aboard. As I sank onto the padded seating, I heard Dellafiora instruct Tech Sergeant Bonilla, "Keep an eye on him, Ray. He doesn't look good."

Perhaps Bonilla should have followed those orders more diligently. But he also had the task of searching for signs of the missing aircraft. And I had no desire to remind him, just sitting there jostling in my seat, eyes closed, feeling miserable. When Bonilla did remember to check me closely, about two-and-a-half hours into our flight, it alarmed him.

"Dom!" his startled voice echoed up to the cockpit. "You'd better come here and check on our airman!"

Dellafiora left his co-pilot in charge and rushed back. Noticing my flushed face, he quickly touched my forehead and confirmed what he suspected. "You're burning up, Taylor," he told me, something I already knew. "We need to get you back to Alamo now. Just wish we had a blanket for you." He smiled a caring grin when he said it.

"Want me to sweat off ten pounds in a hurry, Dom?" I responded feebly. He laughed slightly on his way back to the cockpit.

Back we flew to Alamo, where an ambulance awaited us to take me to the base infirmary. With military precision, something I was thankful for at the time, they admitted me with a diagnosis of pneumonia. I stayed there for four days before the doctors deemed me well enough to return to Carefree.

As I improved, I even made a vain attempt to have a date. A particularly vivacious blond first lieutenant, Karen Howe, tended to me more than any other nurse. I suggested that before I left Alamo, we go to the base theater for a movie. True, the movie was The Green Berets, starring a 60-year-old John Wayne pretending to lead men in battle in a strongly pro-military film. But I deemed it worth the sacrifice to spend some time with luscious Lieutenant Howe.

Upon my proposal of such an evening, she immediately switched into military mode.

"Uh, remember, Airman, I'm an officer. Or haven't you noticed my lieutenant's bar?" she asked, becoming quite formal.

"But I have a college degree," I protested meekly, hoping that our similar educations would make us equals.

"But this is the Air Force. . ." She paused. "Airman." That dashed my dreams. For the rest of my last day, another nurse replaced Lieutenant Howe. A major obviously several years older than I, so I didn't even consider trying.

The next morning, hospital personnel placed me on an air transport that had climate control, so I flew back to Carefree in relative comfort. All in all, despite the Lieutenant Howe disaster, my treatment by the Air Rescue crew and the staff at the Alamo infirmary gave me my first positive impression of the military since Sergeants Washington and Downing had pulled strings to save me from the jungles of Vietnam and their resident Viet Cong.

Back at Carefree, Lieutenant Hesse would see to it that the positivity died a quick death.

Chapter 7

"Screwed things up royally, didn't you, Forsbie!" Hesse growled upon my return to the office. Using my military nickname and blowing more Camel smoke in my direction, the lieutenant hinted at what he had in store for me. Since I had barely entered through the door, I figured he had to have been waiting there just so that the first thing I would hear would be his chewing out. Secretly, I appreciated that he didn't disappoint me. I needed his obnoxiousness.

"Hi, Lieutenant! Did you miss me?" I responded in mock cheerfulness.

He caught it. "There you go with your flippancy again," he responded, his face reddening in restrained fury.

Deadpanned, I replied, "But sir, I'm just noting that you're the first person here to greet me after my wonderful stay at the Alamo infirmary. You should know that I'm serious here. The staff there treated me well. So did Major Dellafiora and his crew, as a matter of fact."

Hesse seemed confused. And I thought I knew why. "Major Dellafiora?" he asked.

I realized that he did not know the Major. I hid a burst of triumph that I had one-upped him in a way. "Yessir. He and his men were the crew of the Albatross I flew in."

He made the connection of the name to the HU-16B. Either that, or he already knew it. Nonetheless, he felt compelled to comment. "Surprising, since you screwed up their mission."

"I did? How?"

"By going on the mission unprepared," he growled. "Underdressed for the aircraft you flew in."

"Begging your pardon, Sir," I answered, not knowing whether I would strike a nerve or not, but I would try. "I've only been in the Air Force half a year. So I'm not familiar with some of its aircraft, especially those not quite so vital to the mission here. It would have been nice if someone with a little more Air Force background would have enlightened me."

Hesse glared at me for a long time, knowing full well what I had implied. But again, he did not press the issue. "Your impudence will be your downfall, yet, Airman Forsberg. We sent you on an assignment from which we received no press releases because you, you decided to go unprepared. And the other men here," he waved his hand back toward my fellow enlistees, all of whom pretended not to pay attention. "The other men here had to cover your ass and do double work those days you lay in the lap of luxury at Alamo."

"It was an infirmary, sir," I came close to crossing the line. "I did not luxuriate during my time there." I proceeded, unable to resist. If he wanted flippancy, I would give it to him. "I also asked a nurse for a date."

Hesse's jaw dropped. "What?"

"Don't worry, Lieutenant. She put me in my place. Reminded me of my lowly airman's status compared to her elevated rank of first lieutenant."

"She should have written you up."

"She was too sweet to do such a thing, Sir." I hoped we would not proceed any further. I figured it best for him to have the last word.

"You're fortunate, Forsberg." He did not have to say what he would have done if I had gone too far in military etiquette with him, although I had come close in this conversation. "I'll talk with Major Otto to find some projects for you to do here to make up for your lost time." Again he waved toward the others. "And the burden you put on them." Finished, he marched down the hall to his office. I followed up by biting my thumb.

Once he was out of earshot, the others, as if they had rehearsed their reaction, bent over in unison, then pretended to lift heavy weights from their backs. They laughed as Mitchell said, "You nearly broke our backs with all the work we had to cover for you."

I started to apologize in seriousness, but they waved me off.

Mike even reassured me on other matters. "I stopped by the barracks a couple of nights ago. Long told me that all was fine there. No one had come to inspect," he turned his head toward George's cubicle. As usual, Long had decided not to come in that day. "We had a nice chat," Schlaeger continued. "I might have to sneak over there more often just to socialize with the guy."

"I'll have to join you," I added. "After all, he's been covering my ass at the barracks. But I hope he gets out soon. He's been a short-timer way too long. But I'll have to find some way to get officially off base. George might, as they say, be here today, gone tomorrow."

"Long would like that," Mitchell assured me, although he had admitted once that he had seldom said even one word to George. Chuck belonged to that vast majority of Carefree servicemen who steered clear of George Long, alias Anathema.

Then, Mike asked me, "I've noticed you bite your thumb after engagements with Hesse. A nervous tic?"

"Ever read Romeo and Juliet?" I asked.

"Good God, yes," he moaned. "The girls loved the tragedy over their romance. But it didn't interest us guys, even with all the sword fights and bloodshed."

"I had the same reaction in high school," I continued. "And we really didn't learn much other than rhyme schemes and other literary terms. But in college, I had it again. And the professor enlightened us in so many ways as only a college education can. You remember the opening?"

"No."

The others were listening in, wondering what I was about to reveal.

"Well, in the beginning, guys from the Montagues and Capulets start talking trash, and one of the men bites his thumb at those of the other family," I explained.

"So?" Schlaeger responded.

"As our professor explained, that was the Shakespearean way to flip someone the bird," I educated my partners to their laughter. From then on, whenever Hesse would turn to leave us, we all bit our thumbs. A tradition of disrespect was born.

Hesse soon returned to end our reverie, lugging a thick bound notebook with him. He plopped it on my desk, then addressed me through a cloud of Camel smoke. "This is the latest volume of the base story from our historian." The chronicler, certainly a brother of

Methuselah, had his own alcove near that of the base commander in another wing of our building. My workmates had told me when I first saw him stumbling through our office that he probably had been at Carefree since it opened just in time for World War II.

"He has updated a portion of the work with several hundred new pages," the lieutenant continued. "Excellent work, I might say."

I doubted Hesse had even opened the notebook. Yet I also surmised he may have found it engrossing reading, a riveting page-turner of dull minutiae for the lieutenant.

"Major Otto says you are to proofread this, since you have a journalism degree," he added. I thought I noted a hint of sarcasm from Hesse. "Says you are to look ONLY for misspellings, punctuation mistakes, grammatical errors of that ilk." He could not hide his contempt for me as he finished with a glare. "You are NOT to rewrite history."

I couldn't resist. I had to get at least one punch back in the verbal sparring. "If need be, should I consult with Meth... uh, the historian on anything questionable?"

Hesse did not catch my near jab at the chronicler's age. "That would be wise, Forsberg." With that, he pivoted to return to his lair while I plopped down at my desk and opened the volume. It would turn out to be the most boring compilation of facts, names, numbers, and gibberish I had ever labored through in my life. Even more than reading Crime and Punishment and struggling with Russian names in a college world literature course just a couple of years earlier.

But before I began that tedium, I realized that Hesse, for whatever reason, would not discipline me harshly, if at all. Perhaps he believed that poor airman proficiency reports would suffice, preventing promotion from a lowly one-stripe airman to higher rank and with it, a few extra cents per month added to my meager pay. I could care less about a second stripe, or even more. Like a convict, I merely wanted to serve my time. But be a piss ant while doing it. I would have to exercise caution and do my best to stay within safe borders with my sarcasm and cynicism. The lieutenant did have the rank to screw me royally if he chose.

I did not have to rein in my scorn everywhere, however. So I put it on display that evening when the group of us gathered en masse at the enlisted men's club for a few beers. We decided upon it because the beer was cheap, a local brew that would make horse piss taste good. Or so we assumed. None of us ever had drunk horse piss or admitted to doing so. Not even Mitchell, our resident farm animal expert.

The club had no atmosphere whatsoever; drab tan walls, square tables with chairs randomly spaced around the highly scuffed ages-old linoleum floor. Obviously, the base did not want to waste entertainment funds on the enlisted men, the four-and-done crowd, especially during Vietnam. We enlisted to avoid the Army, and we would disappear back into civilian life once our time of voluntary involuntary servitude ended.

Then there was the girl in the leopard skin bikini on stage, trying her best to look sexy for the few airmen in the hall, but needing to stay within the Air Force level of decency far removed from debauchery. After all, none of us were fighter jocks. Not that it mattered. The girl failed miserably, although my reaction caused her to think otherwise.

She would do some pirouettes and other moves along with a smile she must have thought fetching. But watching her reminded me of when I was ten, and my parents forced me to accompany them to a dance recital where my eight-year-old cousin performed. Fortunately, her family moved out of state shortly afterward, and I never had to endure that pain again.

But there danced Miss Leopard Skin, and every time she looked our way with her obligatory theatrical smile I broke into mild laughter. Apparently, she thought I found her performance enticing because after twirling to Born To Be Wild, she took a break and headed straight for our table. And me. And I knew the guys knew, but they hid their amusement.

"You liked my dancing?" she asked in a failed attempt to purr. Even her tone reminded me of that nightmarish, albeit innocent, evening at age ten.

"Not particularly, Sheena," I replied in the gentlest tone I could muster, although my reference to the 1950s television series about the Queen of the Jungle came from my sarcasm. The girl showed no recognition of my reference.

"What? But you laughed like you enjoyed it."

Obviously, I had offended her. My refinement disappeared in a flash. Remembering that I sat in an Air Force club and had visions of my little cousin whirling and twirling, my antagonisms burst out.

"My laughter was derisive. Your performance, if you can call it that, was pathetic." I had not had too much beer; I just felt grouchy. Plus, I had visions of how fetching and inviting Angela had been on our trip west until she left me near Black Canyon City. "You looked like you were trying to please your mommy at a little girls' recital. That dancing wouldn't get you a man, let alone a job at one of the downtown strip joints." My last comment had no basis in fact. I knew nothing about any Phoenix adult entertainment.

"Do you know who I am?" she huffed, face reddened.

"Well, I know you sure as hell aren't an officer." The rejection by Lieutenant Karen Howe was still fresh in my mind. "You wouldn't lower yourself to perform for airmen like us. And you sure as hell aren't a dependent. No military parent would allow their daughter to play the vixen at an airmen's club. So, no, I don't know who you are."

"I'm someone trying my best to support our troops while so much of the country turns its back on them. That's who I am. A little entertainment does no harm."

"Well then, why don't you go dance with Bob Hope in Vietnam? Guys are just dying to see him over there," I said, hoping she would sense my sarcasm. "Maybe they'd do the same for you.

"Besides, you're hurting me with your attempt at a sexy show," I continued. Those were the last words in our exchange as she stormed away to the ladies' room to collect herself.

Fortunately for me, she had no boyfriend there to come pummel me. And none of the few airmen at other tables had even paid attention to our exchange. But my companions, who had been amused initially, now were bemused.

Petersen spoke for all of them. "C'mon. Let's go. We've been here too long."

"Fuck it," I moaned, rising from the table. As we exited, Somebody to Love by the Airplane started playing. I turned and saw the girl go back on her stage and resume her routine. None of the remaining airmen bothered to watch, too engaged in raillery or boredom, whatever had brought them there in the first place. "You'll never get somebody to love with your routine," I silently scolded Sheena as we left.

On the quiet ride with Mike back to our apartment, I started to rue how I had treated the girl. I told myself I would have to go back and apologize to her. The only thing she had done to me was to be present while I felt pissed at serving in the military.

But I never did acquit myself with her.

The group of us returned to normal office routines the next day. George Long decided to appear and sat alone in his cubicle, perusing a Playboy magazine. Joe Gianelli worked on a droll feature about an enlisted man at the base whose last name had him high in the alphabet and thus "first in line" for so many occasions in which men had to wait. Schlaeger was out with a photographer somewhere working on a photo spread for the Combat Crew Courier. Petersen worked on some old files that Hesse had decided needed rearranging. Klein and Cline were in the radio stall doing who knows what. And Mitchell tried his best to stay awake while doing repetitive articles to send to the Hometown News Center at Blankenship Air Force Base outside Oologah, Oklahoma. Chuck's work all said the same thing, only the names of people and places and maybe ranks differed. I would talk with him about that later.

As for me, I continued wading through the update of the base history. Like Mitchell, I tried not to drift off while doing my mundane work. I had slogged through a few pages over the space of nearly an hour when I came upon a problem that I could not determine if it were a historical mistake or a grammatical error.

The historian had made reference to a B-6 aircraft. I knew that Carefree trained only fighter crews for some years, and his notation placed the planes and the training for them just a little more than a decade before. The letter B designated a bomber; The Air Force used F, P, and A for fighters at different times. Certain that this was a grammatical mistake, I diligently strolled down the hall to the chronicler's cubicle to seek clarification. Unfortunately, I found him leaned back in his chair, nearly tilting over, fast asleep. I decided not to disturb him, instead opting to consider it a mistake of history. Since Lieutenant Hesse had ordered me to correct only grammatical miscues and not rewrite the story of Carefree in any way, I chose not to change the obvious error. I wondered if anyone knowledgeable would ever catch it. But I didn't give a damn.

But I did care as to why Mitchell, like me, showed signs of boredom. So after I closed the historical update, I went and sat across from Chuck.

"Bored?" I asked the obvious.

Mitchell looked up with a sigh. "Yeah." He paused. "And no. It could be worse."

"How do you mean?"

"You do know what I'm doing, right?" he asked. Without waiting for my answer, Chuck continued. "Standard, boring, routine, never-ending blurbs for as many newspapers in the good ole US of A as each item can."

"Sure, I get it, but..."

Mitchell interrupted. "Do you know how overblown this is? Especially since so many guys in our age group are entering the military in record numbers?" He thought for a second before continuing. "Oh yeah, some women enlist too. They get equal space."

I knew Chuck would give me a thorough education on Hometown News, so I encouraged him. "Tell me more," my face exhibiting mock curiosity.

Mitchell didn't miss a beat. "Oh, I planned to. You're a captive audience, especially since you so obviously desire a break from reading another stirring bit of Carefree history.

"First of all," he continued, "I'm lucky I'm doing this here. The Blankenship center has become so overwhelmed with these choice items that the Air Force has issued temporary duty orders for enlisted men from information offices throughout to help. They've been sent to Oklahoma to process these hot news items.

"I lucked out because I have only a couple of months left before I become a civvie again. So Major Otto was able to get my orders rescinded. But plenty of poor schmucks aren't, so they're buried under mounds of this shit in beautiful Oklahoma," he continued.

"Okay, there's lots of us in the service right now, but..."

Chuck interrupted me yet again. I wondered if he did so because he could pull rank. Or maybe he merely wanted to tell his tale. "The problem is," he continued, "the Air Force puts out a news release every time a member does something, no matter how mundane. Take me, for instance. One about me went out after I completed basic training. Then another after I completed defense information school. Then another when I arrived at my first assignment. At Otis Campbell Air Force Base in Massachusetts."

I caught his humor by adding the name of the town drunk in The Andy Griffith Show to the base on Cape Cod. "You're quick," I congratulated him.

"Then, there was another one. I wrote it myself when I arrived here. You lucky bastard. You only have two, seeing as you didn't have to go to propaganda school, what with your journalism degree and all.

"But with hundreds of thousands of folks in the Air Force, every time one of us farts, a hometown news release goes out. Just imagine all the small-town newspapers dotted across the vast American landscape that uses these."

I had to admit the numbers had to be staggering. I also had to admit, "Yep. Stories about the hometown folks, no matter how trivial, are the bread and butter of so much small-town journalism." I told Mitchell about all the riveting stories of street paving and religious revivals I had done in my brief stay at the Garrettsville Bulletin.

"See what I mean?" Then he smiled. "Better hope you don't get TDY to Blankenship after you finish your historical editing of the base history."

I cringed at the thought. Following up that assignment with a mountain of work at a base in Oklahoma with others burdened with the same task could destroy my morale or turn me into an even more bitter cynic. I hoped that Lieutenant Hesse would not consider doing that to me. My hopes rested with Major Otto, who, of course, outranked my nemesis and who also seemed impressed with my journalism credentials even though they had been vastly underused thus far. Still, I wondered if we could do something that might get past Hesse.

"You know, Chuck. You ought to make up some fictitious airmen to send releases about," I suggested. "Just the name would suffice. Everything else would be real."

Mitchell raised his eyes to the ceiling and pondered my idea for a moment. "You know what? You're right. How about Nately?"

Chuck disappointed me, bringing up our recent endeavor from the office signout board. "That name would raise a red flag with Hesse," I cautioned, even though the lieutenant probably never set eyes on hometown news releases. They oozed repetition and enough nothingness that he would not need to check them for accuracy. They just went out in the mail.

"You're right, Forsberg," he replied. Then he deliberated in his mind over how to achieve our new goal. "I know," he slapped his hand lightly on his desk. "We need slight variations of recognizable names but not too obvious." He returned to thinking mode for a moment. "How about Bob Krieger, a slight change from Robby Krieger of the Doors? Subtle, but I'm sure it would get past Hesse if he even happened to see the release. I could have him come from Dyersburg so that I would know if it makes it through. I'd ask my folks if they saw it in the paper."

I nodded in agreement. He had come up with a superb way of making our subversion, such as it was, work. So Chuck typed out a hometown news release for one Bob Krieger of Dyersburg, Iowa, in a matter of minutes. This fictional airman had just come to the Seventy-seventh Ordnance Maintenance Squadron at Carefree after completing rigorous training at Ordnance Maintenance School at Minton Air Force Base, Illinois.

We sat back, smug smiles on our faces until I thought it best to return to my proofreading, and Mitchell went back to grinding out legitimate copy. Except for the usual short breaks and what passed for lunch at the enlisted mess, I spent the rest of the day with the base history update. Shortly before work ended, Mike came and stood over me. "Let's drop by the barracks and visit George. Make sure everything is fine. Maybe he'll let us ogle the naked broads in his Playboys," he suggested.

I thought it an excellent idea. I had not seen any scantily clad or totally nude female skin since the encounter with Sheena. And even if some of the pictures in Playboy needed airbrushing, I would see sufficient female nakedness to end my drought. "I'm game," I agreed.

Long was in our barracks room when Mike and I arrived. Unlike when he supposedly was on duty, he now looked human, dressed in a polo shirt and jeans. He even had his locks combed as neatly as he could, considering their length and his overdue need for a haircut. He guessed the main reason for our visit.

"Come to look at my Playboys, didja?" he cracked a smile.

"We won't lie," Schlaeger admitted. "Yes. But we also appreciate you looking out for Taylor here in your own way." I nodded in agreement. Mike's orbs averted to a couple of Playboys on George's desk. I, on the other hand, could not stop staring at the dent in Long's head. He noticed and reached for a baseball cap sitting on his bed.

"S-Sorry," I stammered, but also defended myself "But seriously, I am amazed that you didn't have any permanent brain damage."

George chuckled, a bit too slyly. "How do you know I didn't?"

139

I started to explain myself, but Long held up his palm to silence me. "It's okay, Taylor. I know you don't think I'm a freak. . . Maybe." Another chortle.

"Seriously, Long, I do thank you for covering for me," I said, now at ease. "But we also don't have the need to shun you like nearly everyone else here feels they must. Have you heard anything more about your separation?"

"I won't hear anything until it's here. Then I'm gone." He could have a subtle sense of humor sometimes. "But if you fellows from the office aren't shunning me, why don't you invite me somewhere when you all get together? Off base, of course. You say you don't have to avoid me, so you wouldn't have to sneak around to pick me up."

"What fun would there be in that?" Schlaeger asked, uncreasing one of the Playboy centerfolds for a full view. "Not sneaking around, I mean. You're right. We will invite you and come pick you up for our next venture off base. But we will come cleverly disguised so that no one can accuse us of breaking the Carefree George Long taboo."

We laughed about that and visited a while longer, with Long lamenting that he had not had any communication about his release from the service in months. "I just want it to end," he admitted, but then added, "however I've found new purpose in being a pariah. I can flaunt my disdain for the absurdities of the military and get away with it.

"But you guys..." he paused. "I see the subtleties you guys have started to do since you arrived, Forsberg. Just enough to irk people like Hesse, but not enough to really create problems for yourselves." Again he laughed, "But I think you went a little too far when you contracted pneumonia."

We kept our word to Long. Since Cline lived closer to the base and likewise did not think of George as a plague, he picked up the Carefree outcast that Saturday to join us for a game of football at a park adjacent to a nearby junior high school. On their short trip to the field, they developed a bond when they discovered they both came from Maine; Alan from Augusta and George from Caribou.

"We talked about Maine stuff," Long beamed when they joined Mike and me at the park. Obviously, he was feeling like a member of society again. "You know. Lobsters. Moose. Blueberries."

"Blueberries?" Mike queried.

"Yep. We supply most of the blueberries in this country. Remember that the next time you have blueberry pie."

"It'll be a first," Schlaeger responded. "Never had it before."

"Don't take Long too seriously," Cline broke in. "He's from so far north in Maine I suspect he might be a Canuck," explaining that Caribou sat near the border with New Brunswick.

We joked about all things Maine until the others arrived, the rest of our office enlisted men and two from the base photo lab. The guys from the photo lab were hesitant about George because of his reputation, but after we assured them they would not contract leprosy, they decided to stay.

We had played for about half an hour with three touchdowns for each team when a group of six parents and ten children approached us. In the lead marched a woman whose air immediately suggested to us that she thought of herself as royalty and of us as peasants. For some reason, she strode up to me.

"We're taxpayers here," she announced. "We've come to use what we pay for so our children can enjoy themselves. So kindly leave," she ordered, not too kindly.

Emboldened by his newfound status as a member of at least part of society, Long stepped up and wedged himself between the shrew and me. "And we're serving in the military to preserve your right to pay those taxes and reap their benefits."

The woman looked around at the rest of us with our military haircuts, then back at George and his long tresses. She scoffed, "I know enough about the air base here to know that you're not in the service. Maybe they are," she indicated us others, "but they'd never allow you to look like that."

Long didn't hesitate, but he did become somewhat deferential. "Au contraire, Ma'am," he countered. "I am in military intelligence. Attended training in Monterey, California. Looking military would hinder our work, so we can grow our hair and also beards if we want, and dress as we like. If I were older, I might infiltrate your PTA to see if anyone has anti-American tendencies. If I'm to infiltrate anti-war groups of people my age, I can't look like my buddies here." He nodded toward us, all trying not to look amused by Long's performance.

"Well, I...", the woman stammered. I quickly prevented her from finishing. After all, it had become my mission to counter people who thought they were authorities. Much as he seemed to relish it, George couldn't carry the full burden in this case.

"You never know, Ma'am. Our intelligence might determine that kicking military personnel out of a public park might be subversive." I paused, figuring that we had made our point.

142

The woman did seem flustered, apparently looking for her next move in our argument. Finally, it came, another laughable one, although none of us laughed. "Well, these are local taxes I'm talking about. You're in the national military."

None of the others said anything, although I knew they thought the same as I did. I wanted to remind her that we were protecting her right to pay all taxes thrust upon her for whatever reasons, but decided not to press the issue further. "Look," I tried to sound kind but knew that scorn permeated my response. "We've had a good time playing football here. But like he said, we're serving so that your little kiddies can play in this one particular paid-for-by-your-local-not-federal-taxes place. So we'll leave now so that they can frolic. Glad we could protect your freedom to kick us off public property. Don't forget to support us as some of us die for that in Vietnam."

So we left. Smiling. Not because we had given the woman a comeuppance, but because we looked back and saw the children having a good time together. Just like we had. We really didn't mind ceding the field to them. Just the circumstances.

"Hope she learned something from that," Petersen observed as we reached the parking lot, then went our separate ways.

On the way back to our apartment, I kept thinking about how Long handled himself despite his long period of Air Force-and-self-imposed quarantine. Schlaeger apparently was thinking the same as he turned the car onto our street. "You know," he offered, "we need to keep treating Long the way we have recently. I think we're good for his sanity anyway." He said that with conviction, and I had to agree.

"I agree," I said with conviction. "So what can we do about it?"

"Let's drive over to the base early tomorrow, hope he's in the barracks, and invite him over to have a few beers with us. Get to know him better. If he's not in the barracks, we still should not have much trouble finding him unless he's wandered off base. Most everyone else will either be nursing hangovers or in church or both."

"Great idea," I said. And meant it. After all, George was covering my ass big time insofar as living on base was concerned.

Finding him the next morning was no problem. We woke him up. And unlike much of the base personnel, he was sober. Nor was he planning on seeking redemption in church. But he opened up back at our apartment after a few beers.

Although he was only slightly older than Mike and I and the others, he came from a different world altogether. The war had not yet become the divisive issue when he enlisted that it had by the time we joined up. Just a couple of years, yet it was like the generation gap.

"I was fucking idealistic as fucking hell," he started telling us. I soon thought that I had returned to Kent and found myself among either the Societe or Undraftables, so punctuated with the ultimate of curse words was Long's vocabulary. Guess it really was more than a sign of the times.

"Believed in Kennedy," he explained. "Then when fucking Oswald shot him, it stoked my Kennedyesque patriotism. You know. 'Ask not what your country can do for you. . .'" He went on. "So I enlisted. Vietnam wasn't much to worry about other than stopping Communism until it conquered all of Asia and that fucking shit.

"Joined up in Sixty-four and stayed stateside until early Sixty-seven when I got orders to Nam. Went over there still fucking idealistic as hell. Even had every intention of making the Air Force a career. For most of my tour, I was fairly safe at the base, until I got this." He tapped the dent in his forehead.

"But I started hearing and seeing all sorts of fucking shit. Heard about soldiers fucking killing women and children in sweeps. Heard soldiers in downtown bars fucking laughing about raping women and girls in the villages. Saw all kinds of military personnel treating the people of Saigon like fucking pieces of shit. Started questioning my desire to re-up. And then, this fucking happened to me." Again he tapped the depression in his forehead, then continued with the tale of his wound. He told us of the Viet Cong assault during Tet, of being hit, of his long recovery.

"But then, the Air Force put me in this fucking no man's land. Deemed me unfit for further service. Shuffled my fucking medical discharge papers in the fucking bureaucracy. Intentionally or not, it turned me into a fucking leper. So I decided 'fuck them'. That's how you see me now. Except you guys," he paused, gathering himself. "You guys didn't fuck with me."

Again, he halted briefly, but this time with a gleam in his eye. "Unless you fucking befriended me just so Forsberg here," he jabbed me lightly with a fist, "could fuck them."

Mike and I laughed with him. His glint and poke convinced us that he believed we had done what we had as much for him as for me. Although he cursed up a storm in his tale, we knew his wound had not damaged his brain. It also became apparent to us as we palled around with him even more until we took him back to the base that his cursing came only when he was angry about the damage the Air Force had inflicted on him. And in a way, although I had come into

145

the service under far different convictions than Long's initial ones, I sympathized with him. But unlike Kennedy's assassination inspiring George's idealism, it furthered the dissolution of mine. Certainly, we both held the same antagonism toward the Air Force. Mine primarily centered around Lieutenant Hesse, who could fuck it.

Although the Arizona desert remained almost continually dry, Hesse loomed consistently as that rain cloud that could dampen my spirits. He had only drizzled, had not yet become a monsoon, and I hoped to keep things that way.

Fortune broke through the Hesse cloud the Monday after our weekend of the taxpaying mother and the revelations of George Long. I had been at my desk only about fifteen minutes when the lieutenant appeared, complete with his customary scowl, his cigarette, and a sheet of paper. He handed it to me and I quickly saw that it contained information on the wing parade that would ruin the morning of the following Saturday for all us enlisted men. Instead of sleeping late, sobering up from the previous night, or prepping for some activity we would enjoy, we would be marching and standing at attention on the Carefree flight line. All to please the wing brass.

"I don't know why Major Otto wants you to do the story on the parade," the lieutenant mumbled. "You haven't shown me the military bearing to merit doing this piece."

I couldn't resist getting in a dig. "Questioning the major's judgment, Sir? That could be dangerous. Maybe he hopes to rehabilitate me."

"Flippant as usual," he retorted. But that was all. He did his usual about-face, then disappeared back to his office. He didn't even bother to leave a cigarette butt in my ashtray.

Petersen, seated at the desk across from me, whooped. "This might be your ticket, Forsberg," he exclaimed with a more rapid than usual tapping of his pen.

"Whaddaya mean?"

"If you were to write a positive article about the parade, especially if you can say something complimentary about some high-ranking officers, you might get the approval you want to move off base," he informed me. "You need to go over to squadron headquarters and fill in a request. It will need the squadron commander's approval, but if you do what I just suggested, you'll get it. Despite all the shit officers dump on us enlisted men, they find ways to reward us when we kiss their asses. Directly or indirectly.

"And... "he paused. He could be a damn good actor at times. "The paperwork will come to the major, not to Hesse."

"Done!" I shouted, leaping from my chair and signing out for squadron headquarters. Within fifteen minutes, I had seen the squadron's first sergeant and filled out the necessary paperwork. Being the noncommittal lifer that he was, he offered me neither encouragement nor discouragement

"We'll see what we can do, Airman Forsberg," he informed me, reading my name on the request. Otherwise, he would not have any idea who I was. A lot of faceless airmen came and went through his office in the course of a day. At least by his count. I doubt if more than a handful came by during his office hours.

Of course, I had to endure Saturday's parade in order for my hopes to come true. And then write up the best parade story I could muster And find some way to inflate the ego of some important officer in my story. But Petersen had given me hope. And fate, in the form of our squadron commander, Captain Howard Plunkett, would play a major role.

The rest of the week went excruciatingly slow, primarily because of the monotonously dull narrative I continued to proofread. But I also looked over it carefully, fearing that the slightest overlooked grammatical error would catch Hesse's eye and I would pay for it. Certainly, he would look for something, anything, to retaliate for my comment about his concerning Major Otto's selection of me for the parade coverage. I did have a brief interlude on Wednesday when I did some editing help for the base newspaper. Then came Saturday and the parade.

The parade! Here I thought that they occurred only in basic training, a way to teach discipline and marching in lockstep. How naïve of me.

"Oh no," Mike corrected me as we searched the gathering troops along the flight line, looking for our squadron's guidon bearer. No greater shame could occur than to march with the wrong group of men.

"This'll be my third since Lackland," he continued, eyes still scanning for our squadron. "I think they occur whenever our scrambled eggs lordships get hairs up their asses or think they may need to boost morale."

"Got a problem with marching on a Saturday, Airman?" a burly master sergeant scowled at Schlaeger. I guessed his grumpiness came from him having to march on a weekend. Either that or he just wanted to flaunt his lifer rank over one of the enlisted peons.

"No, Sergeant," Mike answered crisply. I had to give him credit. He could be quite the airman when it suited him. I still had a few things to learn from him about timing. The master sergeant left us with no further comment.

So we continued waiting for the call to squadrons. I noticed that, of course, the Nicaraguans did not have to march. Nor did the fighter jocks, either instructors or trainees. Royalty did have its privileges. Just the support squadrons of the wing mission had to, so their officers mingled with one another, displaying the decorum their ranks required. Lifer NCOs engaged in raucous conversation, probably a carryover from Friday night at the NCO Club. Or a prelude to Saturday night. We one-term enlisted men, at least most of us, gathered in small groups mumbling and grumbling. All we wanted was to get the damn ceremony over and get the hell out of there and into civilian clothes and more worthy weekend pursuits.

Finally, the call came to formation for each squadron. Obedient servants that we were, we lined up in neat rows and columns behind our guidon bearers and officers. None of us enlistees were allowed on the outer fringes. After all, when each squadron passed the reviewing stand, those on the right edges had to sharply turn their heads to acknowledge our leaders viewing from that exalted place. No one in a squadron leadership role trusted a mere enlisted man with that task. Squadron pride was at stake, and with some of the enlistees having limited education and others having boundless disdain for all things military, the officers and NCOs would take no chances. So we enlistees were fenced in by a wall of lifers.

Once all squadrons had assembled, I finally noticed that we would have a fifty-yard march to our spot before the assembled hierarchy laden with scrambled egg headgear and ribbons galore on their left chests. Just beyond their regal perch, facing toward us, stood the Carefree band fixing to toot and drum our way to our designated spots where we would stand at attention for however long it took for the ceremonies. Ho hum!

That went smoothly enough, although our squadron, being first, had to stay at attention for what seemed a god-awful long time. Finally, the order came for parade rest, and I thought, "Great, We're almost done."

Wrong.

Now the band had its task of prolonging this agony. It started into a military march, natch, and proceeded down the length of the flight line to where we originally had assembled and back again, blaring and drumming a few more marches along the way. I had no idea what was the band's purpose in doing this, but probably its director and a few people on the reviewing stand did. I also wish we would have been able to clap along in cadence with them as they passed twice before us. Or maybe they could have played Country Joe's I Think I'm Fixin' to Die Rag as one of their tunes just for the sake of diversity. But they didn't.

After a few more about faces and other military moves, the wing commander, Brigadier General George Armstrong, made a few comments, mostly commending all of us for our fine military bearing on a Saturday morning and that it was the least we could do while some of our brothers were fighting and dying in Vietnam. "All the more reason for Country Joe," I thought. Then he announced that our squadron had won the supposedly highly coveted award of Best in Parade.

"Hallelujah!" I nearly shouted but caught myself. The general had just handed me what would be my ticket out of the barracks.

If I played my cards right.

Chapter 8

Knowing well my who-gives-a-shit attitude, the others were somewhat stunned by my quick attacking of my assignment on the parade story at the office Monday morning. So intent on organizing my thoughts and putting them on paper for Thursday's Combat Crew Courier, I didn't notice when they apparently came to a consensus on my eagerness. Mike probably suddenly remembered that I had high hopes of my story being my ticket to officially live off base. I had told him the clincher came when General Armstrong announced our squadron as the best in the whole damn parade, the elite of marchers, the epitome of military precision.

I won't give the whole story here, but I will highlight some crucial details. First, remembering that our squadron commander was the one to sign off on my housing request, I used my journalism training to ensure that his name would appear most positively and quickly in my lede. It began thusly.

"Under the dedicated command of Captain Howard Plunkett, blah blah blah . . ." I figured using *dedicated command* right before the captain's good name would clinch it with him. But I also wanted to show my appreciation for Major Otto selecting me to do the story and, yes, suck up to General Armstrong, too. Although I really didn't expect any feedback from him.

So I did some flowery phrasing as well, such as:

"neat, orderly rows and columns," and "smart stepping to the crisp martial music of the band," and "starched 1505 uniforms". And my best effort, journalistically speaking anyway: "low cut dress shoes so heavily polished that they brilliantly reflected the deep azure cloudless Arizona skies warming the flight line Saturday morning. It was as if God Himself were blessing the men and mission of Carefree Air Force Base." I added that last piece because I had seen a photo in another base's newspaper showing a parade float with Jesus predominant on it and the phrase "Power for Peace" emblazoned on the side. So I figured it never hurt to include religion with war and carnage if I could. So I did. It was all bullshit but oh, what an effort on my part!

"I'm sure our squadron commander and several other higher-ups will appreciate this excellent piece of writing," Major Otto, accompanied by a sullenly silent Lieutenant Hesse, congratulated me. He had returned with my article, having made a few inconsequential changes to it. I couldn't tell if the piece needed them or if the major merely wanted to remind me of his rank versus mine.

"Thank you, Major," I said, making certain to eye him directly and avoid Hesse entirely. My compatriots smirked slightly and gave me thumbs-ups as the officers turned back to their den.

Come Thursday's distribution of the Courier, to my disappointment, the day passed with no reaction from any higher-ups to my masterpiece. So I sulked on our way back to the apartment until Mike reminded me, "C'mon, Taylor. Not everyone, not even the brass, stops everything to read the base rag. You'll probably hear something tomorrow."

And so I did. Around mid-morning, an underling from squadron headquarters came to our office with the paperwork I needed to sign. After using my trusty black ballpoint pen to enter my off-base address and telephone number, I was legally no longer a barracks resident.

Captain Plunkett had already signed the form. I could clear out my few things from the barracks before Mike and I headed home. Home. That sounded great to me. And legal. But I wondered how George Long would take losing his roomie who never slept there. Mike and I found him in the barracks, reading an article in one of his Playboys.

"Whaddaya mean, how do I feel?" he shot back after we told him my good news. "It's not like we became bunkmates or anything?" He paused. "What's your name again?" he asked, then broke into laughter.

"I'll help you pack and get your ass out of here," he continued. "After all, you guys have treated me like I was human and not a leper." Another pause. "What are we gonna do to celebrate my return to solitary?"

"We'll help you escape for one night," Schlaeger offered. "Come back with us, spend the night, and we'll talk over a few beers about how to celebrate tomorrow."

"If we're sober enough to enjoy ourselves tomorrow," I warned.

We collected my meager gear and a change of clothes for Long, loaded them in Mike's trunk, and headed back to the apartment. While staying clearheaded despite those few beers, we decided that we would spend part of Saturday hiking around nearby Black Mountain. We called our PIO cohorts, but only Gianelli agreed to meet us there. The others said they had made other plans. Still, I looked forward to the next day's activity.

"After all, I've been here nearly five months and have not really seen the dry, dusty, nondescript scenery up close," I chirped.

"Sounds like you're already doomed to a dull day," Long rejoined.

154

Doom, if one wanted to be pessimistic, almost described that Saturday morning. In early 1969, even with snowbirds from Ohio and Illinois and other points north wintering there, the area around Carefree and the air base was sparsely populated. One couldn't go out and about without having a strong likelihood of seeing someone they knew.

Our someone was actually two people. Gianelli had barely joined us as we started to unload some water and snacks when he sounded an alarm. Quietly. "Uh oh," he muttered. "See who's here." He pointed to a car about twenty-five yards away where a familiar woman was getting out with a group of children. Our chasing-us-from-our-football-game nemesis had come to Black Mountain, too.

"Big fuckin' deal," Long chirped. "We have enough open space here that if she gets bitchy, we'll just find another part of the mountain for hiking. I could care. . ." he paused. We could see something in the opposite direction had caught his eye. We turned to see what, or who, had halted his speech. There, just out of the driver's seat of his four-door Ford Galaxie, stood Lieutenant Hesse. He opened the rear door behind him and crisply called, "Fall out!" Sure enough, two preschool children dutifully climbed out from their perches and stood almost at attention next to the rear fender while their father closed the door.

"I bet those two boys had to sit straight up with their hands folded in their laps for the ride over here," I observed. "His wife probably had to as well."

"Shit!" Gianelli grunted. Referring to the two people we least wanted to encounter on our outing, he warned, "If those two see us and somehow get together, she could make trouble for us with the lieutenant."

"I'm not sure Hesse would come near us," George noted. "After all, the whole base except for you guys treats me like I have bubonic plague."

Mike was not as confident. "I don't want to take that chance," he said. "We can always come here another day or go to another nearby mountain. Whaddaya say, Taylor?" he turned to me. "You're the one who wanted to enjoy the desert sandery."

I agreed that we should not risk those two antagonists somehow joining forces and making trouble, no matter how slight, for us. "What say we just go back to the apartment and hang out? Although deep depression will set in because I didn't get to hug any cactus. I may never recover."

"We'll come some other time," Mike assured me, patting me on the shoulder. "Just hang in there, kid."

Not wanting to give in to boredom and yet with only three television stations out of Phoenix, this Saturday morning now looked unpromising as hell. Once back at the apartment, Mike came up with an idea. "I have my old Monopoly game," he offered. "Let's play it."

Despite initial groans, we decided that Schlaeger's idea had merit. He, Gianelli, and I still had good feelings about American capitalism despite our leanings to the left. And we laughed about the irony of our participating in such a reflection of one of the worst sides of that system, mostly the cutthroat greed reflected in gobbling up competition and property.

Long, despite his treatment by the Air Force since the concrete chunk had caromed off his head more than a year ago in Vietnam, looked at the game as an opportunity. "Nothing wrong with building an empire," he opined. And he wasn't kidding.

Shortly, Long had gained control, through lucky rolls of the dice and shrewd maneuvering, of the properties surrounding Go. We might pass Go and collect two hundred dollars, but we could not make our way through without likely landing on Park Place, Boardwalk, Mediterranean Avenue, or Baltic Avenue. We would pay either a premium or pittance in our passage. But we would still pay Long. And with strategic purchases on the other sides of the board, he quickly bankrupted the three of us. I went first, probably because I had had no training whatsoever in wheeling and dealing.

Mike lasted a couple of circuits longer, but when he landed on Boardwalk with its hotel, he, too, ended up broke. "Fucking capitalist!" he screamed in mock despair at Long.

"Screw you, Ho Chi Minh!" George shot back as Mike and I headed for the refrigerator to retrieve beers for all of us.

Gianelli held out a bit longer, but he eventually succumbed to Long's lust for money, power, and status.

"Maybe we should have let you rot in the barracks after all," Mike growled as soon as Joe had gone belly up. I couldn't tell if he was joking for a moment. Then he burst into laughter. "No way would I do that, George. If anything, we should apologize for not befriending you sooner."

George finished counting his stack of Monopoly money before holding it defiantly in his hand. He thrust it toward Schlaeger. "This. . .is my revenge!" he roared.

"Damn," I responded. "I'd hate to see you avenge yourself against the Air Force."

"I won't bother," Long replied. "When those papers come, I'll be gone. Period. My smoke will put the Roadrunner's to shame," he added, alluding to the cartoon character. He would hold to his word.

With plenty of time still on our hands and with the weather being its routine pleasant way for March in Phoenix, minus the smog, we all finally agreed to try to satisfy my hunger to experience some desert. By this time, Chuck had joined us at the apartment, So we all piled into Mike's Valiant and headed for Squaw Peak in Phoenix, hoping that we would not encounter anyone of the ilk of Hesse or the taxpayer woman.

Our experience there would be quite different, yet a reflection of some aspects of the youth culture. We had been leisurely hiking up the mountain for about half an hour when we saw three people around our age descending toward us. Even when we first saw them approaching, I noticed that the girl looked slight and downright frail. The two men with her looked muscular enough that they could well have been linemen from Arizona State's football team.

The girl greeted us when we met up. "Hi guys," she said coyly, her body language suggesting flirtation. Her companions merely grunted hellos. We helloed back, but I noticed that her eyes were dark and sunken.

We continued to talk for a few minutes, even the men with her joining in. We had trouble following the girl's train of thought. Her impaired concentration, distortion of sentences, and constant yawning perplexed us. But then, her thinking became as clear as the Arizona sky.

"I fucked these two this morning," she said, turning toward the two behemoths beside her. "How about you guys coming back with us, and I'll fuck all of you." She was a forward lass, going straight to the point.

I noticed her two friends did not grimace or object or say anything. But I had a flashback to when my basic flight got to go into San Antonio. A couple of fellow recruits and I were standing on a street corner idling away some minutes when I noticed a young lady get out of an old Chrysler from the Forties. I had noticed it because it looked like the one my grandfather had when I was growing out of diapers. Its driver was bigger than the car. I thought nothing of it until suddenly the girl was standing next to us.

"Y'all want a date?" she asked.

None of us needed to guess or ask her for clarification of what that would entail. Even had we been so inclined, being basic trainees, we all knew we did not have enough money for the frolic she was implying. After we politely declined, I told my companions about the bruiser who had let her out of the Chrysler. They thanked me with pats on the shoulder and paid for my Coke when we stopped for drinks at a stand near the River Walk.

I had the same feeling about this opportunity. The two hulks could have easily pummeled and robbed us once we entered the girl's chamber of delights to delight in the chamber between her legs. I had not had sex since the night before Angela left me and was horny as hell. But I valued my body too much to risk it

"No thanks," I replied, with the others quick to agree. This may have been the era of free love and my scruples may have been in question, but I still had standards.

"Your loss, men," she answered. "Or maybe I should say, boys. Well," she nodded to her two friends again, "these guys will get the ride of their lives again today. Sorry for you."

She nodded disdainfully. The two giants grunted. And our groups went on in opposite directions.

"God! She was a mess," Gianelli said once he was certain they were out of earshot. Coming from St. Joseph's in Philadelphia, he had seen much of the burgeoning drug culture of the Sixties as it grew. "My guess is she was on psilocybin," he explained. Then he gave us a bit of education on the drug scene. We had seen some minor indications in each of our experiences and had stayed clean. Joe had seen much more in that large Philly urban area, but had also managed to steer clear. "But I can assure you guys, it wasn't easy," he added.

"Even at a religious school?" Mark asked.

"Yep. They do keep a close eye on the morals of their students. But the big city drug scene is not quite like corn liquor, is it, Mitchell?" He gave Chuck a scornful look.

"You shouldn't assume, friend," Mitchell quickly retorted. "Iowa is the Midwest. We provide you with your wholesome breakfast corn flakes. We don't have thousands of Robert Mitchums swerving over hills and dales on Thunder Road peddling moonshine." He paused. "Besides, I never drank until I joined the service. The Air Force drove me to liquor."

"Of course you don't act like Mitchum, Mitchell," Mike argued. "You live in shitty Iowa, for Chrissakes. You don't have any hills and dales to swerve over. It's all flat."

160

Chuck quickly replied, "Ah! But we do have occasional curves to swerve around."

I then changed the course of our conversation, telling them of the San Antonio episode, and they agreed that we all may well have received a battering had we taken up the girl's offer.

After that, our visit to Squaw Peak went smoothly, with me finally getting my first real taste of the Arizona desert. I did not hug a cactus, but I nearly got stabbed by a prickly pear. Such can be the hazards of desert hiking. That and solicitation by a woman most likely strung out on mushrooms.

The next week would bring the end of Chuck's tenure in the Air Force. On Thursday, he would receive his separation papers and become a civilian again. So he began it with his short-timer calendar now in the low single digits. The rest of us showed jealousy just so we could rib Mitchell about his successful survival of military life. But mine had a tinge of envy. After all, he was nearing zero days. Yet I still had days of servitude numbering in four digits.

"I have no sympathy for you," Chuck taunted me that Monday when I brought up our differences in fortune. "You enlisted. Just like me. It's not my fault that you showed bad timing. Besides, while I wiled away the hours shucking corn and milking cows, I had a lot of time to contemplate my future. Not my fault you grew up in a city."

"Excuse me for thinking college would enlighten me more than raising cattle," I shot back. "Pasture patties never intrigued me as a part of my livelihood."

"Then you've never known the thrill of that first breath of country air, have you," Mitchell bantered back.

Petersen joined in, switching us from agriculture to our present work. "I don't care how little time you have left, Mitchell," he offered. "But it sure would be nice of you to do some work and take some of this crushing burden off us."

That would become our theme for Chuck's few remaining days. Like most short-timers, he found no reason to do any of the tasks assigned to him as time ran out. If he received any. Mitchell had become a miniature image of George Long, but Long had mastered the craft of idleness out of bitterness. We added extra verve to our bitching by usually saving our complaining for when Lieutenant Hesse was among us.

"Jesus, Chuck!" Mike moaned later that day when Hesse had brought an assignment down to Gianelli. "I've gotta cover your ass while you just sit there doing nothing. And the lieutenant can't do anything about it because you'll be gone Thursday. Won't mess up your APR and hurt your chances for promotion. You might as well read one of Long's Playboys."

Wanting to add to this minor maelstrom, I chimed in. "Must really bother you that you can't write ole Mitch up, huh?" I asked as I stared directly at Hesse.

Hesse could only reply, "Sergeant Mitchell must not think much of you guys. Some friend, forcing more work upon you." He stared coldly back at me, the ever-present cloud of smoke coming from his lips to my nostrils. "Although work might not be the right word for some of you. It's more like dawdling."

And so it went pretty much for Mitchell's last days with us, keeping the tension with Lieutenant Hesse just below his boiling point. So we were in a celebratory mood when we feted Chuck at our apartment Wednesday night. All of us enlisted men, including Long, gathered for Mitchell's sendoff. George admitted he wanted to see how one actually commemorated separation from the service. "It's been so long, I can't remember," he joked.

Chuck had barely settled into our recliner, the seat of honor for this occasion, when I started the digging. "What the hell are you in a rush to get home for?" I asked. A spring snowstorm had hit Iowa the night before. "I see there's twenty inches of snow on the ground there."

"I hate to contradict you," Mitchell contradicted me. " That was Des Moines. We only had eleven inches in Dyersville. Just a dusting. Dad'll have me plowing fields almost as soon as I get off the plane. If it doesn't land in a snowdrift."

"They have airports in Iowa?" Cline deadpanned.

"Good thing you didn't go to Nam and get killed," Long interjected, a glint in his eye. "Your dad would have had to use your remains as fertilizer." He paused, looked down for a moment, then raised his eyes to Mitchell's and rested his palms on George's shoulders. "Sorry, bud. I apologize. That's no way to think. Maybe I let jealousy get the best of me."

Chuck grasped Long's hands and squeezed them. "I feel for you. Have patience. Your day will come. In the meantime, you have these morons to keep you sane."

"To Mitch!" Cline shouted, raising his beer over his head. We all joined in unison, erasing the awkward moment by saluting Chuck with his military-issue nickname. We celebrated the rest of the evening till about ten with just enough raillery and too much beer.

None of us were hung over the next morning, but we all felt a bit woozy. All except Chuck, who flew high from the euphoria of knowing that before noon he would be a civilian again. And he would fly later that day to Dubuque, where his father would pick him up and drive him back to the farm. There, Chuck would reacquaint himself with the scent of cow manure and prepare to work in their snow-covered fields.

I wondered if Mitchell would even think of us that day. And how long, if ever, any of us would hear from him back in his world.

"Oh, you'll hear from me," he assured me with a sly grin. "I want you to come visit once you're out. But give me advance notice. We do, despite what your mind might conjure up, have indoor plumbing. But we still have our old outhouse a couple of hundred feet from our modern facility. You let me know a few days ahead and I'll be certain to use it so that it'll be ready for you. I want you to get the real feel of fresh country scents."

"Just as long as your mother has clothespins I can use to block out your stench," I taunted back.

"You most certainly will sit out there long enough for a shit, Shithead," Chuck retorted. "You'll have to breathe through your mouth eventually. That'll do you in. And don't expect me to come resuscitate you. Hopefully, you'll remain conscious enough to crawl yourself out of there."

"You're such a friend, Mitchell."

Little did we know then that I would visit him sooner than either of us thought.

164

Not much later, Chuck returned to the office carrying civilian clothes on a hanger, entered the office latrine, and emerged a few minutes later carrying his wadded up uniform in his hands. We said our final goodbyes, then he exited, not looking back, leaving his military service behind him.

Our routine became anything but once Mitchell left. By week's end, understaffed with no replacement for him and Long continuing in limbo, assignments piled up. We made certain that items for the Courier made it into the weekly rag, but our enthusiasm for all the other mundane work ebbed below their already squat levels.

Major Otto intervened mid-afternoon that Friday.

"Men," he addressed us. I thought it nice that he considered us men. But after all, we all were in our twenties. "I'm going to think about things here this weekend. Monday, I may have to tell you that you will need to work overtime to catch up. I know we're short. But this is your duty. I expect you to do your professional obligations." Then he paused and smiled, "I have confidence in you." Otto then left, returning to his office. Lieutenant Hesse remained.

"I hope you fellows understood the Major," he addressed us, but looking longest at me. "You will get these things done."

"Yessir," I replied. "He was nice to us," I added, suggesting by my wording and tone that kindness was not a trait of the lieutenant's. It went over his head.

"See you Monday, Lieutenant," Petersen chimed in, suggesting that Hesse leave the room. He ceased his tapping so he could pull over a notepad from a corner of his desk. "Guess I'll get back on this article," he noted as he put a fresh sheet of paper in his typewriter.

Hesse did not reply as he turned and headed toward the back office.

The next couple of weeks were a mixed bag. We found ourselves overloaded with work because no replacement for Mitchell had yet arrived. But with Lieutenant Hesse gone most of that time on a temporary duty assignment, we felt no pressure nor animosity toward anyone. Major Otto, when he did appear in our area, merely checked on our progress without becoming tyrannical like his absent assistant. We, in turn, made certain, as usual, to put our primary efforts into finishing the base newspaper by deadline. Other items took more time and sometimes missed their deadlines, but only with slight delays. Without Hesse-initiated tension, whether by himself or one of us, the office functioned as smoothly as we wanted. We still remained our mostly undedicated selves.

And I finally became owner of another car, purchasing a 1961 Chevrolet Bel-Air coupe from a single technical sergeant who had received orders for overseas. Even though it would become my auto, he insisted that I take good care of it, and I promised him I would. A small obligation to make to get the car I wanted. It certainly was a sporty car, a far cry from the Creamsicle, which had died a few months before. Because of its primary color, I christened it the Bronze Bomb, using just a hint of sarcasm. It was no bomb in the figurative sense; it ran well, unlike the Creamsicle in its last days. But it did belong to an airman, albeit a reluctant one. Now I could share driving duties with Schlaeger and not have to help buy gas. But of course, it added a greater burden to my meager airman's wallet with a car loan and insurance payments and my own gasoline purchases. I felt renewed independence nonetheless.

But change and an addition to our staffing did come about two weeks after Chuck's return to his cow manure and other farm amenities. I was sitting at my desk that mid-morning, next to a partition that prevented me from seeing anyone who came in our main door until he or she stood practically before me.

Someone entered and stopped short of coming into my view. I noticed Gianelli and Schlaeger looking up in surprise just as I heard the newcomer slapping his cheeks.

"Lawdy, lawdy!" a voice screeched from just the other side of the partition. "Jes as Ize 'spected, Ize gwana be yer token Negro!"

Something about the speaker's expression and tone caused my cohorts to burst into laughter. With that, the person came into my view, a one-striper as black as any man I've ever seen. He wagged his finger at Joe and Mike. "Don' you honkies go thinkin' Ize some meek little shit." Then he turned to me and grinned. "You one of dem?"

I felt the same as I thought my buddies did. I hoped this fellow was putting on an act. I raised my hands in mock defense. "Only if you say so."

That caused him to chuckle, moving his gaze back and forth among the three of us. "I'm John Smith, reporting for duty here at the information office."

"John Smith?" I questioned, my expression suggesting this fellow was lying. Not even white guys had that name, let alone a Negro.

"Who y'all 'spectin'?" his voice reverting to stereotype. "Booker Smith, mebbe? Or Roosevelt?"

167

Before I could respond, he pulled out his wallet and took his military ID, waiving it in my face before turning to do the same with the others. Indeed, the card said his name was John Smith. Then he added, "And if you like, I'll show you guys my degree from Columbia."

I couldn't help myself. If any ice still needed breaking, I blurted out, "Ohmigod! An Ivy League Negro!" Smith erupted in laughter. We followed suit instantly.

At that time, Mark returned from an assignment dealing with some of the Nicaraguan student pilots on base. He gave Smith a quick glance, said nothing, and sat at his desk next to mine. Our newcomer pulled up a chair between our desks and rested his right elbow on mine as he faced Joe and Mike. We followed quickly with the obligatory introduction of ourselves, much like the others had introduced themselves to me a few months before. We also told him he would be on his own remembering Cline from Klein in the radio room if he couldn't see their nametags. And even then, confusion often would reign.

"I'm John Smith," he reintroduced himself, following our pattern. "I grew up in the Bronx and have a journalism degree from Columbia. I can tell you all you need to know about headline writing, story placement, and copy editing."

"I've already done that," I interrupted.

Smith looked at me in mock scorn. "Remember, I'm from the Ivy League. You're from a land grant school.

"My parents worked hard to get me that education," he continued. "Dad's a driver for the manager of a Manhattan skyscraper, and Mom clerks at our neighborhood grocery. I received damn good schooling, and I'm happy to know I can use it here."

Mark tried to interrupt, but John kept speaking. "I know this is PR rather than real journalism, but. . ."

Joe interrupted, "We're able to sneak some in from time to time." Then he asked, "You really feel fortunate to be with us? Like Taylor here?'

Smith laughed. "Hell yes! You know how computers are. If my first name had been Booker or Roosevelt, you know where I'd be? I'd be in the motor pool, or worse, laboring at the Officer's Club." He then switched back to his stereotype dialect for an instant. "Yassuh. Nosuh. Would you lak more coffee, suh?"

He continued, "I'm certain that the computer saw John Smith and said this guy can't be a Negro. Not with a name like that and a Columbia education. If my schooling even showed up when the computer went to work. Here, I can say yessir, no sir, and not give a shit about someone else's coffee. I'm a liberated token Negro!" He raised his fist in a Black Power salute. "Don't worry," he assured us as our expressions suggested concern for his doing such. "I looked around and didn't see anyone who looked remotely like a lifer. Just you guys. As your troubadour Dylan says, the times they are a-changin'."

"Indeed they are," Mike echoed as the rest of us nodded in agreement.

Before Mike took him to the back office to meet Major Otto, Joe informed him that we all considered Lieutenant Hesse a prick but that the major, more often than not, treated us fairly. But as per usual, Otto was not in his office. And with Hesse on TDY, the shock of a Negro information specialist would have to wait for those two.

In the meantime, I took Smith to the squadron headquarters so he could officially process in and receive his barracks assignment. Noting that he received a key to my former luxury accommodations with George Long, I filled him in on what to expect on our way there.

He did not get what I expected. John opened the door, started to step inside but paused, surveying the whole room. "Is this the right place?" he asked, finally entering the room. I followed.

"Holy shit!" I exclaimed as I, too, looked around. The beds were made, the desks and floor were cleared of debris, and the floor shone brightly from a thorough waxing. But then we both noticed the wall over the desk that had been George's. He had left a message in bold, black capital letters.

ADIOS MOTHERFUCKERS!

A knowing smile came to my face as I realized fortune had finally blessed my friend.

"Hallelujah!" I shouted, my words echoing off the walls. "Long is long gone!"

Smith and I thought it wise to inform the squadron office of Long's farewell note, but learned when we went back that they already knew. Crews would come in to erase the graffiti before John had to move in. So we went back to the office and surprised our fellow airmen with the news.

After the initial hubbub, Petersen offered Smith a place to stay. "My roommate is out of town for another ten days. So if you don't mind living with a honkey, you can stay till they force you into the barracks."

"You think I never lived with a white guy before?" John chuckled. "How many brothers do you think get into Columbia?"

Mark jokingly guessed one. Smith. But then he offered a great idea. "We need to get together at my place Saturday and celebrate Long's release with a Hairy Buffalo party."

"A what?" Gianelli asked.

"Hairy Buffalo," Petersen reiterated. "It's a drink that'll knock you crazy. Its ingredients are nearly every intoxicant known to man. And some that aren't. And the kicker is the sweetener. Hawaiian Punch. We mix them all in a large bucket, then just dip cups to get our drinks. You guys will love it. It's perfect for an intoxication occasion."

Unanimous accord cemented the celebration. We felt we owed some tribute to our office buddy, now freed from the shackles of Air Force bureaucracy. So we all gathered at Mark's early Saturday evening. Good judgment or not, Gianelli brought his girlfriend, and either Klein or Cline brought his. Without their nametags, I could not be certain. Even after a few months in the Carefree PIO, I still got the two of them confused at times. They just spent too much time in the radio room.

We had all been there for little more than an hour when things began to deteriorate.

"Bastard could at least have said goodbye," Mike moaned, beginning the onslaught of verbal abuse for our departed cohort.

171

"What a son of a bitch," I chirped. I would not allow Schlaeger to be the only one to express his displeasure at Long's exit. No worries. The others joined in.

"Asshole didn't even let us know. Just left," Joe complained. Then it all steamrolled. Everyone, including the girlfriends, had to carp.

"Shithead."

"I hardly got to know him."

"I didn't get to know him."

"Did anyone really know him?

"What'd he look like?"

"How the hell should I know? He was never around."

"Wonder if he thought of us as the motherfuckers he said goodbye to."

"Did he even know us?"

"Who gives a flying fuck?"

This could have gone on until we all passed out, but Mark suddenly raised his cup, spilling some of his drink. "To absent friends!" he toasted.

The rest of us lifted our cups in unison and chorused, "To absent friends!"

"The word's been said," either Alan or Allen added.

"He was my friend too," Smith offered, even though he had already admitted that he had never met him. That made John basically the only one of us who had told the truth.

We all echoed "absent friends", even though we had no idea what that had to do with the salute to our departed compadre. And so the toasts and curses to George Long continued until the last of us passed out. When I awoke the next morning, most of us were stretched out on the floor or the couch or slumped in chairs. I finally realized it was Klein who brought his girlfriend when Cline reminded me which one he was. Allen had left with his date sometime after I blacked out.

But Joe's date, I soon discovered, had stayed. I was still the only one awake when she, Alice Swann, waltzed out of a bedroom wearing only her black lace panties. As she paraded past me, her shoulder-length blond hair, tits, and ass all swayed with the grace her last name implied. This was a parade I could enjoy much more than the one I had endured on the flight line a few weeks before.

"God, Alice! You're a wonderland all by yourself," I complimented her. I tried to sound casual about it, but I guess my drooling gave me away. At least Alice thought so, rather than believe it was the aftermath of my hairy buffalo indulgence.

"Dream on, Taylor," she teased. "I'm monogamous." It seemed she meant it. Still, she stood there erect before me in all her near-naked glory. I was erect elsewhere but trying to hide it from her. Sort of.

"That's okay, Alice," I replied, my eyes roving up and down her gorgeous body. "I'm celibate." Then I told her about Angela and about how she had left me up at Black Canyon City months ago.

Trying to make me feel better, she asked, "Would you be celibate if Angela were here?"

I just shrugged my shoulders. Yes, I ached for Angela, but she had left me. Left me most certainly for an uncertain unknown.

"And you have no idea where she is now?" Alice asked with genuine concern. "Bummer."

"Nope. No word. She might be all right, but her parents never replied to any of my inquiries. They didn't approve of our relationship. And my folks didn't ask. You know how the older generation is."

Alice tried to reassure me. "I bet she got a ride from some kind soul and she's now somewhere safe."

"Or vultures are pecking at her remains off some lonely road after some pervert raped and murdered her," I lamented.

"Don't be so negative," she tried to persuade me. She bent over to plant a light kiss on my forehead, folding her arms across her breasts I guess in case she thought I might try copping a feel. If I did, I would have stopped because right then, Gianelli came into the room bare-naked. I could surmise from his equipment that I couldn't compete with him for Alice's charms anyway. It swung from his torso like a buffalo bull's snout pummeling dirt after he had picked up a cow's scent during the rut. Joe gently took her arm and they returned to the bedroom, coming out fully dressed a few minutes later and said their goodbye to me, still the only one awake. As they walked out the door, I stared at her body, fantasizing about the desire it had induced in me just a few minutes before. Yet Alice had planted a seed, rekindling my never totally lost longing for Angela and hoping for her safety.

Those of us who remained spent the better part of Sunday nursing hangovers. Mark called Klein early that afternoon and learned they had made it safely home, although his girlfriend had spent most of the night throwing up.

"Such are the hazards of Hairy Buffalo parties with the uninitiated," Petersen noted.

As for George, I received a postcard from him from somewhere in Oklahoma a couple of days after our farewell to our absent friend. He apologized for leaving without saying his goodbyes, but invited us to come visit him in Caribou if we ever got the chance. The fact that Long had addressed the card to only me slightly pissed Mike off.

"Hell, I was just as kind to him as you were. Or any of the others," he complained.

"You forget," I reminded him with a poke on the upper arm. "I was his roomie. We never shared a lot of time together in our barracks room. That has to count for something. You were just some meager acquaintance."

Laughing, Schlaeger grudgingly agreed.

Things reverted to normal in their abnormalcy at the office. Lieutenant Hesse returned from his temporary duty and quickly reminded us of how little we had missed him. After he had met Smith, he had returned mumbling to his lair. Klein swore that he had heard Hesse grumble, "Great. A damned nigger," as he passed the radio booth.

None of us were surprised and an amused Smith just shrugged his shoulders. "I've heard that all my life from whities, present company excluded."

175

But the lieutenant would turn his scorn toward me again. The opportunity came compliments of Dwight Eisenhower.

The former president had died at the end of March and several of us were talking about him when I referred to him as "Ike" just as the base commander, Colonel Latham, passed by.

"That's General Eisenhower, Airman," he scowled without even looking in our direction.

"With all due respect, Sir," I replied with all due respect, "when I was growing up, he was a hero to kids like me. And so when he ran for president and re-election, I had my "I Like Ike" campaign buttons to wear. He was that for me and a lot of my friends. The World War II hero."

Latham said nothing as he continued on through our office. But a few minutes later, Hesse came storming down the hall, puffing on a Camel. He stopped just inches from me.

"You just can't stop being flippant, can you, Forsberg?" he grunted. He then told me that the base commander had complained to him about one of his personnel, namely me, having shown him disrespect. To the lieutenant's credit, he assumed the right airman among us.

"Sir," I said coldly, "the others can vouch for me that I fully respected the colonel, even beginning my remarks with such." My fellow airmen all nodded their heads. "And frankly, Sir, I'm surprised at the colonel. Eisenhower was president, the colonel's commander-in-chief just a decade ago. What is the proper military protocol? Shouldn't *he* have referred to Ike as President Eisenhower?" I purposely said "Ike" to irk Hesse, but I held back on suggesting that

176

Latham had shown disrespect by not acknowledging his presidency. I trusted my judgment once again in my dealings with Hesse. Once again, I was rewarded with a harmless rebuke.

"Just watch your flippancy, Forsbie," he finished, then turned and walked back to his office. I did a little wince of appreciation once he left. He had used the dreaded standard military nickname for me. Chalk one up for Lieutenant Hesse. Even though I didn't keep score.

My next chance to irk the lieutenant came a little more than a week later. But it backfired. Hesse had told me that Major Otto wanted me to do a special job on the weekend. I had a feeling that the major had told him to select one of us for the assignment, and the lieutenant had decided that who better to select and ruin his weekend than me. The wry smile on his face as he told me suggested that strongly.

"Forsbie," he addressed me, puffing on his ever-present Camel. "Chaplain Hicks is hosting a group of students from a Carefree church on Saturday and he wants them to see a film about the Air Force mission. So go find one in our library in the radio room. You've been selected to show it. Get to the chaplain's main office no later than 10:30." He paused. "In uniform."

If he expected a reaction of disappointment from me, I let him down. Expressionless, I merely asked him where that meeting would occur.

"Doesn't surprise me that you wouldn't know where the chapel is," he said, thinking it would dig into my conscience. It didn't. I didn't give a damn. I knew damned well the chapel's location, but I wanted to remain contrary with Hesse. So he told me, then stubbed out his cigarette in the ashtray he always managed to make sure was on my desk. Conversation over.

I waited until Friday to venture into the radio booth and leafed through the small library of Air Force films in search of an appropriate one for a group of youngsters all gung ho to spend their Saturday at an air force base celebrating God and country. I found the perfect one.

When I arrived at the chapel Saturday morning, about twenty pimply-faced teenagers and Lieutenant Colonel Hicks awaited me. We went through the obligatory salutes and hellos, then I set up the projector and screen. For the next twenty-three minutes I treated those youngsters to a barrage of color carnage, napalm turning villages into orange and yellow fireballs, trees being blasted out of the ground, falling in flaming heaps back to earth in a barrage of butchery. I remember as a kid thinking these "jelly bombs", as I called them, were fantastic. I had outgrown that years ago. It seemed these youngsters, even though they were in their teens, might still be in that stage. They all watched like they were at the movies; only no one provided popcorn. Hicks thanked me when the film ended.

"Glad to oblige, Sir," I replied, then quickly departed.

"Chaplain Hicks appreciated your film Saturday," Hesse told me early Monday. His expression suggested that he despised complimenting me. I hated it too. I had hoped the chaplain would have complained about the mass destruction I showed those teenagers for twenty-three minutes.

Maybe I just didn't understand some concepts of God and country.

Chapter 9

Maybe I didn't understand some concepts of sex, either. I had had none since my virginity breaking trek westward with Angela nearly six months ago. That certainly did not sit well with this man in his early twenties. With her, it had been love, and I ached for the passion and also the tenderness of our union. But I had no idea where she was since she climbed that highway ramp near Black Canyon City. Letters to her parents asking about her never received the courtesy of a reply. They probably detested me for turning their daughter away from Catholicism and into hippiedom. Even though they had done plenty themselves to accomplish that. I tried not to think that she may have hitched a ride with a rapist/murderer and that her body might lie in some desolate desert or mountain spot only miles away from her scribbled goodbye.

But I still had the urge for sex and it was growing stronger. Masturbation could only go so far. And prospects with a woman were practically nil.

Most of the women at Carefree did not interest me. Not subject to the draft, the majority of the few there were enlisted women. I found those females either unattractive or made the prejudiced decision that they were not my type merely because they most probably had no education beyond high school and I didn't want to find out otherwise. I noticed a couple of attractive female lieutenants, obviously with college degrees, but I remembered my experience with Lieutenant Howe at Alamo. Thus I knew the probability of any kind of intimate relationship with a female officer as nil.

As for the local area, Carefree sat far enough away from Phoenix that only a few bars dotted the nearby landscape. Women frequenting them mostly had set their eyes on officers, married or not, or belonged to the cowboy-booted yeehaw country music crowd and held no attraction for me. Arizona State was too long of a drive to warrant going to Tempe and trying to find a coed who didn't get plowed every weekend. Some airmen in other offices had talked about free love fests at Encanto Park in Phoenix. But taking part in an outdoor group orgy wasn't my bag, nor was the prospect of being busted by cops for public fornication. And I had long ago stopped attending church. Besides, I still believed regular churchgoing women had no interest in removing their panties for a man until marriage.

"I've been here longer than you have, Taylor, and I've had no luck," Mike moaned the last time I brought up the subject of meeting women. "And it's too far to drive to Nevada to take advantage of their legalized women of the night."

Gianelli and Klein, the two who had girlfriends, offered no help. "We were lucky to find them," Klein told me. "And I wouldn't say this in front of my girl. I want to keep her, but none of her friends or Gianelli's girl's friends would turn you on. You have to trust me, as desperate for a lay as you are."

Smith offered no sympathy. " I'm as hard up as you, Forsberg. You think I'm gonna find a sister around here?" he asked, waving his hands in despair. "Are there even any black women in Arizona?"

All the others finished the conversation by echoing Mike.

A few days later, fortune seemed to smile down upon me when a grinning Lieutenant Hesse stopped by my desk. "Lucky you,

Forsbie," he said, too happily for my thinking. "Got word from the squadron that you will have base locator duty Thursday night."

I quickly learned what base locator entailed. I would sit in a lonely room in another building on base beginning at 4:30 that evening and through 7:30 Friday morning. Just me, a bed, a chair, a desk, and a telephone. My duties would consist of answering the phone whenever someone called during that time and answering their inquiries as to how they could reach specific base personnel, either with a barracks number or a home one. I would find out the truth that Petersen warned me about. People would call at all hours. But on the bright side, I would have Friday off, basically a three-day weekend. I was sure Hesse did not realize that perk when he happily told me of my locator duties. Else he would not have smiled broadly.

Fortunately, I would not go hungry for that assignment. Mark brought me a bean burrito and Coke from the base bowling alley. "Enjoy yourself, Forsberg. Parting is such sweet sorrow," he chirped, then left me to my sparse environs. I didn't even have any good reading material, just a few old, old issues of Sports Illustrated, Time, and Field and Stream. At least there were no Air Force periodicals among my choices.

I soon learned that my involvement as base locator became more intense and bizarre the later the night progressed. Beginning around eleven, I started handling calls from obviously drunk officers seeking the numbers of other officers, most likely to get drunk with. Others came from apparently upset wives wondering where in the hell their husbands were this late on a Thursday night. How the hell was I supposed to know? I tried politely to tell them that I merely had the usual contact numbers for base personnel and that they did not have to sign a checkout sheet with me. That did not go over well. To keep

181

things on an even keel, then there were the inebriated NCOs wanting to contact enlistees and chew them out for one reason or another.

The highlight of the evening and the chance for sexual release came sometime after midnight when the calls lessened and I managed to nap. The ringing of my telephone interrupted my sleep. I arose and went to my desk.

"Base locator. May I help you?" I asked in the required polite voice.

"Are you hard?" a female voice cooed on the other end.

Still groggy, I asked, "What?"

"Are you hard? I'm wet, horny as hell, and I want you."

This started to sound interesting, certainly the most fascinating call of the night by a long shot. "Well, I could be," I replied. Such an offer can make a guy wake up in one hell of a hurry.

"Oh! So you want me to talk dirty to you so you can pull it out of your pants and shoot it all over your bed? Wouldn't you rather shoot your cum into me?"

My interest was growing, as was my cock. "Only problem, sweetheart, is that I don't want to have someone walk in on me in the act. And you aren't here to help me with your second option."

"Well, I know enough that I know you won't have to work tomorrow," she purred. She sounded more enticing as the conversation went on. "You want to come into my panties tomorrow?"

Granted, the risks were starting to accelerate. As I noted earlier, I had not had sex with a woman in months, but she did sound worth a shot. I did not hesitate. "Sure. Why not?"

"Oh good," she sighed. "I want you so badly." Her vocabulary sounded somewhat juvenile and I should have pressed the issue, but I didn't. "Only thing is, I have classes, so you'd have to come in the evening. But then, that would be after dark, so that would make our sex even more fun."

"I'm with you there," I replied, hopelessly ready to go for broke.

"Good, Love," she hummed. "By the way, I'm Carol."

Somehow, I sensed she had not given me her real name. So I responded with the first name that came to mind, "I'm Dick."

"How appropriate," she sighed. Only then did I catch what I had done. "By the way. I have a friend, Maxine, who would love a man as well. We can make it a foursome."

I immediately thought of Mike. I was about to venture into territory far removed from the innocence of love only with Angela. "That can be arranged," I promised.

So Carol, or whoever she was, gave me directions which I dutifully, excitedly wrote down. "See you tomorrow, stud," she finished and hung up before I could reply.

It took awhile for my erection to subside, but finally, I felt normal in my crotch area again. The rest of the night went with only a few interruptions to my off-and-on sleep. But when relief came shortly before 7:30, I rushed over to the office and cornered Mike, telling him the good news.

"Hell yes!" he exclaimed.

"Good. Pick up some rubbers on the way home tonight. And by the way, I told the girl my name was Dick. I know what you're thinking, but it was what popped into my head. Don't know if you want to be Tom or Harry, but I'd use a fake one, too, if I were you. Just to play it safe."

Mike laughed slyly. "I'll be Peter."

To which I groaned, "Just because I was too slow to come up with anything other than a double entendre doesn't mean you have to," I called over my shoulder as I left the building.

When dusk came, Mike and I went to my Chevy for the drive to our highly anticipated rendezvous. At the same time, I felt some unease about this upcoming date, although neither I nor Schlaeger mentioned it as he acted as a navigator, reading my directions faithfully.

Shortly we arrived outside the address Carol had given me, a stucco one-story with an arched exterior. Lights shone through the draped front window and Doors music reverberated at a decent decibel level from inside. Carol probably didn't want the neighbors paying attention, so she didn't have the music blasting.

We strode up and I rang the bell. When the door opened, there to greet us were two females in short shorts and tee shirts, no bras underneath. Their nipples pressed against the cotton fabric and their breasts hugged the shirts. But those attributes seemed too immature for who we expected.

When we looked at Carol and Maxine's faces, my unease became more certain. Their skin was too smooth and several pimples dotted Maxine's, a sure sign of underage.

"Hey, Stud. I'm Carol. You must be Dick," the clear-faced one hummed as she approached me. I backed off and turned to Mike, who had an 'uh oh' look on his face.

"What's the matter?" she asked. Fortunately, she did not yet offer any insults. Those would come later.

I decided to get straight to the matter. "Carol, how old are you?"

"Nineteen," she responded immediately, but it sounded rehearsed like she had prepared herself for my question even before we hung up on the phone the previous night.

I surveyed both her and Maxine and also spied a textbook on a table behind them, the same English textbook I had used in high school only a few years before. "You're lying. What's the truth? Fourteen? Fifteen at most?" I did not wait for a reply, instead pointing to the textbook. "That's for high school sophomores."

Carol looked over her shoulder to where I had pointed. "Oh!" she paused, seeming to search for an answer. "That's my sister's."

"Then she's your twin," I called her bluff. "Sorry, but we're leaving."

"What?" Carol huffed. "You decided you're not men enough for us?"

"Not that," I replied, trying to be polite. "But we don't go around having sex with underage girls."

185

"What makes you think we're too young?" Carol persisted. But her tone suggested that I had guessed her age correctly and knew that she had no sister. So I repeated for her.

"We can tell by looking at you. And the way you're acting, like the schoolgirl you undoubtedly are after someone catches you in a lie. You're going to have to get laid by someone else, not us. Statutory rape is not our thing." Mike and I turned back to the Chevy. We could hear Jim Morrison finishing "Light My Fire" from the stereo inside. But Mike and I would not be igniting any flames of passion that night. As he started to climb into the passenger seat, Carol called to us, "What are you afraid of, little boys?" I had to credit her for not giving up easily. But Schlaeger offered the best response.

"Jail time!" Mike shouted back as he closed the door. I turned on the ignition and we drove off, heading back to the apartment and a weekend of beer and moaning about our misfortune in not getting laid and good fortune in not bedding a couple of teenyboppers. Even when I proposed driving into greater Phoenix for a major league exhibition game, we ended up nixing the idea. We would consume only beer and boring television that weekend.

The sexual release would have to wait even longer. I had gone nearly half a year. I could go longer. Not that I wanted to, but sometimes life crosses you up and you have to show patience. And morals. Yes, morals. Even in the free love era.

Life returned to normal Monday as we started a new week of mundane work and the presence of our nemesis, Lieutenant Hesse. The normalcy lasted until late that night.

When we left at 4:30, we dropped by the commissary to buy the makings of spaghetti and meat sauce. We didn't cook that often, but

Mike was hungry for some pasta and quite frankly, was a decent chef with some items. Such as spaghetti.

Our meal tasted slightly different that evening, but we thought nothing of it until just about bedtime. I started to feel queasy, but fortunately, we had some Pepto-Bismol on hand and that seemed to settle me. For a while.

Shortly after midnight, my stomach went into major upheaval and I rushed to the bathroom where luckily, we had an empty waste basket so that both ends of my unfolding disaster were serviced. In the midst of this, Schlaeger suddenly appeared outside the door.

"I heard you were upchucking," he moaned, his face pale. "I don't feel so good myself."

I tried to be humorous. "You'll have to get your own basket," I answered. "Hopefully, you won't need the pot until I'm done."

Somehow we managed to make it through the evening alternating shifts on the toilet but making more use of our buckets than we would like. We determined we were in no condition to go to work, so I called the office and informed Lydia.

"I'll let them know," she replied, "but they won't like it. Especially the lieutenant."

Sure enough, within a matter of minutes, Hesse was at the other end of our phone. Experiencing a respite from his intestinal troubles, Mike answered.

With full officer's authority, without asking how both of us felt, the lieutenant informed Schlaeger, "If you're sick," the emphasis on sick, "you must report to the infirmary." Apparently, Hesse thought we were faking our illness. Plus, Air Force regulations required such a visit.

"With all due respect," Mike replied weakly, with no respect whatsoever, "we're both vomiting and shitting nonstop. If we tried to drive to the base, our car would be full of puke and shit and our uniforms would be soiled beyond repair."

The lieutenant did not press the issue. "Very well, then," he retorted and hung up. Close to an hour later, our doorbell rang. We had an inkling that Hesse had come to check on us, so I answered in my shorts and a t-shirt while holding a puke-filled basket in both hands.

"Lieutenant," I grinned weakly, not lowering my vessel. "Thanks for caring about us and stopping by." I knew full well that he didn't give a damn about our health.

Hesse jumped back from the stench. Clearly audible in the background, Schlaeger was expelling his poison from both ends. Breathing as little as possible, Hesse mouthed, "I guess you both really are sick."

Before he could say more, I replied, "Why would we lie, Sir?"

The lieutenant resumed where he had left off. "I expect you back at the office tomorrow," he suggested just as I spewed a fresh amount of vomit into my basket. He turned back to his car without saying another word.

As he drove off, I shouted with the little flippancy I could muster, "Thanks for your concern."

The next day, weak but able to function, we returned to the office, ready to resume our normal humdrum tasks.

"Justice is served," a smiling Smith greeted us. "I'll let Lydia tell you how."

So Schlaeger and I strode back to her desk. "What's up?" he asked our secretary.

"Glad you boys are feeling better," she smiled. She felt like a mother to us younger men in the office. We appreciated that. "Looks like Lieutenant Hesse suffered your fate. He's out sick today. Believes it's bad beef from the commissary."

Just in case Major Otto was nearby and would not like our reaction, we held our laughter until we joined Smith and the others back in the main office.

When I first saw Hesse the next day, I could not help but ask, "Did you make it to the infirmary, Sir?"

Too weak to muster more than a slight scowl, he yapped, "Flippant as usual, aren't you, Forsbie," and shuffled feebly back to the comfort of his den. He did not bother us anymore that day.

* * *

If my white companions and I used our writing and radio skills to a minimum, Smith went in the opposite direction. He had no desire to be considered that token Negro he joked about. His first shot at excellence came to a couple of days after Hesse's return from his sickbed. Although Major Otto treated us kindly as a whole, he had doubts about John's ability. So when the base band director told him about a newsworthy sergeant there, Otto, who could not give a shit

189

about the band, decided to have Smith write the feature. He told the lieutenant to assign John to do the article. Although Hesse loved everything military, especially the pomp and circumstance of bands and marching, he grudgingly did so. The lieutenant believed that John would write a subpar piece, being a Negro and all, and not do the justice a talented band member should deserve. Apparently, neither officer believed Smith's Columbia degree was legitimate.

Smith's interviewee was a technical sergeant who had recently transferred to the Carefree AFB band.

"I don't know why he's in the middle of nowhere here," John said as he marveled at us about the impresario. "He should be in the highest echelons of military banddom."

Smith's article turned out to be a journalistic masterpiece. It went into great detail about the man's passion for playing several woodwind instruments and his success at composing more than three dozen pieces in various genres. John captured how the sergeant developed a deep love for music inspired by a teacher way back in elementary school and how playing in Air Force bands had helped him achieve his goals.

"My god, Smith, this is a great piece of writing," Major Otto admitted in a meeting after he had read John's draft. He wanted us deadbeats, although he was always too kind to call us that, to take note. Lieutenant Hesse could always handle the insults, which he willingly did.

But John, staying respectful in tone, nevertheless, reminded the officers who had not expected much from him because of his race, "Well, I am Ivy League educated. Columbia School of Journalism, as a matter of fact." As if Otto and Hesse didn't know.

The major didn't flinch. He knew a prize when he had one. "I'm submitting this to Air Force Magazine under your byline. It deserves it. And you needn't remind us in the future of your Columbia education. " Otto's stern look suggested that he had just issued a warning. The lieutenant didn't flinch because he had no clue that Smith had spoken a subtle insult nor that the major had reminded Smith of their differences in rank. And color.

For the rest of our time together in the Carefree information office, John composed journalistic masterpieces that reflected his education. Each time he received praise from the major, he would jokingly taunt us, other lowly enlistees, "Yassuh, see what y'alls token Negro kin do? It's cuz I wents to Clumbya." Then for emphasis, "You nee verse it tee!"

And we all would have a good laugh.

Shortly after his musician-centered triumph, he made a proposal to us as we all were having beer and pizza at Salvino's. He showed us a newspaper he had brought to the table.

"This is West Side Stories, an underground newspaper based over in Glendale. I've had contact with its editor. Talking with her about writing some satirical articles. She's game. You guys want to join in?"

After we all leafed quickly through the issue, Mike and I said we would be glad to join in. The others declined, if only because they had other pursuits.

"We'll be a triumvirate!" Mike declared, raising his glass. We all joined in on the toast.

So over the next couple of weeks, we started our work for Stories. Mine was a satirical look at the occasional love-ins at Encanto Park.

Somehow it worked to the editor's satisfaction, even though I had never been to those festivities. John and Mike also submitted humorous pieces that the newspaper published. All of them carried our chosen byline, Donald Duckworthy. It certainly was a lame take on the then moniker of a Mickey Mouse operation, one mired in bureaucracy or ineptitude. Or both since they often went hand in hand. We must have been drunk when we chose it, but it stuck. I know we had had a few beers each.

"Well, he did cause a ruckus in the openings to The Mickey Mouse Club," Schlaeger noted as we cast our final votes for our pseudonym for that icon of animation, Donald Duck.

John objected to the name at first. "Shee-it," he moaned. "I stopped watching that show when I realized none of the mouseketeers were brothers or sisters. And Spin and Marty? Maybe if it had been Spin and Roosevelt, Roosevelt being a home boy from the ghetto trying to fit in with the white dudes. Maybe then I would have watched it."

Nothing like deciding on something from our childhood to, only a few years removed, show our maturity. We had considered Eldridge Hoffman but decided we didn't want to sound too revolutionary. Eldridge Cleaver and Abbie Hoffman would have to fend for themselves. Eddie Haskell's name came up as well, but fear of a lawsuit from any of a number of sources associated with Leave It To Beaver eliminated him rather quickly. With our limited frame of reference and narrow perspective and John finally relenting, Mister Duckworthy seemed like the safest bet.

Then came The War of the Flies.

We had not tackled anything dealing with Carefree to that point. But when our office suffered a severe fly infestation, we could not pass up the opportunity. On this endeavor, the three of us worked in concert. We decided to play up inflated body counts, which much of the press was now accusing our leaders of doing regarding enemy deaths in Vietnam. As if they would do such a thing. West Side Stories printed our article as follows:

Their infiltration began surreptitiously. First, a solitary, then a second housefly appeared on the window behind an airman's work station with a view that stretched to the Carefree Air Force Base flight line and its contingent of aerial weaponry.

Then a third fluttered back and forth from an ashtray on another desk to the water fountain and the pale green wall behind it. Shortly, a few more made their entrance, suddenly appearing in various spots around the office. By the first day's end, the airmen were aware that more than a dozen of the creatures had invaded their work area. They thought no more of it as they left for the day.

But when the men arrived for work the following morning, they discovered a large number of the pests had joined their companions, a major enemy infiltration.

"They must have flown in via the Musca Domestica Trail," cracked one airman before he and his fellow workers deemed ridding their workspace of the nuisances a necessity. The problem demanded quick action, but the office had neither flypaper nor flyswatters in its inventory. Fortunately for the besieged airmen, there were plenty of periodicals available.

"We each armed ourselves by wadding up copies of the base newspaper," commented another airman. "Then we started swinging and swatting everywhere and the carnage began."

In keeping with their military training, they kept an inflated body count. "There were so many of them. It was hard to tell how many we'd hit in any one swipe," that same airman continued. "You'd splatter the enemy against a window pane, for example, and there'd be a leg here, an antenna there, another body part somewhere nearby. We didn't know if all those came from one fly or more, so in this example, our body count was three. Just to be safe. And to show that they incurred heavy losses while none of us suffered the injury. That's how it's done in war, you know."

Whatever the case, the men saw the light at the end of the tunnel by the end of that second day. By midday of the third, they had totally annihilated their nuisances, which they decided to call the Housefly Cong. The final body count was 7,362 killed HC, none wounded or missing. A complete massacre in what they jokingly called The War of the Flies.

The office staff suffered only one minor casualty. One of the men sustained a bruised thumb when he swung hard and obliterated a pair of flies on his desk. Or at least the body count said two were killed by that action.

Of course, somehow, Lieutenant Hesse obtained a copy of the edition that carried our story. And, of course, he immediately assumed I was the author.

"At it again, Forsbie?" he accused me as he set his copy on my desk.

"You buying subversive newspapers, Lieutenant?" Smith asked him, looking over my shoulder at the folded underground periodical. Hesse's stare at John was not one of amusement.

The story was on the front page, so I took my time pretending to read it. Well, actually, I did read it so that the pretend time would be legitimate. "Sir, I haven't seen this before," I told the lieutenant, looking him in the eye. And I was telling the truth. I had not seen that particular sample of our story before, as it was Hesse's own copy. In fact, the last time I saw the article was on the galley reading for printing.

"It has all the earmarks of your flippancy, Forsbie," Hesse continued. I knew I would have to endure his usage of my military nickname during this confrontation. "So much like your first piece of shit here on the dead coyotes after the Nicaraguan air crash."

"How is that, Sir?" I questioned. "My piece of shit, as you called it, stuck to the facts as they were presented to me." I decided not to remind him that he had been the one to give me those facts. "This story," I pointed to our masterpiece, "has an apparently inflated body count. You know, like some people claim we're doing in Vietnam about enemy deaths. And other parts of this seem to satirize aspects of the war."

"You certainly seem to know much about this story," the lieutenant accused me.

"Well, I am a trained journalist, Sir," I reminded him. "I've learned to observe and absorb quickly and accurately. And I did just read this article. So, yes, Sir, I do know much about it."

My response flustered Hesse, something not all that difficult. He picked up the newspaper and read the article again, apparently searching for anything that might help indict me.

"Well, this first paragraph describes this office," he offered as proof, turning his gaze towards the window noted in that paragraph. Our eyes followed his.

"With all due respect, Sir," Smith interrupted, "that describes numerous 1505 offices on this base." Fifteen-oh-five was the number designation of the tan uniforms worn by office personnel in warm climates throughout the Air Force. Quickly, John defended himself before Hesse could accuse him. "I picked up a copy of the newspaper last night from a hippie selling it outside the bookstore where I went to buy a new copy of Catcher in the Rye. My old copy had become a bit torn and frayed."

"Reading subversive trash, Smitty?" Hesse asserted. The poor man used those damned military nicknames whenever he could.

"Freedom of the press, Sir," John shot back. Politely. "But you have a copy, too, Sir," he reminded the lieutenant.

Hesse's reaction came swiftly. "You getting flippant, too, Smitty?"

"No, Sir. Merely stating a fact. Unless accuracy is flippancy. If so, then yes. But I still say no, Sir."

I had to give the lieutenant credit. For once, he was quick with a reasonable reply, at least from his point of view. "I'm an Air Force public relations officer. It's my job to protect our image from trash like this." Still believing that I, or maybe a few of us, had something to do with the article, he turned to Gianelli. He pointed to Joe's black and blue thumb, which we had referenced in our casualty list. "Get that from swatting flies, Gianelli?" he asked. There was no way he could come up with a nickname from Joe's surname. Though I wouldn't have put it past him had he used any one of the derogatory terms bigots used for those of Italian heritage.

"No, Sir," Joe lied outright. "I jammed it when I slipped getting into my car yesterday afternoon while leaving work."

Mike finally chimed in. "Sir, I know it looks suspicious, what with the fly infestation we had here. But we weren't alone. I heard from friends elsewhere here at Carefree that they had them too." He then added, "Must have been in this immediate area. My friends and I talked about it while swatting away flies at Salvino's. Not much fun trying to eat pizza with flies buzzing around your food."

"I just may check around to see if those bugs bothered others here," Hesse threatened. "I still think you wrote it about this office, Forsbie." With that, he returned to his lair. Whether he checked elsewhere or not, we never found out. Nor did he come back and accuse me, one of a trio of authors of the piece, of being the sole wordsmith.

We celebrated that evening with a flyless meal of pizza and beer at Salvino's. And the swelling in Gianelli's thumb had already started to subside.

While we saluted our War of the Flies coup, Klein suggested an even more daring activity. I knew it was him because I had finally learned to tell who was who between him and Cline, even when no girlfriend was present. Besides, Cline had not joined us.

"I heard that students at ASU will hold an anti-war demonstration on campus tomorrow night," Allen observed. "You guys want to go?"

We considered his suggestion for a couple of moments. I, for one, thought we should until Mike came up with objections. "Look at us," he noted without motioning his arm around our gathering.

"Our short hair is a dead giveaway," he said, stroking what little he had on his head. "If the FBI is watching, we'll stand out like sore thumbs. Or—" he paused, "the students will note our appearance and probably beat the shit out of us as spies."

"Even the coeds?" Gianelli inquired. Then he fluttered his eyebrows like Groucho Marx, "I'd like that."

In the end, we all agreed that Schlaeger had a point, that we should steer clear of any anti-government demonstrations. Smith clinched it for us when he observed, "Hell, I don't even go to any civil rights marches anymore. Same reasons as Schlaeger's here. My absence of the requisite Afro would give me away to the wrong people."

But our discussion caused me to decide to come up with another way to possibly get under Hesse's skin. Why not get a map of Sweden and place it under my Plexiglas? With some American servicemen deserting to that heaven of no extradition and plenty of nubile blonds,

I figured the lieutenant would have some snide remark to make about it. He would not disappoint me.

That night, I wrote a letter to the Swedish consulate in Phoenix, noting my surname and requesting a map of the country. Within a few days, it came. The following morning, I took it to the office... I immediately unfolded the map, took out a yellow highlighter from my center drawer and marked Ystad, the coastal town from which my paternal grandparents had immigrated late in the nineteenth century. Then I proudly placed it under the Plexiglas on my desk. I then cut out a small Swedish flag from some additional literature they had kindly sent and taped it to my Plexiglas. What a beautiful sight! What a great trap for the lieutenant to bite on.

Shortly afterward, Lieutenant Hesse was standing over my desk, blowing his cigarette smoke my way as he so often did. "What's this, Forsbie?" he inquired out the side of his mouth as he surveyed my new desk adornment.

"A map of my ancestral homeland, Sir." I decided to insult his intelligence by stating something I was certain even he knew. "Forsberg is Swedish. Proud of my heritage." The pride statement was sort of a lie. Thanks to my friction with my father, my feelings towards my Swedish legacy were lukewarm. If the lieutenant had asked me the difference between a Swedish meatball and a Swedish massage, I would have had difficulty telling him the difference.

Instead, he directed his attention to the flag.

"Ah, Sweden. I notice the yellow stripes on your flag," he said, thrusting a finger and billow of smoke at my cutout. "Guess they stand for the cowardly deserters who have fled there." The contempt flowed out the side of his mouth along with smoke residue. "You didn't think of doing that, did you, Forsbie?"

I decided if he could be a prick, then so could I. Especially since he had used his chosen nickname for me. "Not yet," I answered coldly. "We all can't be perfect, Sir."

He stood there, speechless. I could not tell if he was searching for an answer or even had the capability to do so. I added, "It is the homeland of my grandparents, after all, Lieutenant. That's why I answer only to my full last name, Forsberg, sir. Not the militarized Forsbie that tries to establish camaraderie. Sir."

"But you just did answer to Forsbie, Forsbie," he noted with a satisfied smirk. He had me there. And he had to rub it in. Chalk one up for the lieutenant. "Flippant as usual," he scowled.

He wasn't done yet, noticing the small yellow highlight of Ystad. "That where you're running if you do high tail it to Sweden?" he accused me.

I wanted to plant my fist in his jaw but wisely held back. "No, Sir," I replied with obvious contempt. "That's where my ancestors boarded the boat for America."

"Ah! Tired and huddled masses yearning to breathe free?" he asked. He surprised me that he knew part of the inscription on the Statue of Liberty. I decided to play along.

"No, Lieutenant. They weren't huddled or tired in Sweden. And they were breathing free. They just saw America as the land of milk and honey. You know, green pastures of plenty." Maybe my references paled in comparison to Hesse's insofar as patriotism was concerned, but I also believed he had little knowledge of the likes of Pete Seeger and Woody Guthrie.

It must have worked. He stood there awhile, unable or unwilling to produce a comeback. Then he turned away and addressed the whole office. "Time for our meeting. Major Otto is waiting."

And so we receded into our usual wearisome routine.

Only a few days later, I started to digress from that normalcy through no fault of my own. And Lieutenant Hesse took what advantage from it that he could.

When I was growing up, I sometimes heard, why I don't know, that the Arizona climate was good for a person's allergies. I assumed that meant improved health because of drier air and little vegetation. You name it. My case became the opposite. Arizona brought mine to the fore. Frankly, I don't know why it took nearly six months before they went berserk.

My troubles started early one morning when I suddenly started sneezing and could not stop. My handkerchief quickly became soaked from all the snot I was blowing into it, sneeze after sneeze. The sound of my discomfort echoed down the hall, finally causing Hesse to come to our work area to see what was happening.

He immediately blew smoke from his Camel my way, adding to my misery. "What seems to be the problem, Forsbie?" he asked gruffly before blowing another puff in my direction.

"No idea, Sir," I admitted. "Just can't... " Sneeze. "...stop sneezing." Sneeze. Blow my nose into my handkerchief.

I know it pained the lieutenant to make the suggestion he was about to make, but it probably would have smarted him even more to hear and endure my constant sneezing. Plus, my discomfort was distracting the others in the office.

"You need to go to the infirmary, Forsbie. You know, where you should have gone when you and Schlaeger were so sick," I sensed sarcasm in his tone. "Get one of the doctors to help you."

Normally, I would have balked at going to see the Air Force doctors. Sure, they had all received their degrees from legitimate medical schools, I think. But I still didn't want to trust any of them. Yet I did want relief. So I trooped down to the infirmary, saluting a few passing officers on my way in between sneezes.

After a quick visit and talk about my medical past and present, a kindly captain prescribed Phedriphed for me, each dose being fifteen milligrams. I took my first one there before he sent me on my way. Within minutes, I had an inkling. Although I had never smoked weed, I started feeling high from my antihistamine, my head hovering about three feet above the rest of my body, each seemingly dancing in different directions. I felt as if I were in Hendrix' Purple Haze but without any color. Just an ethereal fog. Even before I returned to the office, I thought with a laugh, "so this is what I've been missing," although I had no temptation for harder, illegal drugs. More importantly, I had stopped sneezing.

Lieutenant Hesse was waiting for me upon my return. "How'd it go, Forsbie?" he asked coldly while dropping some ashes from his cigarette into the ashtray he once again had placed on my desk.

"Fine, Sir," I replied with a noticeable lilt in my voice. Hesse picked up on it.

202

"What's with you, Airman? Sneak a joint somewhere between here and the hospital?" he accused.

His question prompted me, in my drug-induced state such as it was, to use my impudence that he so often correctly accused me of having.

"First of all, Lieutenant, I don't smoke pot. I don't like inhaling the smoke of any kind," I continued, directing my eyes to his cigarette, hoping he would get the hint. If he did, he seized upon it to blow another blast of smoke in my direction. "Though I must say that at every rock concert I've attended, as soon as the lights dimmed, it was impossible not to breathe in that natural wonder." Thought I'd throw in a term or two to remind him how aware I was of the counterculture, no matter how shallow my involvement within it.

"And secondly, I wouldn't be stupid enough, despite the opinions of some," I continued, this time looking him in the eye, "to light up a toke here on base. I like to leave here at 4:30, not sit in the brig awaiting discipline for being a pothead.

"No, Sir, it's just the Phedriphed working its charms, all legally prescribed by an Air Force physician. Have you noticed I haven't sneezed once since I returned? Light-headedness is a small price to pay if it keeps me from blowing mucus all over the office, wouldn't you say?"

Hesse stammered a bit. "Well, just make sure you can discharge the duties we assign you, Forsbie."

"Yes, Sir. I'd rather do that than discharge snot. I should be able to maintain my usual quality of work." I immediately regretted not using *high* to describe that caliber. Even so, I put in another shot. "It's bad enough the Air Force is trying to kill me, assigning me to a place where my allergies overwhelm me. And then it sends me unprepared into an unheated plane where I catch pneumonia."

Hesse ignored my health concerns. Only me doing my Air Force public relations job mattered to him. "Phedriphed or no, try to actually improve that so-called quality," the lieutenant suggested as he blew one last puff of smoke before heading back to his office. As usual, he got in the last word, sort of. Like many other times, I waited until he was out of earshot before saying more.

"Dickhead!" was my rejoinder, this time right after I bit my thumb.

My Phedriphed turned me into only one of two so-called druggies in the office. All the others were as clean as I had been. Except for Smith.

"What the hell did you expect?" he asked when most of us gathered at our apartment that afternoon. "I come from New York, the trend-setting city in the trend-setting East. Hollywood isn't the only hot spot for drugs in this country. And I went to an Ivy League school, for Chrissake. We have to be in the vanguard of society. So I smoke pot. But that's it. I've seen too much bad shit result from the other shit."

Mike couldn't resist a dig. "So you smoke shit, do you, John?"

"Shit, yeah, man!" Smith laughed. So now we knew a little more about our token Negro.

Only a few days later, John's weed habit almost caused a catastrophe for him, Schlaeger, and me. But he came prepared. Apparently, he had had close calls before.

After work that day, we escaped the normal Air Force drudgery and headed for West Side Stories with some articles. Not far from the base, Smith asked us if we minded if he smoked a joint. We had no problem. Shortly after he lit up and the aroma wafted throughout my car, I noticed something disturbing in the rear view mirror.

"Guys, I don't like this," I cautioned. "I think there's a police car tailing us."

"Don't act or drive suspiciously," John instructed me immediately. He then rolled down his window slightly, then stubbed out his reefer. Certain that he had extinguished the flame, he put the remainder of his joint in a front pants pocket. Then he pulled a Marlboro out of a pack in his shirt pocket, lit it, and began puffing casually. Soon enough, my car smelled like a crowded bowling alley instead of a jammed rock concert.

And soon enough, the sheriff's deputy came alongside us and motioned for me to pull over. I felt confident we were safe, so I complied. I lowered my window as he walked from his cruiser to my car. Schlaeger sat nonchalantly next to me. John sat in the back seat, continuing his smoking. I complied with the officer's request for my license and registration, which he perused and then handed back to me. I noticed that his name tag read Hesse.

"You were weaving between lanes back there," he charged, although I recalled quickly that I had changed lanes only once. And legally. But I wasn't about to argue.

"I wasn't aware that I was, officer," I replied, trying to sound contrite.

Apparently, it worked. After he looked over at Schlaeger, who was admiring the empty desert scenery, and at Smith, who was puffing on his Marlboro, he warned, "I'll let you go with a warning. But just be more careful."

I was about to reply, but John had noticed the deputy's name tag. "Hesse!" he exclaimed. "You got a brother at the air base? A cousin maybe?"

The officer did not like Smith's interruption, probably because he was a Negro. Or maybe he felt John was being insolent. Or maybe trying to get me off without a ticket even though Deputy Hesse had already promised that. "No," he said coldly. Without a further word, he walked back to his cruiser.

"Must be a Hesse trait, then," Smith laughed. "Like the lieutenant, he just walks away. Seems to leave the conversation hanging."

"Jesus, John! Why did you do that? He could have turned on me thanks to you and given me a ticket," I complained, giving him a cold stare.

"But he didn't," Smith smirked. "Besides, he probably thought you were cool, putting me in my place at the back of this bus," he joked. And we let it go at that.

As we started back on the road, John told us he always carried a partially filled pack of cigarettes just in case of encounters like we just had. "Put out the joint, light up a regular cigarette, and puff away. Blows out the evidence every time," he explained while taking another drag on his Marlboro. He was considerate enough not to take out his marijuana and relight it. I thanked him for that. Who knew how many police officers cruised this highway looking for pot-smoking airmen?

We arrived shortly thereafter at the offices of West Side Stories, a storefront in a strip mall. Those milling about reminded me of the section of Phoenix Mike and I had experienced with Ed Begay as our guide. We were the only gringos in sight. I never felt comfortable as a minority. But although we still wore our uniforms, those around us were savvy enough to realize that since the most stripes any of us had on our sleeves were Mike's two, we had not come as a threat to the underground newspaper.

Once we were inside, a young woman greeted us. Latina, with long mid-back length raven hair parted in the middle, wore no makeup but was pleasantly pretty anyway. She gave me a sense of déjà vu as she was dressed in the uniform of the Societe de la Renaissance from Kent, complete with light blue denim long-sleeved shirt and stone-washed jeans. Of course, I had become more worldly by now and surmised that this outfit of rebellion had probably originated on the West Coast, and the Kent students had merely picked up on it. So the déjà vu passed quickly.

She greeted me with a warm smile, extending her hand. "So—" she paused momentarily, pretending to try to retrieve from her mind what she already knew, "you must be the last of the three amigos."

Since we three were still in uniform, I quipped, "What gave it away?" evoking a pleasant laugh from her. "Taylor Forsberg."

"Duckworthy One, Two, or Three?" she asked.

Quick with a quip, Schlaeger jumped in, "We rotate, Consuelo."

Oddly, I had not heard her name before. "Consuelo?" I asked, a bit confused.

"We Mexicanos can be that way with names," she explained. "You probably expected Consuela because I'm female." She jokingly thrust out her chest to make certain I knew her gender. "The name means solace. Or consolation. We sometimes interchange the *o*'s or the *a*'s, depending on the parents' moods. My father apparently wanted a boy, so instead of me bringing him solace, I became his consolation prize. Second place. Hence the *o*."

"And how is your father?"

She smiled. "Oh, he loves me. I'm his estrella brillante." She was serious.

We four exchanged some more pleasantries before we three amigos left our latest articles. Then we retired to a nearby cantina where we feasted on, what else, Mexican food with Conseulo and an associate. Once done with that camaraderie, we headed home, dropping John off at the barracks. He smoked neither marijuana nor a Marlboro on the return trip, for which both Mike and I were thankful.

If any law officers were tailing us, we couldn't tell in the darkness. None pulled us over for any real or imagined infractions. Certainly, Deputy Hesse did not reappear.

But one aspect of our after-work adventure carried over into the next day at work. As usual, shortly after 7:30, Lieutenant Hesse, the paragon of punctuality, appeared in our area to see that we had arrived on time. For some reason, he didn't blow smoke in my direction, perhaps because Smith jumped in with a question even before Hesse could give us his usual lukewarm welcome.

"You have any relatives in the area, Sir?" John asked. I cringed, wondering in what direction he planned on taking this.

"None that I know of, Smitty. Why?" the lieutenant responded.

Smith paused for a moment as if considering his options. "Nothing really, Lieutenant. I just saw someone yesterday who reminded me of you."

"In what way?"

John hesitated again, toying with Hesse. "Positive, Sir. He just seemed to have that confidence that authority can give someone." It almost sounded complimentary. To Hesse, it did.

"It goes with being an officer," the lieutenant observed.

"Yeah, like being a prick," I thought to myself.

Hesse's words ended the conversation, although he did add, "Major Otto doesn't need a meeting today. You airmen know your assignments."

"Yessir," we all replied in unison. We could be uniform and compliant when we wanted or needed to be. Our response satisfied the lieutenant, but as he turned to leave, he picked up the ashtray on Gianelli's desk, stubbed out his Camel, then placed the receptacle on my desk. I flipped him the bird from under my desk as he walked away.

Joe noticed where I had placed my hands. "Playing with yourself, Taylor?" he demanded.

I responded by rolling up a Courier and tossing it at him. Then I pulled my vial of Phedriphed from my pocket and went to the water cooler to wash one down. It was my time to fly.

Chapter 10

Over the next few weeks, my flying time met with a lot of turbulence, often rising to the edge of space. Other times it would dip to where my fuselage skimmed the ground. Whatever I was allergic to, be it palo verde, Bermuda grass, Saguaro blossoms, dead fly remains, or maybe even Lieutenant Hesse, the histamines played havoc with my system. Finally, I marched down to the infirmary, where the kindly doctor doubled my dosage to thirty milligrams.

I soon discovered that if I drank Coca-Cola with my increased potion, I became even loopier than I had been in the initial days of fifteen milligrams. I decided that as long as I could get away with it, that would be how I would perform in the office. That aroused suspicions in Hesse's mind and concerns in my colleagues'.

"On your Phedriphed again, Forsbie?" the lieutenant queried after the double dosage took effect upon my return from the hospital.

"Yessir," I said, nearly slurring my words. "The kindly doctor at the infirmary said we needed to increase my potion—" I chose that word deliberately for Hesse's benefit—"to keep my sneezing in check."

Ever suspicious but totally unaware of the added effect of my soft drink, he accused me with another question. "Sure you're not getting some drugs from a pusher?"

"Don't need to, Sir," I answered calmly. No need to increase the antagonism to a dangerous level. "I'm this way legally. All compliments of Uncle Sam. I don't like how it inhibits my performance any more than you do, Lieutenant," I lied. Getting under his skin always brought me satisfaction.

"Who knows?" I pressed on. "Maybe if this continues, the Air Force will have to give me a medical discharge."

"You wish."

"Ah, Lieutenant. To hope. Perchance to dream."

He ended the conversation with, "Dreams can become nightmares." I had no intention of that becoming the case.

But I did risk increased friction by a foolish thing I did a couple of days later. Buzzing from my Coca-Cola and Phedriphed combo that morning, I butchered a piece of writing I had done for the base newspaper. Using my reliable black ballpoint pen, the one that never would run out of ink, I did major editing on an article about a sergeant in a maintenance squadron who excelled in archery. I crossed out words and phrases, whole sentences, and rewrote them in the margins so much that by the time I finished, the whole paper was a blur of black ink with a few typewritten letters peeking through. I set it in my outbox just as Hesse came into our work area. For once, he didn't have a Camel dangling from his lips.

Petersen had noticed my frenzied slashing and scribbling, so when the lieutenant arrived, he casually walked over to my desk and picked up the article. Pretending to scrutinize it in preparation to do some editing himself, Mark returned to his desk and sat down. With his trademark tapping, he held the paper so that Hesse could not see my carved-up work. While the lieutenant was there, Petersen acted like he was deep in thought on changes, even laying the sheet down a time or two and making a few marks of his own.

Once Hesse was out of earshot, Mark lit into me, punctuating his remarks with a louder tapping than usual. "What the hell are you doing here, Taylor?" he fumed. "This was an excellent article. Maybe you ought to come down from your perpetual highs and realize that sometimes you want to be your own worst enemy." Without waiting for my reply, which I did not give, he put a fresh piece of paper in his typewriter and began trying to rescue my now-butchered masterpiece.

I fumed for a few minutes. But once I realized that he was right about the article, I went over and sat next to him. Together, we restored the archery article as near as we could to its original form.

But I kept on with my high-flying potion. No need to drop it, I reasoned. Just control it.

Even though we seldom interacted with Major Otto, he either noticed my Phedriphed-induced actions or Lieutenant Hesse tried squealing on me. In any case, one day shortly after my editing frenzy of the archery story, he called me into the office. Hesse wasn't there.

"I wanted to talk to you when Lieutenant Hesse isn't here," the major informed me, pointing to the vacant desk of the lieutenant. "This is just between you and me."

So, of course, I believed I was about to get reamed big time by our usually absent boss. He proved me wrong.

"I know that even if you weren't flying on your antihistamines, you would not be putting in your best effort. But with your talent, you should. You're gifted, Forsberg. So why don't you accept that you're here for three more years and try to meet your capabilities?"

I kept my jaw from dropping, but I guessed that the major had no intention of making my life more miserable by becoming more like his assistant. So I used a little honesty with him.

"Sir, most of what you expect me to write is nothing more than public relations and ego-inflating drivel. I got my training in journalism, not selling ideas and the ilk. I honestly feel like much of the Air Force's expectations contradicts my education," I noted. "Nothing against you, Sir."

"But you do have plenty against the lieutenant, don't you." It was a statement, not a question.

"Trying not to sound juvenile, but he started it almost from day one," I offered. "I don't think he liked me from our first meeting, and I wasn't about to let him treat me as scum and get away with it. I would, and will, fight back. I think I know my boundaries, Sir."

For the first time in the meeting, he gave me a stern look. "You need to remember certain things about rank and superiors, Airman. You're lucky that I'm not coming down hard on you. You say you know your boundaries, but they have a dangerous edge. I'd rather sign off on a good airman's proficiency report and get you a rank and pay raise than autograph a severe disciplinary action."

"Rank and money mean nothing to me, Sir. I'm just biding my time here."

Major Otto could have used his rank to press the issue. To this day, I don't know why he didn't. "It's your choice, Forsberg. But if I ever do have to agree to or instigate discipline for you, I will follow through."

"I understand that, Sir. You have to do what you have to do. I feel the same about me."

"And another thing about something you mentioned earlier," he added, pausing to give thought apparently to his phrasing. "Not everyone who is here for a career needs his ego boosted. Yes, the nature of the beast is that some fighter jocks have self-conceits that make even my stomach turn. But many of them are doing a necessary job, whether we like it or not, in the unpleasantness of war."

"But that doesn't mean that I have to do my best to glorify it, Major," I countered, shaking my head.

"You well know that we do other, shall I say, house organ, stories. What's wrong with feel-good stories, Forsberg?" he wondered.

"People are dying in a useless war, Major," I replied with a frown. "Everyone here, directly or indirectly, is a part of that."

The first part of his response seemed absurd. But the rest...

"People are always dying," he countered but then continued. "But think about the article you wrote about the POW wife. That had a feel-good aspect to it. And many people, even you, in how you excellently wrote it, showed empathy for her and others like her. They have a right to feel good any chance they get. God knows they have a right for people to care about them."

Major Otto had a point. I couldn't dispute it, nor did I want to. I merely nodded in agreement. That ended our discussion.

"Very well, Airman. But I do expect you to somehow do your duty. Dismissed."

So he had me confused. Was he trapping me? Or had he acquiesced to my working below expectations? I respected him for what I perceived as his honesty, so I gave him probably the sharpest salute I had done since learning how to do so properly in basic training. It was far from any grudging salute I had or would give to Lieutenant Hesse. The lieutenant still embodied all that I loathed about the war and the military, and people who abused their authority.

Of course, the lieutenant seemed to work overtime to keep our mutual disdain at full throttle. Another episode occurred later that same day. Hesse had come to our work area while we enlisted men were talking about the insanity of war.

Taking a drag from his cigarette, he interrupted us, "You fellows don't seem to appreciate all we're doing for the people of South Vietnam in addition to saving them from communism."

"With a corrupt government under Thieu?" Mike asked.

Before Hesse could reply, I jumped in. "Yep, we're bringing great things to South Vietnam. Be sure to ask the peasant farmer whose daughter now gets paid by GIs for a fuck in Saigon. And Mike's right. You could call the South a banana republic, like our Nicaraguan friends flying here, but I don't think they grow any bananas in Vietnam."

"A lot of bananas grow there," the lieutenant sneered. "Shows what you know."

"You miss my point, Sir," I shot back. To myself, I added, "as usual."

"And those banana republicans, as you call our friends from Nicaragua, help keep Castro from taking over Latin America," he

216

asserted, blowing another mouthful of smoke my way. He stood quietly, shaking his head at our apparent lack of anti-communism.

At least he didn't directly accuse us of being red sympathizers. It wasn't like we went around chanting "Ho! Ho! Ho Chi Minh!" in our off hours. Not that at least some of us had considered it if we thought all it would do would piss off Hesse. But as active duty military personnel, we knew the serious consequences we would encounter had we done so. Plus, despite our opposition to the war, we did not think of Ho as "uncle" like many anti-war people our age did. We still considered Sam, in all his red-white-and-blue garb, as our true uncle.

Then Hesse directed a comment to an earlier one of mine. "You know, Forsbie, most of those so-called peasant farmer prostitutes are actually VC. Many of them insert razor blades in their pussies to slice the dicks of your fellow servicemen when they pay for their services."

Smith, undoubtedly more worldly than the rest of us combined, immediately broke into hysterical laughter, nearly falling from his chair onto the floor. He took nearly a full minute to stop, nearly erupting again as he looked directly at the lieutenant.

"Jesus, Lieutenant!" he exclaimed. "You can't actually believe that shit. Think about it. They'd self-mutilate trying to insert the blade in themselves."

Hesse stared back at John, dumbfounded. He knew what Smith said was true and felt brainless when he realized the veracity of the statement. Without any further comment or blowing of smoke, he turned and went back down the hall to his office. Probably to sulk. We didn't dare break into all-out laughter, but our smirks and chuckles punctuated the rest of our day whenever we recalled the razor blade fiasco. Once again, I wondered how anyone as dense as Hesse could ever become a military officer. Surely the services had ways of weeding out leadership candidates such as the lieutenant. Maybe not. Or maybe the Air Force noticed how much he reveled in parades, their pomp, ceremony, circumstance, and ritual. Maybe it realized how totally committed he would be to giving orders, something I had noticed in his handling of his family at Black Mountain. Who knew?

I also became more suspicious that he had some kind of listening device in our work area. Granted, Hesse was the assistant public information officer and thus needed to be near us often. But he seemed to have the knack of appearing whenever we talked freely, ready to inject his own thoughts into our talks. So often, he would come strolling down from his office, shrouded in a cloud like Pigpen in Peanuts, only the lieutenant's was laden with carcinogens.

A case in point came the Monday after our razor blades symposium, if you could call it that. Our conversation this time had turned to beer. I had just started to speak when suddenly, there stood the lieutenant and his cigarette-induced smog.

"You guys ever hear of Rolling Rock?" I asked as I tried to fan the smoke away from my nostrils.

"Sure thing," Gianelli chirped. "Great beer. Smooth. Loved it when I could get it."

"Whaddaya mean?" Petersen queried.

"It's a regional beer from western Pennsylvania," I chimed in. " Comes in green bottles. Got a horse head on the label. And Joe's right. It's smooth. Real smooth. They don't ship this far."

Apparently wanting to feel superior, Hesse interrupted. "You do know that beer's brewed from polluted water, don't you?"

I couldn't resist. "Have you talked with the surgeon general lately, Sir?" I asked, an overt reference to his habit as he took another drag from his Camel.

Typically dense, the lieutenant replied, "Didn't need to. It's common knowledge to anyone with the remotest interest in beer." He then showed his so-called grasp of brewing by extolling the virtues of a local beer we all had agreed on weeks before that tasted like horse piss. Even though none of us had drunk horse piss ever. At least, not that I know of. Certainly not me. If Mitchell had still been with us, he might have been able to verify our assertion.

"Now, that's beer!" he proclaimed, taking one last drag before stubbing the butt into the ash tray that he once again had placed on my desk. As I decided I would no longer remove the offending receptacle from its spot, Hesse turned and left us to our own musings.

Early the next week, he apparently had his listening device working again as he waltzed into our work area shortly after we began discussing politics, anti-war protests, LBJ, and Nixon.

"Nixon's a great president," Hesse interrupted, as usual uninvited. "He's getting things done here and in Vietnam. Doesn't care what the protesters think."

"He should. They . . . er, we gave Nixon the presidency," I countered.

"What? How's that?" I knew he would bite.

"We chased Johnson out of office with our youth movement and war protests," I explained.

Hesse was so caught up in plugging his own thoughts on the matter that he ignored my use of *we*, for which I was immediately grateful. "No, they didn't. Sirhan Sirhan did that by killing Bobby Kennedy. Enough people would've voted for that asshole son of a bootlegger had he lived cause everyone knows he would have gotten the Democratic nomination."

I seethed, but inwardly. Didn't want to give the lieutenant the upper hand. But my next words gave it to him unintentionally. "I left a previous job because my boss thought Bobby, all the Kennedys, as a matter of fact, were pieces of shit."

"You can't leave this one," Hesse smirked. "Besides, even you aren't that stupid."

I wanted to retort that I could, point to my map and flag of Sweden, and say something about returning to my ancestral homeland. But I had no intention of desertion, even in the heat of an argument with my nemesis. Besides, I did not want him sometime later on referring to me having a yellow stripe as he had before about those who had deserted to Sweden.

Smith finished the argument, getting in the last word. "The Democrats gave you Nixon, nominating a milquetoast like Humphrey. There probably weren't five independents in the whole country who voted for Hubert. I don't know any brothers who did." John admitted later that he didn't know any brothers who voted, period. This occurred shortly after Hesse left our area, apparently believing he had made his point.

John's comment took my thoughts back to when Rufus Hill and the Kent United Black Students had walked out on the then Vice President at my alma mater. What was it with Negroes and Humphrey? So I asked. "I understand Humphrey was quite a champion of civil rights. Where'd the Negro vote go?"

Smith did not even hesitate. "It's the old 'what have you done for me lately?" he said, shaking his head. "He wasn't doing anything for us." That blanket coverage of all blacks nearly caused a fight.

"No wonder you all look the same to us whites," Mike chirped, forgetting to smile. "You all vote alike."

John gritted his teeth and became serious. "I hope you're joking, honkie." It sounded like a threat. Schlaeger immediately caught our companion's gist.

"Jeez, I'm sorry, John," he apologized, extending his arm for a handshake. "I forgot to smile when I said that. We know each other, but not well enough yet for me to joke like that."

Smith grasped Mike's hand, squeezing it tightly. "You'd better be, white boy." His pause seemed forever, although it was only a few seconds. We didn't need racial friction in what was primarily a harmonious office except for whenever Hesse made his all-too-often appearances. Then he grinned, "Besides, you all look the same to us, Joe." He looked at Schlaeger directly, and we knew that John knew we knew that he had misnamed Mike with Gianelli's name to lighten the mood.

Gianelli, silent until now, closed the discussion with a comment that caused the rest of us to groan. "I wish a bad guy would get

221

assassinated sometime." Sometimes our talks could end insipidly. Like this one.

For the next week or so, the humdrum routine of the office returned. If we talked of anything outside work, it lasted too short for Hesse's eavesdropping device to prompt him to join us and contribute his expertise, opinions, and overall general nonsense. Or maybe his monitor had malfunctioned. Or maybe it didn't even exist. Maybe he merely had a knack for arriving among us at inopportune times too frequently.

So we went on with our mundane stories about such newsworthy events as big doings at the current NCO Leadership School or promotions in rank that would make their way through the labyrinthine maze of Air Force public relations to hometown newspapers. In small-town America like Chuck and I had discussed, these releases would probably get played on some inside page. In the big city newspapers, they probably found their way into waste baskets.

Even though my Phedriphed dosage had risen to 60 milligrams per pill, apparently Major Otto had Lieutenant Hesse assign me to do a story on a batch of Nicaraguan bigwigs visiting the base. They had come on a junket to see the progress of some of their pilots training to bomb the shit out of Castro if he decided to get revolutionary somewhere in Latin America. Apparently, they didn't think he had learned his lesson from the Cuban missile crisis a few years before.

Somehow I had managed to write a decent piece on their visit. Maybe it was because I felt a certain respect for Major Otto because he had treated me well, contrary to his subordinate. And I also did well despite having to endure the nonsense spewed by my accompanying photographer, Sergeant Frank Sargeant.

"I should have joined the Army. That way, I'd probably be killing me some Cong right now instead of taking snapshots of a bunch of wetbacks," he complained after we had followed the visitors around for awhile. Then he added, "But at least I got a nice bonus to re-up. Gonna buy me a Triumph with that money."

Maybe I was too doped up from my Phedriphed, but I didn't have the heart to remind him that quite a few of our fellow Americans who thought they would kill themselves some Viet Cong had themselves come back in body bags. Nor did I tell him that by re-enlisting, he just upped his chances tremendously of going to Vietnam, where the Cong bounced concrete off George Long's head. Nor did I educate him that a dignitary from Nicaragua had not swum across the Rio Grande to get to Carefree, so he could not be a wetback. Some conversations are better left one-sided.

And then, when the monotony seemed unending, the opportunity for another satirical piece for West Side Stories fell into my lap. Or, more specifically, it stopped on a railroad crossing near the small town of Maricopa, just a few minutes south of Carefree as the jet flies.

Our official news release, written by Gianelli, merely stated the usual minimum necessities prescribed by public relations. It reported that an Air Force jet en route from Pima Air Force Base near Tucson made an emergency landing on a two-lane highway but that the pilot was uninjured. The usual "board of inquiry will investigate the incident" completed the blurb.

The following article, part fiction, part truth, came to West Side Stories courtesy of my cynicism plus my sixty-milligram Phedriphed-

223

induced state at the time. It would, of course, catch Lieutenant Hesse's attention and cause him to accuse me of being its author. I was, but again I would deny any involvement on my part. I alone was not Donald Duckworthy. I was only one-third of him.

Thousands of Phoenix area children were denied a day of fun recently thanks to the ineptitude of apparently a number of military personnel.

For some inexplicable reason, an Air Force jet ferrying from Pima Air Force Base in the southern part of the state to Carefree Air Force Base had to make an emergency landing near Maricopa. Fortunately, it descended upon a mostly deserted stretch of two-lane blacktop.

Unfortunately, it did not come to a stop until it came to rest on a railroad crossing.

More unfortunately, the Bryan Brothers Circus train, en route to Phoenix from two days in Tucson, had to stop five miles below the crossing when informed of the trespassing military plane.

Jim Magoo, who saw the jet land ahead of him, expressed surprise. "Sure, I was glad that the plane landed safely," he gave in his first-person account of the incident. "But when I ran up to the jet and saw the pilot standing next to it, apparently unhurt, I asked him what happened. He replied that he had run out of fuel.

"Now I thought that pretty ridiculous. I'll be the first to admit that I ain't the smartest person in the world, but I know if you fill any fuel tank, you have more than enough to get you from Tucson to Phoenix. Why didn't the plane have a full tank?"

Because the jet blocked the tracks for nearly twenty-four hours before it finally became airborne again, the circus performances for the following day had to be postponed. Several Phoenix area schools had scheduled trips to that day's matinee but had to cancel. That left approximately 3,000-4,000 students back in their classrooms for banal work instead of a festive day with clowns, elephants, acrobats, and other circus performers. The one child we asked for comment at a local school broke into tears and was unable to give a response. We did not try any others for fear we would open heartbreaking wounds for them as well.

Spokesmen at both air bases could not be reached for comment.

(That's because I didn't try for obvious reasons). Carefree did put out Gianelli's press release stating that the incident would be investigated.

Naturally, Lieutenant Hesse came looking for a culprit, namely me, among our staff. He thrust his copy of West Side Stories in my face. "Got anything to say about this, Forsbie?"

I edged back in my chair so that I could see what he had assaulted me with. When I gazed at the headline, I innocently asked, "Mind if I read the story first, Sir?"

Hesse grudgingly nodded while as much smoke spewed from his ears as from his mouth. So I perused the article, then returned his gaze. "Doesn't look much different than what was reported in the

Republic." The Arizona Republic was the morning newspaper in Phoenix and had run a story about the incident and its effect on the circus train and the area children. "Just looks to me like these guys scooped the Republic by getting a first-person account from a witness. That's good journalism, Sir. Eyewitnesses always make for interesting copy."

Truth be told, there was no eyewitness. Jim Magoo came from my imagination. He was a combination of the cartoon character Mr. Magoo and actor Jim Backus, Magoo's voice. Remember, in satire, you're allowed to stretch the truth. I took advantage of that.

"So you didn't write this story?" the lieutenant persisted.

"I'm not Donald Duckworthy," I insisted. Technically, I did not lie. Three of us were pseudonymed writers. "And I work here during school hours, so there's no way I could have tried to interview any of those deprived students, including the one who the article noted began crying."

Because Lieutenant Hesse always dealt with reality, he never grasped that the bulk of the story was fiction. He probably had problems reading novels when he was a student. I thought about asking him if he did but ended up thinking better of it. Once again, after hemming and hawing for a few more minutes, he left our work area for his refuge of military truth, such as it was. Slightly smiling at another victory, I went back to proofreading some of the claptrap we had written for the next issue of the Combat Crew Courier.

Chapter 11

For the next several days, serene peace and boredom reigned in the office. Lieutenant Hesse had gone on another temporary duty assignment, and Major Otto was his usual hermetic self, wherever that took him. Each morning, we staffers would trudge back to Lydia's desk, and all exchange greetings.

"And here's Major Otto's assignments for you men today," the ever-pleasant Lydia smiled as she handed us our individual sheets. "Thank you," we all answered in unison like we had been forced to do with our training instructors in basic. All of us, including Lydia, would laugh after that, then engage in some more small talk before we men returned to our work area. Somehow, despite the absence of the two officers and the existence of our indifference, we managed to meet the major's goals. Even the weekly edition of the Courier came out on time and with an amazingly low number of typographical errors. We didn't know whether to be proud of or chagrined with ourselves.

"Maybe the military isn't so bad when we don't have to act like it," Petersen mused as we admired the latest edition of the base rag.

"Don't kid yourself," I retorted. "The military is still military," I reminded him.

"Right on, brother," Smith concurred. I could almost always count on him to agree with me on such matters, somewhat out-of-the-closet revolutionary that he was.

"Don't take me seriously," Mark laughed. So we didn't.

Our tranquility ended when Lieutenant Hesse returned from his assignment. We learned he was back when we trooped back to Lydia's desk.

"Sorry, boys," she frowned. "The lieutenant has come back from Idaho. And Major Otto has appeared as well. They're both meeting with the wing commander across the street. They'll summon you when they get back."

"Summon?" John queried. "Are we on trial?"

"Bad choices of words, men," Lydia replied. "I heard the major tell Lieutenant Hesse as they passed by that the general wanted to commend them. He didn't say what for, but I can only guess that it would be for the work you guys did this past week. That's the only thing they have in common, such as it was since one of them was away and the other in increased seclusion.

"Plus, I've only known the lieutenant to have finished a task, such as it was, twice," she quipped.

I bit. "What's that?"

"He has two kids."

We laughed at her biting words towards Hesse, then returned to our area to await the inevitable meeting.

The meeting went well, with the major indeed praising us for our efforts and making specific reference to areas of the newspaper that the general had singled out. All during that time, Hesse sat like petrified wood at his desk without comment. I smirked inwardly and guessed that the others were doing likewise. I even bit my thumb at Hesse when he wasn't looking.

Toward the end of the session, Major Otto informed us that the base would have a special visitor in a couple of days, movie actress Olivia Starr, a real bombshell of a body, even if she could not act all that well. She certainly could not compete with either of the Hepburns in that regard.

"And you will do our coverage for both the Courier and our news release," the major informed me, a broad smile on his face. Statue Hesse still maintained his stance. "You do your best work on such projects," Otto commended me. I thought I caught a frown appear on the lieutenant's face.

"Don't cream your uniform," Petersen cracked once we were out of the officers' earshot.

Not surprisingly, the starlet's visit opened another front of the war between Hesse and me. It also gave us prime fodder for another scathing article in West Side Stories. Schlaeger was its prime author, but Smith and I and even Petersen chipped in suggestions. The story ran as follows.

> Hollywood starlet Olivia Starr visited Carefree Air Force recently, much to the delight of a large contingent of base flyboys and bigwigs and a few lucky NCOs and enlisted men.
>
> The blond sex kitten pranced around the flight line in a straight-out-of-Hollywood low-cut, high-hemmed flight suit. Her attire might have been more appropriate if she were visiting troops in Nam, but the Carefree fortunate had wives, girlfriends, whores, and pickup bars available to satisfy the urges she certainly elicited from the salivating throng.

The star, if you can call her that since most of her talents are physical, has appeared most recently in the movie "Madman in Beverly Hills." Coincidentally, the flick ran at the base theater the same day of her visit. Good thing, too, because that was the only place on the base where most airmen below the rank of second lieutenant could see her and her attributes. Those qualities were somewhat subdued on the screen as the movie carried a PG rating. They were much more noticeable in her live visit.

After her strutting on the flight line, Starr spent most of her time at the Officer's Club, where she posed for pictures and signed autographs after giving a short speech expressing her support for the already oversexed fighter jocks, paper pushers, and bean counters of the officers' corps. Notably uninvited, even though they held sufficient rank, were the Nicaraguan pilot trainees at the base. Perhaps the rumored excessive sex drive of Latino men prompted Carefree bigwigs not to invite them. Yet surely, some of the American officers in attendance have some Hispanic heritage. Right? Maybe they were asked, or ordered, to eat some saltpeter before attending.

Both her flights into and out of the base came on taxpayer-funded military jets, the kind usually reserved for ranks of colonel and above.

"So, you didn't get your rocks off while Olivia Starr was here, Forsbie?" Hesse accused me, laying a copy of West Side Stories on my desk. I didn't have to read Mike's article again.

"But Lieutenant," I answered calmly, pushing the edition to the front edge of my desk. "I'm not Donald Duckworthy." Which was partially true, as usual. "Besides, Sir, you have to admit that the article I did for the Courier and our own news release was fair and objective. Right in line with military procedure. Major Otto commended me and I'm sure he told you so. And all those things about her attire and her O Club visit with limited attendance appeared in or were suggested by the stories in both the Republic and Gazette. Any good satirist, which West Side Stories seems to have an abundance of, can twist that information to suit their needs. They didn't get anything useful from my official by-the-book article.

"And I didn't write this underground rag's article," I finished with the lieutenant, unable to catch my sarcastic tone about my secondary income source.

"Well, this Duckworthy had information not in the Republic article," Hesse continued his feeble assault. "How did he know that Miss Starr's movie was at the base theater?"

"Part of good journalism that is not public relations is having a wealth of sources, Lieutenant," I countered. "As many personnel, both civilian and military, as we have here, they could find that out very easily. They don't need to rely on me."

Once again, I added sarcasm. "You seem to always come up with copies of this newspaper," I pointed to the West Side Stories on my desk. "Other personnel here certainly do, too, don't you think?"

For a change, Hesse actually had a reply, lame as it was. "Somehow, I think you were involved with this," he suggested, his mouth curling to the side. I didn't have the heart to tell him that he was right to a degree. Why spoil another victory? So off he trudged again, back to his sanctuary, although the major gave him a minor dressing down for accusing me. Lately, I had considered becoming more of an exemplary airman because of Major Otto's more than fair treatment. He was letting me get away with any number of actions that he could have mildly disciplined me for. So maybe I owed him more than I was giving. But I wouldn't stop as long as Lieutenant Hesse kept trying to get the better of me. Maybe the major loathed the little shit almost as much as I did. Or even more. I couldn't tell.

I had to hand it to Hesse. He continually could find some reason to disagree with me or cast aspersions on our band of enlisted men and me. It happened again a few days after the Olivia Starr fiasco when the lieutenant interrupted our talk about attending a concert we had gone to in Phoenix the night before.

"Iron Butterfly, Sir," Schlaeger answered when Hesse asked who we had seen. "And a group called Alice Cooper." The then relatively unknown Cooper band had opened for the Butterfly.

"What are they known for?" the lieutenant queried, emphasizing *they* to indicate he held the names of many rock groups of the time in disdain. We were glad to fuel his scorn, and he obliged.

"In-a-gadda-da-vida, Lieutenant," I answered.

"In a what?" he shook his head, the usual perplexed scowl crossing his face.

"In-a-gadda-da-vida," Petersen repeated. This time his tapping mirrored the song's rhythm. "It's a take on saying in a garden of Eden. You know, a perfect place."

"Then why don't they sing the words correctly?" Hesse complained.

I immediately reached into my past for a replay of my non-argument years ago with Mr. Evers during the formative stage of my rebellious persona. "Well, I bet your mother sang this song to you when you were little, Lieutenant. Mairzy doats and dozy doats and liddle lamzy divey. Why didn't that song use real words? You know, mares eat oats and does eat oats, and little lambs eat ivy?"

I answered my own question before Hesse could respond. "It's creative expression. Common to artists. Even little nonsense ditties like Mairzy Doats."

Gianelli couldn't resist joining in. "Yes, Sir. And you would have found Alice Cooper interesting, too, had you gone. They were guys dressed in wigs, I think, and mini-dresses."

Hesse rolled his eyes. Although a part of our age group, he lived on the other side of the generation gap. "Good lord!" he exclaimed.

Joe felt compelled to continue. "Not quite the Ames Brothers or the Lennon Sisters, eh, Lieutenant?" he mocked.

Unflustered, Hesse replied, "You got that right. Now those are artists!" he countered.

I decided to keep the conversation going. We were having too much fun to quit yet. "You should have gone, Lieutenant. You know, to immerse yourself in the youth culture." I paused for an instant until a vision from that night came to me. "Why, we even passed a lass in a see-through blouse. And she wasn't wearing a brassiere. Got to ogle her boobs and nipples big time," I added, rolling my eyes in mock shock.

Mike chirped in. "Yeah. Taylor here gave her the name Nellie Nipples," he laughed, elbowing me in the ribs.

"Why would a woman parade in public like that?" Hesse mused, more to himself than to us.

"It's the new wave of freedom of expression," I offered. "And we're all wearing these uniforms," I emphasized uniforms, "so that she and other free-spirited women can do it. Much to the enjoyment of horny men like us."

With that explanation, Hesse shook his head in disbelief at our retelling of that night. Likewise, we all uniformly rolled our eyes at his gesture. Klein and Cline, present for the exchange outside the radio booth, vowed to try to find some Ames Brothers or Lennon Sisters records to play on their next local show. Unfortunately, or fortunately, depending on one's perspective, they never found any of either despite their library having a large number of records from ancient singers such as Kay Starr, Frankie Laine, and Perry Como. They certainly had none from contemporary artists that suited our taste, such as the Beatles, Rolling Stones, or Beach Boys. Hell, they didn't even have the sappy Cowsills, probably because that squeaky clean family act had released a single of the title from that subculture musical Hair.

A few days later, several of us decided to gather at a Carefree spot called Lancelot's Buffet, a smorgasbord all-you-can-eat type place a

234

few miles down the road from our apartment towards Phoenix. Our talk turned to the growing unrest on college campuses.

I had received letters over the last few weeks from a colleague who still attended Kent State and worked on the campus newspaper. He had written about incidents there that shocked me mildly.

"You have to remember, guys, that when I attended Kent, it had the nickname of Apathy State," I explained after turning the conversation to my alma mater. "There were some anti-war people, but they didn't have much influence. In fact, we also called it Suitcase State because so many students packed their luggage with dirty laundry and headed home so their moms could put their washing machines to good use."

"Finally catching up to the rest of us," the more worldly John noted. "The shit went down there last year," he added, referring to Columbia.

"My buddy, who's still at Kent, wrote last month that…" I pulled out a letter from him that I had brought because we knew we were going to talk about the growing discontent on the nation's campuses. I quoted, "Even in the morning sunshine, the campus has an eerie feeling of what will happen next. Rumors of SDS and students from other Ohio campuses coming in for a mass demonstration. Also, rumors about a vote Wednesday for a general student strike. All I know is I want to finish and get the hell out of here and start my war with the draft board." My friend was in his last quarter.

"And this was when? Last month? What the hell's going on?" Smith pushed.

"Damned if I know," I admitted. "There were incidents at two buildings over a few days. My friend didn't provide much detail. Only mostly just bare basics. He just wrote the other day about two students just being suspended for their involvement last month."

"And that's it?" John continued. "He's a journalism major, right?"

"Yep."

"Well, was there anything in the school newspaper about any of this?"

"Nothing that he sent me or I know of." Yet I learned from him much later that Kent's student newspaper gave at least adequate coverage.

Our conversation turned to the problem of apparent non-coverage. I knew the Stater adviser and most, if not all, of the journalism faculty at Kent and believed that they in no way would suppress Stater's reporting of the incidents in the buildings on their own. They were strong advocates of freedom of the press. "Maybe, the administration told them not to allow any stories," I surmised.

"Yeah, even the most liberal of universities sometimes get paranoid about bad press," Schlaeger interjected.

"I can sympathize with your friend, Bro," John rejoined the conversation. "I just wanted to get done and get out, even though I knew the military was waiting for my ass. I covered our demonstrations last April, both for the campus newspaper and even a couple of pieces for The Village Voice. What would you have done, Forsberg?"

I pondered Smith's question for awhile. Before I could answer, Mike asked John, "You get tear gassed?"

"What the hell you think? Hell, yes, the pigs tear-gassed me. There I was, black, a student, and wearing press credentials that last night." He paused, then gave a light-hearted laugh. "Of course, the motherfuckers gassed us all. Equal rights when that happened."

After the laughter died down, I answered John. "I'd like to think I would cover the happenings. But I might have been discouraged if we couldn't print anything in the Stater. And I didn't know of any underground press in the area. Some news never made it to Apathy State."

"Or apparently out of it," Smith moaned.

I decided to bring our tone back to a lighter one. "Of course, if I had an asshole like Hesse hounding me, I'd probably have been on the front lines protesting. Just to irk him." That educed another round of laughter from our gathering.

Our conversation continued for awhile longer, some of us saying we would have covered demonstrations, some of us saying we would have been involved, and some of us saying we would just get the hell away. No consensus this time from a usually like-minded group.

For the next few weeks, as we sweated our way into the evaporative-cooled days of summer, peace, and tranquility reigned in the office. Hesse must have undergone some kind of temporary lobotomy if there was such a thing, as he seldom rode my ass or anyone else's. We enlisted men went about our duties at a pace that suited us but also kept the lieutenant's belligerence muted. Plus, we did our duties more and more out of respect for Major Otto. He was fair—for a lifer. But a somewhat surprising, timely, and welcome change in the lifestyle for some of us caught me by surprise.

Schlaeger, Smith, and I were delivering our latest Duckworthy masterpiece when John and Consuelo embraced in a long, and I mean long, kiss.

"Are you two an item?" I asked, pretending innocence despite the obvious signal once they finished.

"Sure enough," Consuelo beamed. "Have been for awhile." That explained why John had been coming to West Side Stories a few times on his own of late.

"And you told me your love life was nil because you couldn't find any sisters in the area," I joked at Smith, jabbing a finger into his ribs.

He laughed and poked me back. "I'm black. She's brown. Close enough, Bro."

Then Consuelo threw a totally unexpected proposal our way. "We've been living together for a few days now. We need some more people we can trust to help pay the rent. John's already talked with Joe and Alice and they're willing."

"Our own hippie commune!" Mike declared. "Is there anything in Air Force regulations preventing this?"

The thought of my celibate self seeing Alice Swann in only her monogamous panties again intrigued me. And Schlaeger's lease would expire in a couple of weeks. The timing couldn't have been better. "I'm game if you are," I announced, turning towards Mike.

"Why the hell not?" Schlaeger agreed.

Conseulo and John told us about the house. Her father owned it, but she paid him rent, and we would have to chip in. But our portion would be slightly less than what we were paying now, and the landlord had already told us our rent would go up with the new lease. Consuelo's was in a neighborhood about three miles from our apartment, with four furnished bedrooms. A little farther from the base, a little closer to West Side Stories.

"About time we find ourselves some women to share our beds with," Mike suggested. "Don't want these two and Joe and Alice making us jealous when we hear them through the walls."

With that, my thoughts turned to Angela and my wondering what had happened to her. I still could not find a good reason to seek another woman, even though I was horny as hell.

It took Mike and me all of two hours to gather our things and vacate the apartment. We didn't bother to clean it. "He'll keep the cleaning deposit anyway," Schlaeger said of our landlord, "so why bother." Sure enough, he did, nor did he refund us the few remaining days on our rent.

"Chalk up another victory for greedy capitalism," I said with disgust.

The house sat in a pleasant, largely Mexican neighborhood, mixed with homeowners with children and renters, some married, some like us free-spirited counterculture-after-work types. Unlike our experience at Cesar's with Ed Begay several months before, we found the neighbors we met welcoming and friendly to the new gringos on the block. We even became immersed in Mexican cuisine. Most of our evening and weekend meals saturated with frijoles, tamales, enchiladas, burritos, you name it. For the first few days, that diet caused a lot of farting by Mike and me, bringing caustic comments from our fellow inhabitants at the house and likewise at the information office. At work, we tried our best to unleash some silent-but-deadliest whenever Hesse was around. Somehow, he never said a word, but his expressions often told us that he had picked up a pungent odor. Eventually, our digestive systems adjusted, and the flatulence subsided considerably.

"Damn, I wish we could still fart on demand or off," I lamented one time after Hesse had left our presence and I had failed to pass noxious gas. "Things have been too quiet here for some time. And now we can't even assault his nose."

But the office tranquility would soon end, oddly enough, because of Tranquility Base.

"We sure showed the commies what America can do," Hesse crowed in our work area the morning after Neil Armstrong set foot on the lunar surface. "We beat them to the moon."

"Thanks to the vision of that damned liberal JFK," I reminded him bitterly. "You know, the assassinated President who said we'd be there before the Sixties were over."

"Don't you airmen feel a sense of pride?" the lieutenant countered. Good question, actually.

"Yes, we do, Lieutenant," Smith answered before I could. "But I'd feel more pride if we cleaned out the ghettos so that my brothers and sisters could live in a decent environment."

"You didn't have it so bad, Smitty," Hesse replied with a sanctimonious tone. "America made it possible for you to receive an

240

Ivy League education, even though those schools are hotbeds of liberalism."

"I'm not talking about me, Sir," John answered, his tone leaving no doubt that he held the lieutenant's words in contempt. "And I'm Airman Smith, Sir. If you're going to address me, I'd prefer that you do it using our military ranks. The only thing we have in common is the space we occupy here. I don't like someone using nicknames for me, especially lifer ones."

"Well, Airman Smith," Hesse retorted, the disdain obvious in his tone. No doubt it was both racial and military, black and enlisted man. "You should be thankful for your opportunity."

"I am, Sir," John continued with proper military address but with his own scornful tone. "But that came about because my parents bucked the system, and I thanked them by working hard to earn my degree from my…" He paused to prove his point. "Fortress of liberalism.

"But I'm talking about my brothers and sisters who keep getting beaten down by the man every single day, living with roaches and rats. You ever live with them, Lieutenant? Ever have them crawl across your body when you sleep at night? Ever have them scurry out of your cupboard?"

Hesse countered with the usual, "Everyone in this country has a fair chance." I doubted that he had ever come within five minutes of spending time in a poor neighborhood, black, brown, or for that matter, white. "I'm honored to live in this country," he continued, his tone implying that John lacked such pride.

241

Smith countered. "I am, too, Sir. That's why, despite my objections and because of my fears of jail time, I'm wearing this uniform for the next few years. But I don't believe in that trite phrase, 'My country, right or wrong'. When I get out of here, I'm going to work my black ass off for change. For the brothers and sisters and others."

"I'm sure you will," Hesse replied without really acknowledging Smith's avowed commitment. "I don't understand you guys. I try to bring a sense of camaraderie here by addressing you with nicknames, and you don't want that. Although Schlaeger doesn't seem to mind it."

Mike responded quickly. "What choice do I have, Lieutenant? The Air Force has shortened my name for my obligatory nametag's sake. So it's not really a nickname. I must bear that cross until I separate from duty. . . Sir."

"What's your real name?" John asked, in the dark as to Mike's true identity until now.

"Van Lautenschlaeger."

"Shee-it, man. That's one whole typewriter line, even with wide margins."

All of us except Hesse laughed at Smith's remark. He could think of nothing more to say, so he did his usual about face and strolled back to his office, mumbling a grudging "good morning" to Sylvia as he passed her desk. She did likewise to him, bless her soul.

"Well, Smitty," Schlaeger addressed our companion with a sly grin, accompanying his comments with a burrito-induced fart. "I can't wait to see you working your black ass for something good."

Those of us who were around chuckled slightly, both because of Mike's comment and his now rare flatulence. We didn't want our mirth echoing down the hall where the lieutenant might hear it and come back for more argument.

"Guess it's taking you longer to adjust to our new cuisine than for me," I taunted Schlaeger. We could not contain our laughter for that comment, but if it filtered all the way down to the officers' lair, Hesse must have ignored it. He did not return.

Even as Schlaeger and I saw our flatulence dissipate, another aroma from our new environment posed potential problems for all of us at the house. Consuelo and John smoked three or four joints almost every night. And although it wasn't as severe as when the lights went out for a rock concert, the sweet smell of marijuana permeated throughout. It didn't seem to stick to our clothing, but paranoia struck deep, especially for those of us who were not potheads. We four feared that the fragrance would stick to our bodies and be discovered. That would not work well for those of us in the Air Force and Alice wasn't keen about it either. So we made certain to shower thoroughly.

That was all well and good, except six people showering daily really could cause our water bill to skyrocket. Our money concerns eased when Consuelo and John decided to shower together with Joe and Alice quickly following suit. Problem was that some of their showers became erotic interludes, depleting the hot water before others could erase the marijuana smell. So we had to set a schedule to which we all would strictly adhere, alternating times in fairness.

"And you know," Alice suggested one evening over our dinner of chicken enchiladas, "you two could shower together." She leered first towards Mike, then me. "That would save some more water." She showed only the slightest of smiles. We caught her drift.

I raised my hands in opposition. "Not on your life," I protested. " Although what that would imply might get us a discharge from the service."

Schlaeger laughed, "I like Taylor, but the equipment's all wrong."

"We could take turns showering with you," I suggested, ogling our tormentor.

"You'll never learn, will you, Forsberg?" Alice asked, tossing her napkin at me. It missed and fell to the floor. "You'll be lucky if you ever see me half-naked again."

"Ah, but I can dream," I countered. "Sometimes the fantasy is better than reality. Besides, you were about ninety percent nude."

"Not likely with your fantasy," Alice rejoined. She was quite adept at getting in the last word. I give her that.

With the move into the house, I found myself more and more surrounded by the counterculture and many of its trappings. True, I had been on the edge of it with Angela, what with her granny glasses and attitude for awhile, but this was much more direct. I had Consuelo and John with their marijuana and both couples with their somewhat open lovemaking. But Consuclo educated me even more one Saturday when just she and I drove to a nearby deli to pick up sub sandwiches for the whole crew.

"Why don't you have a VW van?" I asked her as we headed out in her Ford Econoline.

"What?"

"You know, the requisite youth culture vehicle. A VW bus."

She turned to face me. "Look at me," she ordered. So I did. "A Volkswagen bus? The pigs are drawn to those Hippiemobiles like they are to a trough. And I'm Mexican. That would be two strikes. So I have the Ford. I have to drive under their radar as much as possible. You still have things to learn, gringo," she laughed that light-hearted one of hers that made me like her even more as a friend.

"Teach me," I jostled back.

She sensed that I was implying something more personal. Maybe I was. Sure, I respected John. But we were in the free love culture. "Some things are not my style. Let's keep it that way, Forsberg."

Her use of my last name brought back a bit more formality to our relationship and I realized that. I shrugged a friendly shrug. "No problema, mi amiga."

"Te amo como, amigo," she smiled. At least I was learning more Spanish.

Chapter 12

The recent near misses with Alice and Consuelo, such as they didn't come close to misses at all, brought thoughts and questions about Angela back to the fore in my mind. I decided it was time to take some leave and return to Ohio to see if I could personally track down her whereabouts or whatever I could about her. Besides, it would be a welcome change trading the oven-baked desert summer for the sauna-esque heat and humidity of the northeastern Ohio summer. As it was, I lucked out, as a cold front planted itself back home, with high temperatures hovering on either side of eighty degrees and with low humidity.

Fortune did not favor me otherwise, however. Wanting to save money on my trip, I decided to fly military standby from Phoenix to Cleveland. That meant I had to wear my uniform, which I just as soon would have liked to leave in my closet at the house. Other than my Air Force issue white boxers, that was the only trace of military involvement I took home. Oh, that's right. I forgot my military haircut, out of style for most men my age. So that was a dead giveaway of my status, although I received neither scowls nor smiles from anyone on my trip back east. I had no trouble getting on the first flight available that day at Sky Harbor and all went fine until I deplaned at Cleveland Hopkins.

"Oh Taylor!" my mother gushed as she hugged and kissed me there. "You look so handsome in your uniform."

I knew she was just being a mother, but I couldn't help giving her a mild rebuke. "Please, Mom," I replied, pulling back from her hug

246

and smiling affectionately, but embarrassedly, at her. "You know how I feel about this uniform and the war."

Of course, Dad could not let it slide. With his standard man-to-man handshake and no hug, he contradicted me. "You should be proud to wear that uniform," he scolded. He had served during World War II, although where and how he never said. Once again, I tried to convince him that this war was different.

"A lot of men my age are dying in garb like this," I countered. "All for no good reason."

"Keeping the Viet Cong out of California is good enough reason," he shot back. The domino theory had raised its ugly head.

My return home was off to a crappy start. It did not improve.

When we drove up to our house, I noticed immediately that Mom had slapped a blue star mother's decal in the front picture window. I loved her, but...

"Damn, Mom. Did you have to put *that* there?" I complained, pointing to her patriotic sticker.

Dad jumped in before she could reply. "Your mother is proud of you being in the service. Show her some respect."

He had a point, but it didn't improve my mood. And the tension did not subside even after I half-heartedly apologized to my mother. Dad persisted in keeping the same old tired argument going at dinner, although I kept trying to change the subject by hoping to catch up on news about cousins and aunts and uncles. It didn't work, so we ended the day parked in front of the television and saying little. Mom did come over on occasion and hug me, for which I was thankful. Mothers can be so blindly loving much of the time and that made my first day back home less painful. Dad had already left for work when I awoke the next morning so Mom and I had a more pleasant visit at breakfast. Until I mentioned that I thought I would drive to Austintown to try and learn any news about Angela.

"I don't know why you want to do that," Mom tried to reason. "You haven't heard from her in months. So apparently she doesn't want to get back with you. And you know you're not welcome at her parents' home."

She had a point about the lack of warmth, particularly from Angela's father. But I still suffered from doubts about her whereabouts. I still feared that some psycho had picked her up at Black Canyon City or elsewhere and had taken her into some forsaken wasteland, raped and killed her. I hoped that at least her parents would tell me if she were alive. Since it was a weekday, maybe Angela's father would be at work and I would have a more pleasant encounter with her mother.

I was wrong.

"You've got a lot of nerve," Mr. DeAngelis scowled when he answered the door and my heart simultaneously sank. "Abandoning my daughter as you did."

"I'm sorry, sir," I replied, trying to keep the conversation alive. "But she left me," I emphasized. I repeated for him what I had told him in prior letters, that Angela had taken off when I had gone to the restroom at the restaurant outside Black Canyon City. "The last I saw her she was trudging up the ramp to the highway. I ran out as fast as I could and jumped in my car. But by the time I went up the ramp and onto the highway, she was nowhere in sight."

"Her body's probably been ravaged by vultures and coyotes by now," he said angrily. I didn't need him to remind me of my own fears for her. "She never should have gone west with you." He clenched his fist. I thought he was about to take a swing at me.

For whatever reason, I became callous. I backed off, spitting out, "We were in love. I still love her. I—"

"Get your fucking ass away from me!" he threatened. "Even if I knew where my daughter was, I wouldn't tell you."

I shrugged my shoulders and returned to my car. Yet darkly I thought, "Well, I guess I won't have his blessing if I ever swear allegiance to the Pope." I didn't feel any guilt at getting in a blow at both his and my own father's prejudices. Seems like I engaged in war everywhere with the older generation. With Hesse, who apparently was a young member of that older generation. With war itself.

Whatever happened to the innocence of my youth? Damned if I knew.

When I returned home around dinner time, I found myself battling with my father again.

We argued over the same old things, Catholics, military service, you name it. After dinner, I tried connecting with some old friends. But they had scattered around in the last year, some to jobs too far away to drive, one to Canada to avoid the draft, even one had apparently gone underground with SDS. So I spent the rest of the evening watching tv silently with my parents. When the arguing continued another night at dinner, spoiling my appetite, I decided I had had enough. I would try to fly back to Arizona the next day to the sanctuary of my friends and spend the rest of my leave there. But first…

"Can I have the car keys? I'm going out for a few drinks," I nearly screamed, slamming my knife and fork on the table and rising from my plate of meat loaf and green beans. I wasn't about to stick around for a dessert of Mom's brownies, no matter how good they tasted.

Fortunately, Dad obliged. "Anything to get you out of here," he said more calmly than I thought he would. He reached into his pocket and tossed the keys to me. Maybe he had had enough friction as well.

"Don't get drunk and get in an accident," Mom pleaded as I left through the door. I didn't plan to. I didn't answer her either.

I drove to a bar several miles away, one I had frequented with some co-workers the summer I worked in the steel mills. Hardly anyone else was there. I guess dinners were going much better at most other homes of the tavern's normal set of patrons. I sat down and ordered a Rolling Rock, nursing it and not trying to engage the bartender in conversation. He was more interested in talking with a couple of middle-aged women at the far end anyway. Probably divorcees looking for a one-night stand. This wasn't a bar that married women would frequent just to socialize.

I was barely into my second bottle when a man about my age came in and sat a couple of stools to my left. He ordered a scotch on the rocks, took a large gulp, nearly draining his glass, then stared sullenly at what remained of his drink. Both hands cradled the glass while the rest of him remained stationary for what seemed like forever. Eventually, he took his second drag and ordered another. When it arrived, he turned toward me, expressionless, and asked, "Military?"

I hesitated to answer. His disheveled hair hung to his shoulders, so I assumed he would be anti-war, and I didn't want another argument. But I figured, "What the hell."

"What gave it away?" I answered, staring ahead.

The man also stared ahead as he took another drink from his glass. "Nobody our age has hair that short unless they're in the service." He did not sound accusatory or confrontational. Maybe he merely wanted to chat. Bars do that to people. So what could be the harm. I decided to risk it. It sure beat talking with the two middle-aged women.

"Yep. Air Force," I said lightly.

"Kill anybody in Nam yet?" he asked.

"I fly a desk in Arizona," I replied. Then I tried to lighten the mood. "Not much chance to kill any VC there," I chuckled.

"So you've avoided the war thus far." He was sipping, rather than guzzling, his drink now.

"Closest I've come is working briefly with a guy who got a dent in his head compliments of the Cong."

The man paused, staring at his drink before taking another sip. This one was a bit longer than his most recent ones. "Better than seeing three buddies sliced in two in seconds from machine gun fire." Now he gazed straight ahead at nothing but the various liquors on the far wall.

"Oh, Jesus!" I exclaimed, shocked at his blunt revelation. "Man, I'm sorry."

He didn't acknowledge my apology immediately. Instead, he continued after another sip of his scotch. " Jesus wasn't there," he said bitterly. "Gone like that," he snapped his fingers. "Two others seriously wounded." He paused again. "And me. My mind's fucked up for life," he finished, a noticeable catch in his voice.

I tried to lighten the mood, extending my hand. "I'm Taylor," I introduced myself.

"I'm Bless-Ed. The given name is Ed, but after Nam, after Dak To, I'm Bless-Ed with this curse." His mood did not change, but he did open up without my prodding. He had wounds that continually festered and resurfaced if they weren't there permanently. I suspected they would be. He told me how his squad had been on patrol near Dak To back in 67 "when all hell broke loose. And that ain't no cliché." Before his squad could take cover and return fire, a fusillade of fire shredded his three friends. They fought against the Cong ambush for another half hour or so before it ended. Just as suddenly as it had begun, the VC vanished into the night. His squad suffered no more casualties besides the two wounded. They left the remains of the dead but returned with other men in the morning and tried to make certain they had the right body parts together.

"But who the hell knows?" Another sip and an order for another scotch. "Parts of all three of them may be buried together in each of their graves." He now returned to longer drags on his drink. "But what the fuck? Who the hell knows?" His eyes were watering, but I guessed that he had stopped crying long ago.

"Every night, and I mean every fucking night, I see those guys shredded in an instant. Their lives over." Another pause. The words not coming, although I sensed he wanted them to. "My fucking life is over. I can't go on like this."

Bless-Ed scared me. I felt helpless that any consolation I would try to give him would fail. Bless-Ed had lived, had not even taken a bullet, nor had he been wounded by mortar fire like George Long. But his wounds were more severe than George's. "I don't know what to say, Ed. But . . ."

"It's Bless Ed!" His words echoed throughout the nearly vacant bar, startling the two women and the bartender. They stared at us for a moment, then went back to their barroom banter.

He then spat back at me. "Isn't anything you can say, motherfucker. But you can do me a favor."

"What's that?"

"Get the fuck out of the service. Don't keep this fucking war going. Go to fucking Canada. Or Sweden. Or anywhere."

With that, he slammed his glass to the bar, turned away, and hurried out the door. I sat there and had to wonder. Was my little personal war with Lieutenant Hesse enough? Enough for Bless-Ed and others like him with all those emotional scars from war?

"Damn Vietnam," I muttered, paying for my drinks and Bless-Ed's before leaving. His sorrows had put me in a foul mood. "Now go talk some more to those two bitches," I told the bartender as I turned away. Right before exiting, I turned and apologized, "Sorry. I didn't mean it. That guy's stories from Vietnam just put me in a rotten mood." I didn't wait to see if anyone accepted my regrets.

Thankfully, my parents were asleep when I returned home. The next morning I told them I had no reason to stay and wanted to catch a flight back to Arizona. It disappointed Mom, but Dad just mumbled, "Your mother'll take you to the airport after she takes me to work." We had the usual cold handshake when he left, and I hugged Mom when she dropped me off at Hopkins. I didn't linger to see if she would cry. I hope she didn't on her way home. Even if she did, her sorrows were nowhere as deep as Bless-Ed's.

I caught the next flight back to Phoenix via a plane change in Chicago. On that flight, the woman next to me complimented me on my uniform and service and urged me to "kill some Viet Cong."

"I fly a desk at Carefree," I replied, not bothering to look at her. Then I added, "I put out page after endless page of putrid propaganda." Then I pretended to fall asleep, not wanting to engage in any more conversation. I didn't need to, as she found more compatibility in the pages of some insipid women's magazine. All I wanted was to get back to my friendly sanctuary and rest up before resuming my war with Lieutenant Hesse. Fuck him! I'd be doing it for Bless-Ed as well as for myself now.

John met me at Sky Harbor. "Cut the visit short?" he asked after giving me a mock salute. That's what I deserved for wearing my uniform. Saved money, though.

"Yep. Wasn't much reason to stick around Ohio. Argued with Dad. Argued with Angela's dad. Learned nothing about Angela. Buddies I tried to look up were scattered everywhere out of reach. Ran into a guy royally fucked up by combat in Vietnam. So, yeah, I cut it short." I told him more about Bless-Ed as we walked to Consuelo's Econoline.

To sit on my seat, I had to pick up a copy of Eldridge Cleaver's Soul on Ice and toss it into the back seat. Before I could even ask him about it being there, John offered, "I brought that for you to read. Thought you might want some education on being a Negro in America." A slight grin crossed his face.

"Hell," I replied. Half-jokingly, I continued, "Haven't I learned enough about that just by knowing you?"

John's expression did not belie his mood. "Knowing me? You still know only my surface. Yeah, I've given you some of my background, Bro. But Cleaver and others can give you a lot more about our situation in this country."

"Trying to radicalize me?" I quipped.

"Don't think you need it."

"Okay. Maybe more, as I became after my chat with Bless-Ed?"

"Don't want you crossing any lines, Taylor. We need your money for rent and grub," he laughed.

I snorted at his using *grub*. "Geez, John, when you use white slang like that, you don't sound Negro at all."

"Shee-it, honkie. I have to blend in sometimes."

We joked and caught up for the rest of the ride home. Both of us forgot and left Soul on Ice in the back seat. I'd catch up on the meaning of blackness in America some other day.

Things had changed somewhat in the few days I had been away. Or maybe I had not been that observant before. But as the others greeted me while The Fugs sang I Feel Like Homemade Shit on our stereo, I noticed that some of the books lying around included The Doors of Perception and The Tibetan Book of the Dead. They certainly fit in with the culture of the house, but I had not noticed them prior to my trip.

Schlaeger noted my somewhat bewildered glances at the new literature.

"Inspiration, man," he said, putting his arm around my shoulder. "John and I thought we had become a little stale on our ideas for West Side Stories articles. Carefree can only provide so much. So we're delving deeper into other matters of the day. Broadening our horizons. Or at least mine. John's pretty much already out there."

I nodded. "Fine with me. Gotta keep up the fight." So over sub sandwiches from Salvino's, I told them all how my encounter with Bless-Ed had reinforced my determination to keep battling the likes of Hesse and others of similar mindsets. All within limits. You can't fight a war if you do something stupid and end up in the base brig.

"Did you miss me, Lieutenant?" I quipped at Hesse the following Monday, having returned to the office. He had come and stood over me as I was looking through some background for a story that Major Otto wanted me to do.

The lieutenant dropped some ashes from his cigarette into my ashtray. That would be about as much a greeting as I could expect from him. It also meant to me that he had missed me. You can't flip ashes into a flippant airman's ashtray with much effect if he isn't there.

"Interesting," he replied out of the side of his mouth. I can't say that I missed that or anything about him, really. "While you were gone, there were no articles making fun of this air base by Mister Duckworthy in West Side Stories."

"Not surprising, Sir," I answered, pushing the ashtray to the far edge of my desk. Expressionless, Hesse immediately put it back.

"They do publish only once a week. And that's all the time I had leave. One week. Besides," I continued without acknowledging his ashtray move. "I haven't seen anything in Stories mocking Carefree for several weeks now." Donald Duckworthy's byline had continued on other articles written by some or all of our three-man conglomerate. But they dealt with matters far removed from the base.

Schlaeger joined in. "Maybe this Duckworthy chap separated from the service. Or he received orders from somewhere else. Like good old Nam. You know, the war zone." Mike was becoming more flippant himself. If Hesse noticed, he didn't show it. He didn't turn towards Mike and blew cigarette smoke in his face. Or drop his ashes in Mike's ashtray.

"That would be my guess, Sir. Know of anyone offhand who fits either category?" I queried, my impertinence coming to the fore. God, it was great to be back. At least in that regard. I didn't enjoy my encounters with Dad or Angela's father, but I certainly savored having a go with Hesse.

He had not changed in one week, either. Unable to come up with an answer, he merely flipped a few more ashes into my ashtray, did his requisite about-face, and strolled back to his office. I followed up with my Shakespearian thumb bite.

"Time to dig up something new to ridicule the base," John interjected into the now-dead conversation. I nodded in agreement as

I emptied the lieutenant's ashes into the wastebasket at an unoccupied desk.

One thing about a military environment, even on the peaceful side of warfare such as Carefree, was that opportunities for satire emerged in abundance. Such was the case later that day when Gianelli came back from an assignment about a WAF who sounded just like Rosemary Clooney when she sang. Big news for maybe some of the lifers on base, but certainly not for us. But what he had to tell us wasn't about "C'mon a My House" or any other tune of Clooney fame... It concerned a new arrival to the base, a career officer fresh from Vietnam. Joe filled us in on the particulars, and Mike and I decided to write about it for Stories. It ran as follows:

Apparently, the Vietnam War is so intense day in and day out that it affects even those who make a career in the military. Such was apparently the case of a recent returnee to the States at Carefree Air Force Base from that theater of carnage.

It seems that the blood, stench, and body bags of that conflict stay with even the most seasoned of veterans. That happened with a major who recently went to visit an old buddy of his at the Carefree bowling alley. Things should have gone smoothly with the reunion, but upon entering his friend's office, he noticed a small rocket shell casing perched upright on a desk. The major immediately, witnesses said, went berserk.

"Live ordnance! Live ordnance!" he screamed, grabbing a base telephone book. He quickly found the number he wanted and dialed the emergency ordnance disposal (EOD) unit. "Get to the bowling alley immediately!" he shouted into the mouthpiece. "There's a live shell here!"

As much as the major's friend and others nearby tried to calm him and assure him that the shell was harmless, he did not breathe easier until the EOD personnel arrived and proved to all concerned, namely the major, that the shell posed no danger.

It is not known if the berserk officer was transported to the base hospital or given sedation. But all seems normal at Carefree again. And the only explosions heard are from bowling balls striking and scattering pins on the lanes.

Naturally, Hesse came across the article and came to our work area with West Side Stories in hand, whereupon he began his usual accusations of complicity by any of us, but mostly me. Mike quickly came to our defense. After all, he had written the item with me.

"But Sir," he pleaded with straight-faced conviction. "That story was all over the base in a matter of minutes. Anyone could have let that underground newspaper know about it. . ." He paused. "It does seem to indicate that Donald Duckworthy is still around, though."

"It's a pissing shame that someone would ridicule a fine officer," the lieutenant scowled out the side of his mouth. "I'd like to find out who it was and discipline him in any way I could."

"But, Lieutenant," I argued. "The officer wasn't named. And the readership of West Side Stories hardly knows or cares much, if anything, about this place except that it reflects the American war machine. Besides, we're all here, and so far as I know, none of us knows the man's name." Which was the truth. The panicky major was still anonymous to much of the base, but gossip was full of conjecture as to who. After all, not too many majors had returned to Carefree from Nam recently.

True to form, Hesse shrugged his shoulders, did his about-face, and moseyed back to his desk. We all gave one another slight grins as he departed. No thumb biting this time.

The rest of the week went smoothly, our only encounters with the lieutenant coming in the usual ways of dealing with our work assignments. We airmen did not discuss anything that caused Hesse to somehow magically appear in our area and engage us in some kind of argument. I began to look forward to the weekend, so naturally, one of my mates got it off to a rousing start.

When I entered the kitchen to get my breakfast, I noticed that the copy of Soul on Ice had found its way from the Econoline to my placemat. I moved it aside so that I could savor my customary bowl of cereal and English muffin with milk and orange juice.

I had just taken another spoonful of cereal when Smith arrived and stopped next to me, moving his gaze back and forth between me and the book. He had such a look that I finally broke into a smile. "You gonna say something about brother Eldridge and me out of the side of your mouth like Hesse?" I queried.

John tried not to laugh, but a little snicker came from him. To please me, he did reply out the side of his mouth, "Forsbie, don't you want to be educated about Negro life as I suggested?"

"Forsbie, huh? You want me putting you in the same cesspool as I have Hesse?" I laughed as I set the book on edge in my grasp and pretended to peruse the cover. "Besides, after I finish my breakfast, I have to watch my hero Tom Slick and his other cartoon buddies."

"You're hopeless, Taylor," Smith countered as he headed towards the stove to heat up some coffee for himself. "No surprise that a guy who prefers milk to coffee would want to watch cartoons rather than read something in depth."

I started to remind him of his own love of Saturday morning cartoons when he beat me to it. "I know what you're gonna say, Taylor. Besides, George of the Jungle is more to my taste even though I have yet to see any African brothers depicted with him."

We let it go at that. Later, after Tom Slick and his cartoon cohorts graced our television screen, I did fetch Cleaver's book and delved into it. With temperatures rising to around 115 degrees outside, I told myself to stay inside and like the book no matter what. I made it through about forty pages before nighttime when a guitar-playing friend of Consuelo's came by.

Richie Munoz was his name, and the old adage "if he turns sideways, he disappears" applied to him. Munoz was about as gaunt a person as I've ever seen, thinner than a strand of spaghetti. He had long, stringy black hair that hung below his shoulders a good couple of inches and a stereotypical Frito Bandito mustache. But his eyes troubled me. Sunken and dark, they betrayed no emotion. That is until he started playing his guitar. Still, I deemed for my own safety I would not call him that bandito. Nor would I even mention corn chips.

We had enjoyed a fine meal of beef enchiladas that Consuelo had prepared, washing them down with cold Coors beer while engaging in small talk. Richie contributed little to the conversation, those expressionless eyes peering into each of us as we spoke. All that changed when we retired to the living room and he took his guitar out of his case. Just before he started his first note, it was as if a curtain had been lifted over a brightened stage, bringing those eyes alive.

He broke into I Heard It Through the Grapevine, giving it a slight Latino sound. After singing the third verse with a stunningly soulful voice, Munoz began a guitar solo. Improvising, he carried it for a couple of minutes before I decided to join in. Consuelo kept a tambora as a showpiece in the room. It sat right next to me, so I merely reached over for it, sat it between my legs, and began tapping out a rhythm. Richie quickly realized what I was doing, and we ended up more or less challenging each other on the tempo, speeding and slowing it for more than five minutes. Then he introduced a new riff which I somehow knew meant that we were ending the solo. I stopped, and he went back to the standard song and sang another verse before concluding. We all expressed our satisfaction with what happened. Mike, however, went overboard.

"Groovy! Far out!" Mike exclaimed.

"What?" I said in shock. Schlaeger was not using the vocabulary I normally heard from him.

"I dig it, man! It was far out!"

"Trying to be some kind of hippie, are you, Mike?"

Maybe Schlaeger had had too much beer. "Fuck you, man! I can be anything I fucking want," he spat out at me as he rose and left for his room. The rest of us didn't react much, but Mike's actions dampened the mood for the rest of the evening. He did not return, but we remained subdued in our conversation. Our collective frame of mind was such that Richie and I barely complimented each other on our duet when he left. When Munoz did decide to leave, he did so in his own personal way, stretching out on an available couch and promptly shooting up heroin. Shortly afterward, he retreated to the bathroom. We could hear him vomiting. No one said anything, but I wondered at my wisdom in living in a house where major drug use could occur. Once finished, Richie came back and promptly fell asleep on the couch. The questioning of my intelligence vanished when he started snoring softly.

The next morning, Mike was seated at the table when I entered the kitchen for breakfast.

"Hey," I greeted him weakly, not certain of his demeanor.

"Hey," he returned with a smile. "Sorry, I fucked up last night. It isn't like I came from Haight-Ashbury or a commune or something." He grinned broader. "You know, hippiedom is not my bag."

Okay, some of the counterculture vocabularies had entered our regular words. After all, we were sort of on the fringe. I broke into laughter. "Groovy! Far out! I dig it!" I chirped.

"Let's enjoy the rest of the day," Schlaeger responded. "We go back to Hesse and the salt mines tomorrow."

So we did, lazing around the house with Consuelo and John because it was too hot to go outside. Damned Arizona summers! Although the heat didn't stop Joe and Alice from going off somewhere on their own that day. When they returned late that evening, they informed us they had found their own place. They moved out the next weekend. Joe later told us that Richie's shooting up had caused Alice to insist they move out.

Not to say paranoia struck deep, but I brought up my concern about Munoz and his heroin habit that same day. "We gotta realize that we're taking a risk with the grass around here," I reasoned. "But hard shit like heroin. I don't think any cops would care if they busted him here and we were around. Guilt by association. Dishonorable discharges, Prison time. I'm all for fighting the establishment, but in safe ways."

"Don't worry," Consuelo assured me. "I talked with Richie about it when he left last night. Even if we would have had a disagreement, he reminded me that he was heading to L.A. today. Said he had a promise of a record deal."

If he did, I never heard of him again. Maybe the record deal was bogus. Maybe he overdosed. Maybe he got caught in a drug deal that went bad, or he got busted. Or maybe he just melted into the vast population of Greater LA. If that's even where he went. And marijuana would be the only illegal substance around in Casa de Consuelo, as we started to call our joint rental. I could live with that, although the persistent aroma still got to me more than I would like. It was like being at a rock concert the second the lights went out.

Chapter 13

By August, my mood had soured considerably, although my colleagues and housemates did not wish for me to go away. At least not to my face.

I still pumped in vast amounts of Phedriphed day in and day out to combat my allergies. I was closing in on a full year with no word on Angela, not from my parents and certainly not from hers. I still endured Lieutenant Hesse and all that I hated about him. Which was everything and more.

And now I suffered in the midst of my first desert summer. I wanted to choke anyone and everyone who had told me, "But it's a dry heat." I no longer gave a damn. If the temperature broke 105, it felt like an oven rather than a sauna, still too damned hot. And it was doing it on a regular basis, often hitting the mid-one-hundred-and-teens. That summer, the Phoenix area would also have a number of record high lows. Too many times, the temperature barely dipped below ninety overnight. Fortunately, my Chevy had great air conditioning, and John, Mike, and I almost always took it to work. The original owner had installed the unit on the floor, and it could blast out polar temperatures in a minute or less. That was crucial after the car had sat in the parking lot near our office all day, the inside baking at ungodly highs from the unrelenting Arizona sun.

Our office was barely livable, and we went about our tasks sluggishly. Our system was called evaporative cooling, which I figured out was merely a fan blowing over supposedly cold water to bring our inside temperatures down, but nowhere near what a good AC unit could do. Fortunately, the oppressiveness usually made

Hesse sluggish, too, so we had little friction for most of the time. Of course, that would not last. Our water cooler did not do as advertised, so we did a lot of chugging of Cokes from our machine, guzzling them before they became warm all too soon in our all-too-warm office. That meant we drank a number of them during the day. Consequently, we almost always felt bloated as hell after the first couple of hours in our oven. And the damned heat caused our 1505s to wrinkle in a day or two, which meant more laundry. Fortunately, we had a neighbor woman, Elvira Gatica, who would wash and iron them for a fraction of the cheap prices at the base laundry. Plus, she was much more pleasant than the souls at the laundry, undoubtedly sullen at their misfortune of having been assigned to such a boring task for probably their whole enlistment. I doubt that anyone with laundry duty ever re-upped. Who in his right mind would?

We needed something to create a diversion or to get us back into our usual routine. I, especially, still was pissed at what the war had done to Bless-Ed and who knows how many others like him. He had wounds less open and probably more permanent deep within his psyche. That empathy for him, along with everything else that irked me, added to my need for some kind of friction to make me dislike the Air Force and Lieutenant Hesse even more in my never-ending battle. Fortunately, a movie that some said celebrated the counterculture and a music festival that, dare I say, saluted it did provide the ammunition.

Several of us had seen Easy Rider the first weekend we could after it had come out in July. So we were discussing it when Hesse came into our work area, his secret listening device apparently working again. Or maybe he was related to Edgar Cayce or Jeanne Dixon.

"They got what they deserved," he announced, interrupting Gianelli giving his take on the soundtrack. Joe quizzically asked the lieutenant, "Huh? What Sir? Who?"

"Those two druggie hippies getting blown away at the end of the picture deserved it, being so anti-establishment as they were."

I wouldn't let that pass. "Yeah, their rotten-toothed murderers were fine, upstanding, yeehaw loyal Americans," I said bitterly...

"Well, they weren't trying to rot the country with drugs," Hesse countered.

"Right, Sir," I responded. "They were probably on their way to their moonshine still or a Klan rally when they decided to kill someone just for being different." I could use stereotypes, too, if it suited me.

"They made it so that fewer hippie scum were destroying what I cherish," the lieutenant continued. He did not wait for a reply but turned back towards his office. All of us except for Smith bit our thumbs in universal contempt.

"Happens to us all the time," John said, taking it no further. But we all knew what he meant about Negroes getting shot for no other reason than being unpatriotically black.

I might not have known about the counterculture's festival of peace, love, and music as soon as I did if not for Schlaeger being parked in front of the television watching the national news that Sunday evening in mid-August.

"Hey, Forsberg!" Mike shouted from his perch on one of the recliners in the living room. "Come and see this far-out story."

He had, in my mind, temporarily regressed into pseudo-hippiedom with his use of "far out," so I took my time from reading in my bedroom to see what had caused his excitement. It took me little more than a minute, so of course, the network had gone on a commercial break.

"What's the big deal?" I asked when all I saw on the screen was the Marlboro Man on his horse.

"You should have seen what was just on. There was this big music festival somewhere in New York. Big-name acts. Airplane, Hendrix, Who, and a bunch of others. So many people there that the New York Thruway was closed. Estimates of half a million young people digging the music."

"Sorry, I missed it," I muttered. For all I cared, it might just as well have been on the moon a month earlier with Armstrong and Aldrin. Yet, I admitted to myself that in other circumstances, I might have tried to get there and enjoy the music.

We had plenty to read about the festival at Woodstock the next day at the office when we shared the morning Arizona Republic. And Lieutenant Hesse did not disappoint me when he sauntered into our work area around mid-morning, a newspaper in hand, head shaking in bewilderment.

"So this is what the anti-establishment does," he said out the side of his mouth. "Five hundred thousand idiots," he continued, the disgust obvious in his tone. "Girls running around naked, swimming naked in ponds. Thousands getting high on drugs. Three people dead. What the hell is wrong with them?"

"What?" Smith replied immediately. "You never went skinny dipping with a chick, Lieutenant?"

"No, Smitty. Have you?"

I chipped in before John had a chance to reply. I could not wait to utter my contempt for Hesse and his inability to see some differences and parallels. "Five hundred thousand troops in Vietnam. Thousands getting high on drugs at any one time. And I'm guessing we had more than three dead over the weekend there."

"At least those who died in Vietnam did so for a worthy purpose," the lieutenant retorted. I didn't feel like taking the argument any further. I figured I had made my point. And frankly, from his point of view, so had Hesse. None of the other guys said anything further, either. Too damned hot to argue at length. Eventually, the lieutenant did his about-face and returned to his office. And I went to the Coke machine and got my second bottle of the morning. Time to take another Phedriphed. I would be getting legally high within a matter of minutes.

Gianelli could not resist one last thread of the short conversation. "You ever skinny dip with a girl, John?" he asked our token Negro.

Smith replied with a knowing smile. He did not need to say anything. We all would take him at his word, even though I, for one, had never swum naked. Hell, I didn't even know how to swim. Never got around to learning.

Gianelli did add one more tidbit to the remains of the conversation. "Nothing more beautiful than a human body gliding through water. Especially if it's a naked girl," he sighed, as did the rest of us in agreement.

A couple of days later, Major Otto called me into his office at a time when Lieutenant Hesse was away. I don't know how the major continued to put up with my usual frame of mind, but since Hesse had gone elsewhere, I figured Otto had an assignment for me. Every time he did that, I felt a little guilty about my attitude. But I would not change, even if the major asked me.

"You and I are going down to Cowlic Gunnery Range tomorrow," Otto informed me. "I want us to submit an article about the range and its mission, how the men are dedicated in that wasteland. I know, despite your attitude, that you will do a good job on it. Your journalistic skills will come through. And I want to have a long talk with you."

"Yessir," I replied weakly. I hoped he would not spend the long round trip, I figured at least eight hours worth, lecturing me. I did not want a wedge driven between us. Hesse and the rest of the Air Force were enough.

"Good," Otto nodded. "We'll need to leave early. Be here at six a.m. sharp, Airman."

He called me airman rather than by my name. I began to dread my long entrapment in his car with no escape. I wouldn't dare feign sleep. Too great a difference in rank.

I actually arrived at the office that morning before he did. Had I been forced to arrive that early by Hesse, I would have put in some kind of dig to miserably start what surely would have been a miserable day, long hours passing endless cacti and sand to Cowlic. I had already determined that Cowlic would be the armpit of the world. You don't set up a gunnery range in a garden spot. But since I would be with Major Otto, I decided I would try not to cross any lines.

270

No surprise when he pulled up in front of the office. I had never bothered to notice what kind of car he drove, but I was not startled to see him behind the wheel of a late-model Oldsmobile station wagon with fake wood siding. I didn't dare ask him if he had been influenced by the Beach Boys and Jan and Dean. The Olds was definitely more middle class than surfer chic anyway.

Obviously, he had not. As we drove through Phoenix that morning, Otto had his radio tuned to a station that featured all the old insipid songs of more than a decade ago. I hoped I wouldn't freak out from a steady diet of another generation's music. But, after some blitherer named Paul Harvey gave his take on the news, most of it what I would call obscure sidebars, Otto turned off his radio. Without taking his eyes off the road, the major asked me.

"When are you going to turn it around, Forsberg?"

"Pardon, Sir?"

A genuine smile came to his face. "You don't have to call me sir here, Forsberg. In the car, we're equals. So when are you going to turn it around?"

Perplexed, I responded, "I'm not sure what you mean."

His tone did not change, but at the same time, I sensed increased forcefulness in his approach. "You know damned well what I mean. You have come close to Lieutenant Hesse writing you up any number of times. I could have, too, but you have stayed just on the safe line of insubordination, in my opinion."

"I know." Then I posed a question I didn't think I had the nerve to ask. "Why haven't you done that?"

"Because, as I've told you before, I like your journalistic abilities. When you use them for the good of the Carefree mission and its personnel and families, you're excellent. You wouldn't be helping the base or yourself if you crossed my line."

That bothered me. I had not thought that anything I had written was for the base's benefit. But, yes, I had done a number of stories and tasks without my cynicism showing. Then he dropped a bomb on me.

"Another way you show your excellence in writing is in those articles for that underground newspaper, Mr. Duckworthy."

I said nothing in reply. Figured I would play it safe. Then he hit me again.

"I'm pretty certain you are Donald Duckworthy. Maybe one or two of the others in the office write under that pseudonym, but you do most of it. If I were as uptight about the base's image as most careerists, I would have busted you already. You're lucky that the lieutenant is too dense to put the pieces together and conclude what he suspects."

I sat speechless for what seemed like minutes. I thought of Huck Finn and his attitude towards the slave Jim, a nigger in Huck's words. It reflected his prejudged contempt for a man he obviously was growing to appreciate for his wisdom. My prejudice towards the major now seemed similar to Huck's. Yet here, a career officer had just told me, a one-term enlisted man, that he thought little of one of his own and more of me and my abilities. Was I receiving Jim-like wisdom? Perhaps, but even so, I still felt I had to throw him off the scent. So I lied, sort of. "If I'm as good as you say I am, I would have come up with a better pen name than Duckworthy." For some reason,

I gambled further and chuckled, saying, "Well, Sir, this isn't a court of law, so I won't even plead the Fifth."

Another astonishment. He laughed, "Don't call me sir. And no, you're not in a courtroom. But your disdain for Lieutenant Hesse, a decent man, by the way, despite what I said about his lack of perception, could cause your downfall. Remember, the white whale was Ahab's undoing."

"I never read Moby Dick," I replied.

"But you know about it. Maybe you should read it, Forsberg." The major had me wondering why both he and Smith cared about the depth of my reading material. I pondered whether Otto had read Soul on Ice but decided not to pursue it.

Thinking of John and his journalistic credentials, I asked the major, "What about Smith? Why don't you use him as you do me? He has a journalism degree. From Columbia, no less."

The major stared straight ahead at the shimmering blacktop, but I could see the contempt in his eyes. "He's a nigger," Otto stated.

I considered it in my best interest not to pursue the matter, so our conversation paused for several miles. I didn't need the major turning on me. Though I had a feeling I had betrayed John by not defending him. Finally, I surprised myself by broaching a new subject.

Careful not to call him sir but also certain not to address him by his first name, I asked, "What's your background?"

"How far back do you want to go?" the major responded.

I felt comfortable now. I hoped he wasn't playing me, trying to get me off my guard. But he had treated me more fairly often enough before, so I replied casually, "Wherever you want. It's your story."

"My parents lived in a town called Passau in Bavaria. Ran a bakery. But the minute Hitler became chancellor of Germany, they determined they had to emigrate. They held the belief of many that America was the land of opportunity. So they fled Europe and ended up in Milwaukee."

He went on for some time about their early years there and about his childhood. A standard story that, frankly, I normally would find ho-hum, but the enthusiasm in his voice made it a fresh story. It did remind me of the American Dream stories I grew up with before I became disillusioned by the treatment some men in places of power would wield over "lesser" humans, like the martinets that started me on my path of disaffection. And later came the civil rights movement and Vietnam. I listened, but because I had heard similar tales before, he did not sway my thinking about the country I was now experiencing and supposedly patriotically serving. In fact, it gave me the inspiration to do a somewhat parallel tale for West Side Stories about a fictional officer of Japanese descent at Carefree who also felt that same "my country right or wrong" patriotism that the major was extolling. I couldn't buy it, just like so many of my contemporaries. Thoughts about it kept circulating in my head as I stopped listening to what became a rambling bunch of nonsense from Otto. I realized after a while that fortune had smiled upon me because he did not seem to notice. But he did stop talking after a while, probably because of my silence as we drove on to Cowlic. I also resolved not to submit a similar story of the Japanese until several weeks after our trip. He would be smart enough to make the connection. Especially since he suspected that I was at least part of Donald Duckworthy, a pseudonym I would not use in that story. After all, I still respected the man.

When we finally arrived at the main entrance to the gunnery range, I felt like we were about to enter a labor camp. Except for the security police guardhouse at the entrance, manned by two poor souls who I hoped liked each other for their sake, there was nothing. Nothing but a ten-foot high chain link fence topped with barbed wire stretching as far as I could see. And nothing inside except the endless sand and boulders and some scrawny vegetation that I thought in no way could support any animal life. I had forgotten about the coyote and roadrunner casualties from my first bit of satire at the base.

I tried cracking a joke with the one guard who stopped our vehicle. Nodding towards the man who had stayed inside the hut, I asked, "You guys ever get tired of each other?"

The sentry, an airman first class, scowled, "How would you like to be stationed here, one-striper?" I guess such a duty assignment does tend to turn someone into a grouch. I know it would do that to me.

After we pulled away, Major Otto addressed me without taking his eyes off the road. "I could arrange a transfer for you here, you know." His expression gave me no indication of his seriousness. I decided not to reply. I again realized that although the major apparently liked me, he did hold power over me. "Okay," I thought. "I'm just a temporary serf, and he's my present master. Watch yourself."

We proceeded to the range headquarters, where we interviewed the site commander, another major. He came across as gung-ho for the mission, and I somehow remained attentive enough to write down many quotes in my notebook. Certainly, if Otto checked that work afterward, he would be pleased. But I also felt certain that he trusted me enough that I would get the essentials down and correctly.

Then the major surprised me by taking me to the officers' mess for lunch. Definitely a breach of military protocol. Or so I thought.

"I know what you're thinking," Major Otto affirmed for me. "But I'm as high-ranking as anyone here. So no one will dare complain."

As it turned out, I don't think the enlisted chow would have been any worse. My baked chicken required a great amount of chewing, the green beans were lukewarm and limpid, and the canned corn tasted like the container it came from. Even the apple pie tasted like its crust; I could not discern any tartness or sweetness in the small sampling of fruit within.

"Glad I'm not an officer here," Otto grumbled as we entered his car. "Nowhere near as good food as what we have at the O Club at Carefree."

"I wouldn't know," I responded, apparently successful in hiding my sarcasm. The major neither replied nor gave a disapproving look. So we sat without speaking as we drove for more than half an hour, the tires crunching the desert soil and kicking up just a slight bit of dust. Finally, we came to a halt, surrounded by three one-story wooden buildings about fifty feet long each. Here those who maintained a target area on the range stayed during the day when they weren't working at any of the target sites, the closest one another two miles distant. Best not to sit too close to where the American and Nicaraguan flight crews blasted away with live ammunition.

The officer in charge there fit the assignment perfectly. A rail-thin second lieutenant, he was fired up about the work. "Yep, we make sure the targets are well-maintained so our pilots can get plenty of practice blowing away Fidel's and Ho's boys," he boasted.

His crowing did not impress me, nor apparently, did it do so for Otto. The major's expression gave no indication of appreciation. Or, for that matter, revulsion. He remained difficult for me to decipher.

"Any of your men around here for Airman Forsberg to interview?" Otto asked dryly. "We want to hear from the hands-on airmen." He placed his palm on the lieutenant's shoulder, indicating that he wanted to continue the talk just between the two of them. He was giving me free rein to ask whatever I wanted of some of the enlistees. I gave a slight nod of thanks as he started to turn the lieutenant away from us. I would not let him down, but I determined right then that I might ask some questions that the lieutenant would not want to be posed.

Obliging, he pointed to his right. "The men are in that next building, probably in the room by the far door," he informed me as Major Otto steered him in the opposite direction.

"Tell me more about your overall operation," Otto requested as we parted, and I thanked him inwardly.

I went to the door I had been told of and entered without knocking. Three men, the highest ranking being a three-striper, jumped up from their chairs around a table.

"Oh, geez!" the sergeant exclaimed as he noticed my lonely stripe on each sleeve. "You're not the lieutenant," he continued as they all sighed with relief. "What the fuck do you want?" he asked. I couldn't read his tone. I decided to risk a light answer.

"I'm from the Carefree information office. I'm down here to interview you and find out what fun you have working in this paradise," I smiled. It worked.

"Sarcastic son of a bitch, aren't you," the sergeant replied. His name tag indicated that he was someone named Roderick. "Ken Roderick," he added, extending his hand for a shake. The others, both airmen first class, introduced themselves, but Sergeant Roderick definitely was the one wanting to talk. I know I, with a mere single stripe, didn't intimidate them, so maybe Roderick did. Three stripes can carry a lot of power over those with fewer. But not me. I surmised from his initial attitude that this sergeant didn't give a shit about his work and would leave the Air Force once his enlistment was done.

"So, what's a typical day for you guys?" I asked.

"Mostly, we clean up and dump or burn the carcasses of all the vermin that the pilots shoot up in their runs. Especially after they've been scored by the observing officers, and they still have ammo to waste, so they find the denizens of this garden spot to waste."

"Like what?"

"Coyotes, roadrunners, javelinas. Of course, a few rattlers get blasted, too, but that's purely by chance. No way the pilots can spot them as fast as they're flying."

"Why don't you just let the vultures and other predators clean up?"

"Because this is military, and we have to stay busy," Roderick continued. "Plus, because it's military, even this hellhole has to be spic and span. You never know when some general with a hair up his ass will come in for an inspection. He wouldn't like seeing this

278

beauteous landscape of nothingness looking untidy. And—" he paused, "our lieutenant wants to impress anyone with higher rank, especially those with scrambled eggs on their hats."

"I can tell you the major I'm with doesn't give a shit," I replied.

"There's a major here?" the sergeant seemed surprised. "Where?"

I sensed he felt concerned that someone of such rank would surely look for any flaw in their work. "Don't worry," I assured him. "He went off in the other direction with your lieutenant. Let me come here on my own. So feel free to talk with me about anything you want." But I warned him nonetheless. "We're doing a story about the mission here. So play along. But tell me some things that the lieutenant would not want anyone to know or that show how much you hate your work. I'm in for one enlistment and one only. I do enough to stay safe."

I figured I wouldn't tell them that I had stretched limits on a regular basis. Maybe one, or all, of them bought into the military lifestyle. Judging from what had happened thus far, I didn't think so. But one can't be too sure.

"It's because of boredom more than anything else," Roderick told me as we drove in a pickup truck out to one of the target areas. "So we actually do our jobs well. We figure the brig would be worse." I couldn't argue with him on that. With room for just two in the cab, since I was their guest of honor, I rode in the passenger seat. The two other airmen rode in the cargo bay. "Don't worry about us," one of them said. "We're used to it. We take turns. Another perk of our job." Fortunately for them, Roderick drove slowly enough that they inhaled little or no dust.

Once we got to our destination, they began telling me the intricate details of the tasks they had to perform in their work. I had to admit that they impressed me, but I also remembered their reasoning concerning the brig.

"So I guess you never do anything to throw the jet crews off, then?"

"Actually, we sometimes are ordered to," Roderick explained. "These pilots will have missions in which the enemy has camouflaged their targets, so the higher-ups give us hints. But you can only do so much with what we have out here. Sagebrush, some cacti, palo verde. Usually, we have to put so much together to hide targets that the mound is a dead giveaway in this landscape."

"So what do you do for fun here? What can you do?"

"Well, the movies the Air Force provides us with isn't one of them," he explained. "We see plenty of John Wayne, Steve McQueen, and Jimmy Stewart. Those guys. But you can bet if we want to see Easy Rider, we have to drive all the way to Tucson. Or we go down to Nogales for the cheap beer and tequila and the whores. It sure beats jacking off. Damn glad we have a medical staff here with plenty of penicillin,' he laughed.

"Guess they don't put enough saltpeter in your diet, huh?"

Roderick laughed again. "Isn't enough saltpeter in the world to curb our horniness. I've lusted after a few javelinas in my time here."

"Good thing you're not too far from Nogales," I conceded.

They also told me that some weekends when they stayed in this Godforsaken hellhole, they would go out with some of the security policemen or borrow their pistols to shoot juveniles and coyotes when they could find them. "Even the lieutenant joins us sometimes. Trying to have some camaraderie with us. But we all hate his guts. He's a born lifer."

They ended my tour by taking me farther on the range to where they would pile up the carcasses of the area fauna both they and the aircrews would kill. "We burn 'em here 'cause they aren't edible. Unless the vultures get to them first. Then we just let them have at it."

"Don't think I'd want any myself," I opined.

Roderick looked at me with a slight smirk. "Sometimes, we bring some back and slip the meat into the officers' mess." He paused for a moment. Keeping the smirk, he continued, "You didn't eat lunch at the O Club today, did you?"

I hoped he was kidding. "Do I need to stick my finger down my throat and upchuck? If I do, I'll make sure it gets all over your uniform."

He laughed. "You don't want to walk back from here, do you? If a rattler gets you, they may not find your body for weeks." Another pause. "I was kidding."

"So was I."

We had a few more laughs between the two of us on the way back to the main base. Roderick's companions couldn't join in, still exiled for this trip in the truck bed. At least they had blankets to sit on so they wouldn't get second or third-degree burns from the hot metal. Accommodating fellows, I thought.

The ride back to Carefree with Major Otto passed slowly. We found little to talk about, apparently having covered what he felt necessary on the way down. I managed to doze off for a short while. The major did not bother to chastise me for sleeping on duty.

After we returned, he ordered me to go to the photo lab and ask the NCO in charge there to assign someone to drive to Cowlic to get some photographs that would go with the story. So I explained what we had seen and what I had recorded, giving a rough idea of how the story would go. That way, the assigned man could shoot pictures that hopefully could accompany the story.

"Hell! I'll go do it myself," he said once I was done. "I'll take my own car so that when I'm done, I can drive down to Nogales and get some Mexican pussy."

A couple of days later, we got his prints. "I hope the pussy he got was better than these pieces of shit," I grumbled after one of his airmen dropped them off and before I took them back for Otto to see. The photos he provided showed nothing other than what a completely desolate place the gunnery range was. Even those of blown-up tanks, jeeps, and half-tracks didn't help. Yet at the same time, they reinforced what the major had me calling the range in the story. Freedom's Priceless Wasteland. Freedom? Yep, it was in the Land of the Free. Priceless? Nope, back in 1854 Gadsden forked over to Mexico $10 million for the land it occupied. Wasteland? Yep, I had seen it firsthand myself, and the pictures of nothingness and military vehicles reduced to nothingness proved the point.

"I hope he got the clap from his side trip to Nogales," Major Otto groaned upon looking at them. He obviously had a good read on the photo lab's NCOIC. He gruffly handed the photos back to me. "Do what you can with them. We should have taken one of his airmen with us rather than send that worthless asshole."

I briefly considered humorously suggesting taking the pictures to West Side Stories and letting them do what they want. But I didn't want to join the photographer on the major's shit list. Once again, this was a time when I had more in common with a lifer, namely Major Otto, than I cared to admit. But I also wanted to preserve my fragile standing.

I found myself in a quandary. I didn't want to glorify the training of jet pilots for their murderous missions. But Major Otto had continually treated me kindly, especially letting me push the edge numerous times. He had praised me for several stories, like the one on the POW-MIA wives. So I owed him.

The more I thought about it, the more I felt I could go into some detail about the Gadsden Purchase and then focus on Roderick and his crew as examples of men dedicated to their work without mentioning that they had no choice as to what that work was. With the major's permission, I drove into Phoenix to the main library and found plenty of background on the 1854 purchase, taking copious notes. Back at the office the next day, I foraged through my notes from the visit to Cowlic and organized all of my work into what I considered a workable outline.

As I did so, I sometimes wrestled with the thought that I was selling my soul to the devil of our involvement in that detestable war. But I also felt I could tell the story of those men and make them seem like regular human beings. This was for Air Force Magazine, which, quite frankly, I didn't think cared about human interest articles.

In the end, I was able to forge together the purchase of the land into the present-day mission of Cowlic Gunnery Range and a focus on Roderick's crew. In mid-afternoon, I took the draft to Major Otto.

"I'll read through it and edit and make comments as I see necessary," he told me as I handed the pages to him. "I'll let you know when I'm done."

"Yessir," I responded and fooled myself by actually giving a sharp military salute. But I had no regrets about doing so.

Later on, he came to my desk rather than summoning me. "Forsberg," he smiled, "that was excellent. I made no changes. I'm getting it ready to send to Air Force Magazine with your byline."

As he turned away, I had mixed emotions. Part of me did not want to do well, yet I had. And a careerist had told me so.

Schlaeger had been sitting at his desk when this happened, so he could not help chiding me on our way home, "Going lifer on us, are you Taylor?"

"Those guys I interviewed were decent fellows. I didn't want to make them look bad. And I think I held back on glorifying war. I can live with myself," I replied.

In the end, it made no difference. A few months later, a red-faced, angry Major Otto stormed back to my desk and thrust an open magazine onto it. "They screwed you royally, Forsberg," he fumed.

I looked down at the page. There was the headline "Freedom's Priceless Wasteland." But no byline. No story. Just five photos of the drab landscape with bland captions that I thought even someone at the gunnery range would have trouble recognizing the place. The final product was deader than Cowlic's terrain.

"You deserved better," he added. I noticed behind him Lieutenant Hesse, who had been blowing smoke at Gianelli, smirking. I wondered if Hesse had somehow sabotaged the submission. I almost suggested that to the major but decided that it would not be the best route of revenge on my nemesis.

Hopefully, my cohorts and I would find other avenues.

Chapter 14

For a few weeks after Major Otto had fumed about my article on the Cowlic Gunnery Range, tranquility reigned supreme in our office. Another temporary duty assignment for Lieutenant Hesse made a couple of those weeks possible. I continued to wonder if Major Otto couldn't stand him any more than the rest of us, so he kept looking for such tasks just to get that asshole out of the office.

Nor did any of us come up with any doings at Carefree to ridicule in West Side Stories. We continued to submit different writings on happenings in the Phoenix area and elsewhere in America. And, of course, the war always provided us with plenty of fodder for satire when we so chose. But the Carefree PIO office stayed calm. No truce had been agreed to, but neither Hesse nor any of us stirred the animosity that remained below the surface.

Part of it may have been that the weather had stopped being so unbearably hot, and our evaporative cooling no longer failed to ease our discomfort from the Arizona oven.

That serenity changed around the middle of October when the lieutenant marched into our work area carrying that morning's newspaper and proceeded to stir the pot. At least he wasn't smoking.

"Well, well!" he gloated, obviously for our benefit. He stopped between my desk and Schlaeger's. "Looks like the anti-war movement has fizzled spectacularly."

Gianelli responded first. "How's that, Lieutenant?"

"The Weathermen had called on tens of thousands of anti-war demonstrators to show up in Chicago to protest the trial of those radicals from last year, and only a few hundred bothered." Hesse was referring to eight organizers of the protests at the Democratic Convention now on trial there.

Smith quickly responded. "Begging your pardon, Sir. But the Weathermen specifically wanted the demonstrations to turn violent. Which they apparently did from what I have read," he added, wanting the lieutenant to remember that he stayed aware of current events. "But if you check the anti-war movement, you should know that the overwhelming number of protesters do so non-violently." Smith could not resist another dig. "If anyone should know about such things, I should. After all, I'm a Negro. Martin Luther King, you know. Gandhian tactics."

"Yes, Lieutenant," I chipped in, although Smith didn't need any support. But this was the first time in a while that I could remind Hesse of my flippancy. "Enough Americans are waging war with all kinds of weaponry in Vietnam. We peaceniks don't want bloodshed here too."

Hesse ignored Smith but gave me a cold stare. After all, he and I were the main combatants in our own little war, even though I relished the support of John and the others.

"Nevertheless," the lieutenant countered. "All these anti-war demonstrations have done nothing but divide our country. They're dying now because of President Nixon's leadership."

He said that with a straight face. I succeeded in not bursting into laughter, and from the looks on my cohorts' faces, they did too. We remembered Nixon's secret plan that had yet to materialize. So much for campaign promises.

Within weeks, events would prove Hesse wrong.

"Are you coming?" Consuelo asked at dinner one night in early November, her gaze making the circuit among us airmen. She did that often, making reference to things unclear to us.

"Coming where?" John was the first to ask. I was glad about that. Her lover being the first to show ignorance of where she directed conversation reinforced for me that I had companions as much in the dark as I.

"The march," she said in slight amazement. "There's going to be anti-war marches all over the country on the fifteenth. Hoping for half a million people in Washington alone. And there's gonna be one in Phoenix. So are you guys coming?"

We mulled over the invitation, suggestion, or whatever you want to call it for a few minutes. Mike spoke first. "That would be a risk for us, don't you think."

"Why?" Consuelo questioned.

"Well, certainly the television stations will cover it, and..."

Smith, with his vast knowledge of marches and protests, interrupted. "And, the FBI will be crawling all over everywhere taking pictures. If we show up in either source and we get identified, the Air Force will throw us in the brig quicker than the roadrunner can outrun Wiley."

I loved it when he made references to pop culture.

"John's right," Schlaeger nodded. "We can't carry on our little war if the Air Force locks us up. Then probably dishonorable discharges." He paused. "But you'll have our moral support. We'll watch the local news to see if we can spot you," he laughed.

Consuelo did not laugh with him, but she nodded in agreement. "I didn't think of the risks for you guys with the pigs. Don't want anything to happen to you," she said, reaching over and squeezing Smith's hand. "But Elvira and I are going. And so are a couple of the mothers in the neighborhood. One of them lost her son in Nam in '67. She has plenty of reason to go."

She sometimes irked me with the vernacular of the more radical counterculture. Even though she had never suggested violence in my presence. "Pigs, Feds, FBI. Doesn't matter what you call them. We have to play it safe," I noted. "As for the mother who lost a son, she has reason more so than us here at the table," I added. "Want me to drive you ladies there?"

Consuelo thanked me. "But I can drive. That way we senoras and senoritas will know where to find our way back," she smiled.

The marches would have been enough to stir turbulence with Hesse, but just days before the Moratorium, as it was called, the shit hit the fan at our office.

"Jesus!" Schlaeger exclaimed, even louder than his usual, but rare, outbursts. "You guys see this?" he asked while staring at the front page of the morning newspaper. He did not wait for any of us to ask what and began to read aloud the newspaper article about the massacre of civilians by U.S. troops in a Vietnamese hamlet. My Lai.

Halfway through Mike's reading, Lieutenant Hesse made his entrance into our area as if on cue, puffing away on his cigarette.

"Find that article interesting, Schlaeger?" he asked, flicking some ash into the receptacle on Mike's desk. "It is war, you know."

"But these were civilians—" Mike tried to protest but Hesse interrupted.

"It's war," he repeated firmly, his tone indicating he believed the deaths justified. "Sometimes, there's collateral damage."

I broke in, immediately prompting the lieutenant to turn his gaze, puffing and ashes in my direction. "Yes, some people become, as you say so impersonally, collateral damage. But according to what Mike was reading before you arrived—." I wanted him to at least sense my contempt for his indifference. "—these people, including women and children were massacred. There was no battle. They were murdered."

"That's war for you," Hesse answered me, the frigidity in his tone permeating the room so much so that ice could have formed on the walls.

I wanted to assail him personally, question whether he would have the same reaction if his family were in a similar situation. But I already knew, or at least thought I did, his answer. And I did not want to risk the real possibility that my doing so would cross that boundary that would permit Hesse to make my life miserable. I also believed that, despite his contempt for the lieutenant, Major Otto would not support me if I did.

So the lieutenant and I just stared at each other, our mutual disdain obvious in our expressions. Neither of us broke from our glares, but I sensed the others giving Hesse the same look as I.

Finally, he broke the silence. "You're so fucking naïve, Forsbie," he snarled, flicking some ashes and then crushing the butt in my ash tray. Then, as quickly as he had appeared, he returned to his office.

None of us spoke about the article the rest of the day in the office, but our work pace slowed considerably. We had no desire to help promote the war machine. Fortunately, none of our tasks were urgent, Hesse did not reappear except to pass through while going who cared where, and Otto was somewhere else.

But on our drive home, we discussed the article some more. When we arrived, instead of hanging my uniform in my closet, I flung it in a heap in a corner. And that evening, we spent a lot of time talking about it after seeing the CBS coverage of the story. Our unanimity of disgust and anger echoed throughout the house until we retired. I slept restlessly, my abhorrence preventing me from clearing My Lai from my mind. Guys my age had killed indiscriminately. Maybe Hesse was right. Maybe I was naïve in thinking that we could maintain a sense of morality in war. Chalk one up for the lieutenant. Morality didn't exist in war.

Events turned back in my favor that Saturday. We had to wait until evening newscasts but finally we saw coverage that would prove correct what we had said about the anti-war movement. We received a bonus, but at the same time started to wonder if the lieutenant's surname was as common as Smith or Jones. At least that's what I thought when I recalled the encounter with Deputy Hesse from months before when another Hesse appeared on the screen.

"Look at that crowd," John marveled as we watched coverage of the moratorium in Washington on the evening news. "They easily got their 500,000."

"Give or take a few," I joked, feeling giddy about the success. Then my jaw dropped. The network correspondent was interviewing a middle-aged woman carrying a peace sign. Her name, Evelyn Hesse, who claimed membership in a group called Mothers Against the War.

"Jesus!" I exclaimed. "Could she be related to the lieutenant?" If the Hesse surname was as common as we now thought, why hadn't I heard of it before I started having my almost daily sparring with the lieutenant?

"Maybe it's his mother," Mike suggested. "Wouldn't that tighten his jars."

Light-heartedly, already looking forward to asking the lieutenant about her on Monday, I quipped, "Well, she has to be somebody's mother. She wouldn't be in Mothers Against the War if she wasn't."

John snorted. "You don't have to meet all the criteria in a group's name. You think everyone in the NAACP is colored?"

"No," Schlaeger answered. "And I'm pretty sure not everyone in the Weathermen has a meteorological degree," he joked.

"We will definitely ask the lieutenant about her Monday," I affirmed.

Come Monday, Hesse did not make his customary appearance at Otto's staff meeting. Nor did he come into our work area as early as normal. I began to wonder if he had seen the coverage and could not face my--, our, questions.

I was wrong.

Shortly before noon, the lieutenant appeared. Pulling his pack of Camels from his shirt pocket, extracting, then lighting one of them, he asked, "How are your assignments coming?"

Was he trying to avoid the inevitable questions? Or was he innocently oblivious to them? I was about to find out. But first we obligingly updated him on our individual progress.

Before I could broach the subject, Smith beat me to it. "Say, Lieutenant," he smiled at Hesse, "did you happen to see the half million peaceful demonstrators in Washington Saturday on the news? Quite a microcosm of the nation's mood against the war. Students. People of all ages. Former members of the armed services. Even had some mothers, probably some whose sons were killed or maimed in Vietnam. Or are serving in the military."

Hearing John, I immediately thought of Bless-Ed.. "Or their children came back with unhealed emotional wounds."

"No," Hesse replied indifferently. "I watched some good football games," he announced like the good Nixonian he was. President Crabapple Cheeks had watched a gridiron battle rather than the marchers.

"You have any woman named Evelyn in the family?" I asked innocently. He stared at me with a look I could not read. Had I struck close to home? Or was he merely wondering why I inquired? His silence lasted longer than I wanted.

"Not that I'm aware. Why?" he bit.

Once again, Smith beat me to the next comment. "Well, a tv reporter interviewed a woman identified as Evelyn Hesse who was one of the many mature adults protesting in Washington." John made certain to emphasis "mature".

Again, the lieutenant hesitated. Was he looking to evade or circumvent the question?

"Don't think so. No, not in my family. But Hesse is a fairly common name. Maybe not as common as Smith or Jones. But there are a lot of us around," he finally replied. I thought I detected a faint smile cross his face.

Damn! He made reference to the same frequent surnames I had noted when we saw the Saturday news coverage. Now I started to wonder if he could read my mind, just like my belief that he somehow had a way of listening into our conversations even when he was at the other end of the office. Or maybe he had had the house bugged. After all, he knew where we lived. And he would look for any edge in our tit-for-tat that he could.

"My mother would never protest the war," he affirmed. "She's a true patriot. Besides, her name is Grace." With that, Hesse turned and marched back to his office. He didn't even leave any ashes or butts this time. Nice of him.

Gianelli finally spoke up. "Well, I guess that's that."

I did not reply. I had come into the conversation with the lieutenant feeling like I had first and goal and been sacked three times, putting me out of field goal range. Yes, I grudgingly used a football reference. It seemed appropriate since Hesse and his idol Nixon had watched college football wars instead of anti-war protests on Saturday. Now, I would not acknowledge a forced punt even though Gianelli had affirmed a fourth and hopelessly long situation.

We all went about our duties in a common morose mood the rest of the day. The drive back to the house stayed in the same gloomy humor. So did the evening. Even Rowan and Martin's Laugh-in could not break our dejection. We would have to wait for another day to score a victory.

It would not come soon enough.

Over the next few weeks, I became more difficult to be around.

"You're getting hard to live with," Schlaeger complained several times.

"Remember, the lease is in my name. I can kick your ass out, gringo," Consuelo threatened at least as many times as Schlaeger griped. I did not see her usual humorous glint in her eyes when she did. I learned that I would have to figure out whether she was teasing or pissed off when she called me a gringo. I had my well-being to consider.

"You want me to start hating white people again, Honkie?" Smith would ask me when he had grown tired of my sullenness. I would weakly reply "No." I did not want to push back the progress made in race relations on our local level.

"Glad I don't have to live with you, Forsberg. You haven't been a joy to be around here at the office," Gianelli observed at least three times during my time of moodiness.

Perhaps my grouchy frame of mind resulted from a recurring dream I had several times during its existence. During that nightmare, Bless-Ed would appear in our office and begin recounting the story he had told me that night at the bar. But now, both internal and external body parts and blood would suddenly come gushing out of his head. Yet he would keep on talking in that devastated tone of his. The outpouring of gore would continue along with his story until I would suddenly jerk awake.

Finally, Mother Nature came to my rescue, not so much as to rekindle my war with Hesse. Although it did that, it also gave me a chance to do some serious journalistic writing again. In mid-December, the old girl hit northern Arizona, and especially the Navajo reservation, with a monstrous snowstorm that dumped several feet of snow over the area in a remarkably short period of time.

Once again, Carefree's Air Force Reserve squadron had an important mission. Once again, Major Otto decided that I should fly with them in one of their Albatrosses. Once again, the lieutenant and I had an opportunity to rattle each other.

"I hope you're prepared this time, Forsbie," Hesse chided me, accompanying his words with the usual cloud of smoke. "You better not screw up their mission and end up in the infirmary again," he warned.

"Oh yessir!" I quickly and excitedly responded. "I have a set of fatigues with my lone airman's stripe on each sleeve. And I have my field jacket with its fashionable hood to cover my ears. I should be real toasty warm this time, Sir." I paused, then continued, "And I know Major Dellafiora and his crew will greet me with open arms. They like me despite having had to put me in the hospital last winter. They have such good hearts."

I hoped the lieutenant got what I implied. If he did, he didn't show it. But he did crush his cigarette in my ash tray before returning to his office. So maybe he did catch on.

Not holding a grudge for my recent grumpiness, Schlaeger joked, "You get to see all that beautiful scenery while all I get to see are desks and charts. The major has assigned me to their operations here," he added with unconvincing sorrow.

"Don't worry, pal," I patted him on the shoulder. "I'll have Major Dellafiora put in a good word for you." I put my pointer and middle figure of my right hand together. "He and I are tight like this."

"I see you're prepared this time," Dellafiora greeted me when Mike and I arrived at his squadron's office.

"Yessir," I answered. "Don't want to be a burden on you this time."

He smiled. "If you do become one, we'll just dump you out like we will the hay and food for the livestock and people. But it'll be remote for you. They probably won't find your body until April. If even ever. And don't address me by my rank."

"You're all heart, Sir."

"Think nothing of it, Airman."

Sometimes you could joke with people who outrank you. Especially people like Dellafiora. That had not been, nor would it ever be, the case with Lieutenant Hesse.

"Must be nice being able to joke with officers, Taylor," Mike interrupted.

"Don't worry –" Major Dellafiora looked at Mike's nametag. "Sergeant Schlaeger Once you're here another five minutes, I'll let you joke with me too." He hesitated, then added, "You'd better not call me major either. And I won't mention your rank when I talk to you."

Mike could not pass up the opportunity to test the major's sense of humor. "Actually, Sir, my last name is Van Lautenschlaeger. The Air Force didn't have enough room on my nametag for my full one."

Dellafiora chuckled. "The military likes to mess with people's names whenever it can. Doesn't it, Forsbie?" His eyes glistened as I cringed. Then he laughed. "If you don't start laughing in five seconds, I will forever call you by that standard military moniker." I took the hint and chuckled. He accepted my poor attempt to meet his demand.

The major then took us into a room where a large map of much of the Southwest was pinned to the far wall. Directing us over to it, he explained how the squadron had already marked sections of northern Arizona and the other states of Utah, Colorado, and New Mexico in the Four Corners area. "My crew—" he paused again before directing his comment to me., "will handle this area marked by the yellow pins and string. That is unless you force us to dump your body somewhere up there," he smiled. "Then we'll just have to fly under the radar and lose communication with base ops while we seek an appropriate place to dispose of you."

"We've been hoping for some time that someone would do that with Taylor," a now at ease Mike addressed Dellafiora. I wondered if he were joking or if my recent demeanor had induced some seriousness in his comment. Schlaeger and the major had a good laugh at that one. Mine was somewhat forced.

The major turned to Mike. "You'll be going with Tech Sergeant Hamby to base ops where he will monitor communications between them and those of us in the air if any are needed."

"And what if none are?" Schlaeger asked.

"Then you and Hamby will be shunted into a corner away from the others. After all, he's a reservist, and you're enlisted." Then he glanced at Mike's sergeant stripes. "Well, maybe they'll take you for an NCO since you do have three stripes. But they'll probably think of you as a reservist, and you will have equal shunning with Hamby."

"Nice to know the air branches get along so well," I quipped. My tone must have suggested that some sullenness remained because it produced no response from either of my companions.

Shortly afterwards, Mike remained with Sergeant Hamby and a few others at the squadron headquarters and I left with Major Dellafiora and his crew for their Albatross. Within about half an hour, we were lifting off the Carefree runway and turning north through a clear break in the weather for the bleak, snowblown terrain of the Navajo Nation. And I thought of a now-deceased drunken Indian (his words) named Ed Begay and smiled.

Ed would stay with me for a while because of this trip and the education he had given Mike and me over a year ago. As we flew over a solid white landscape, one of the crew joked, "Where are the teepees?" I wanted to correct him and tell him what Ed Begay had taught me about Indian dwellings. But although I had a good relationship with these men, I decided not to risk being impertinent. If I did, they very well could have dumped me out a cargo door. Even though my name appeared on the flight manifest and thus they'd be held liable if I turned up missing, I took no chances. At the same time, I knew they would not toss me from the Albatross. Yet I still. . .

The first sign we saw of anything other than snow came when we reached the area of Monument Valley where John Ford had filmed so many John Wayne movies. At least, according to Ed Begay. I didn't know how many had been shot there, but I knew there had been several. I recalled Ed's comments about the two Johns as we circled over the Mittens, their red walls topped by snow. Near them sat a group of hogans with perhaps as many as fifty Navajos standing below, waving to us. They beckoned even more as we started to push supplies out the plane's door. With us flying only a few hundred feet above them, the stores landed softly in the deep snow except for one that struck some rocks. Once, a few Navajos had to leap away from a falling parcel. But overall, the relief mission went well, and they waved heartily to us as we banked away.

We then flew a few miles to where we saw a herd of cattle huddled closely together in an otherwise empty setting. We dropped quite a bit of hay near them, careful not to have the bales strike any. I thought of a time when a friend jokingly asked, "How do deer know this is where they're supposed to cross the highway?" as we had driven past a deer crossing sign. How did the cattle know this feed was for them? Somehow they must have because I could see the herd slowly trudging through the deep snow to the dropped food.

Noting the mostly unscarred landscape, I asked one of the crew while we searched for more cattle, "Are they paralyzed?" meaning the Navajo nation. I could see no sign of any roads having been or being cleared.

"Pretty much so," he noted. "These are the wide open spaces of Western lore. And civilization's equipment is where more main roads are. If the Navajos have any road clearing equipment, it's sparse and probably not well maintained." His tone struck me as condescending, but I didn't press the point. "You gotta remember, too, we've had clear weather for only a few hours. But they have to clear the main roads first. I doubt any of the reservation ones qualify. And they're probably all dirt. Not as easy to clear."

Screw the Indians, I thought, echoing Ed Begay. But I knew I had fodder for another article for West Side Stories.

"And once we put it together, we'll put Ed Begay's byline on it," I informed Mike as we drove home that evening. He nodded in agreement.

The next day we wrote our stories for the Combat Crew Courier. The only photograph we had to accompany them was of one reservist pointing to a spot on the map in the squadron's office while another one looked on. Standard crap that did nothing to enhance the story but it gave the photo lab some involvement in the coverage. My story praised the men I flew with the day before as much as I permitted myself to do without becoming too gung ho, staying mostly matter of fact about their efforts to supply the Navajos and their livestock as best they could. No editorializing. No sarcasm. Just straight reporting. Mike's article was similar, although he had some trouble incorporating some coverage from inside the squadron's headquarters to go with the ho-hum photo. After all, he had spent his time at base ops, where practically nothing happened. He had to stretch things out to get eight inches of copy. Mine was more than twice that, almost twenty.

"Great work, fellows," Major Otto congratulated us, and no more. No extra accolades, no pats on the back. But I actually felt a bit of pride for his compliment. He had never done me wrong, so I accepted his praise with a slight nod.

No praise came from Lieutenant Hesse. If fact, I became certain that he made sure that my byline and Schlaeger's never left the base newspaper.

"Get copies of these down to the Phoenix Gazette," the major told Hesse as he handed our stories to the lieutenant. I'm sure that Hesse complied because our stories showed up in the next day's Gazette. No bylines, just a notation as "Special to the Gazette". Even that mundane photograph appeared with the same caption Mike had given it.

"At least they didn't give credit for the stories to that hack Trowbridge," I proudly indicated to Schlaeger as I drove us home, and he read the articles aloud.

"Who gives a shit," he replied, setting the Phoenix Gazette on the back seat when he finished. "We have our bylines in the base paper. We'll cut them out for our portfolios for when we get out of the damned Air Force." Our sourness lasted only briefly. Our sarcasm returned when Fortunate Son came on the radio, and we joyously sang along with it.

Good timing can squelch any bitter mood.

That evening we began drafting our article for Ed Begay's byline in West Side Stories. We finished it the next night, then did some revisions. It appeared in Stories a couple of days later as follows.

WHY ARE WE FORGOTTEN?

By Ed Begay, Navajo Nation

Why are we forgotten?

I ask that because, once again, when we are in a time of need, the white man ignores our plight. Too many of them. But that is not true of all.

Recent massive snowfalls have paralyzed us and our land, the Navajo Nation, in the Four Corners area. It is a vast land, with our people thinly spaced over more than 25,000 square miles of the land that has been our home for centuries.

For the most part, we have been forsaken, left to fend for ourselves in this dire situation. Many of our livestock will die. Many of our people want enough daily food. If not for help from the air reserve people at Carefree Air Force Base, things would be even more tragic. They dropped supplies of food in areas where we had huddled to support one another. And they dropped hay in remote areas where they saw our cattle and sheep. We know that because a few of us have been able to reach some of our herds to scatter some of the hay. For the help of those airmen, we are most thankful.

But we have not been able to reach all of our livestock and scatter the much-needed hay. We can only hope that those animals can somehow pull the food free from the bales and survive before it is too late for them. We know the airlifts have continued.

But other authorities have ignored us. Yes, they have cleared roads where the white men live and engage in commerce. But no help has come to us. We have one snowplow in our whole nation, and it sits in need of repair in a garage in Window Rock. We are not a nation that relies on the horse, like our red brothers in the Great Plains. We are

303

forced to improvise and try to move about on foot, covering many miles in incredibly deep snow and in extreme cold. Our trucks and cars cannot handle the snow. And we have no certainty as to exactly where our livestock is. We have rough ideas of where some are, but this is a vast area we inhabit. Too often, we have risked our lives and come back empty. And I have already mentioned the harsh conditions.

Again we are thankful for the generous souls of the air reserve at Carefree and their help. But it is not enough.

Why are we ignored?

We knew that Lieutenant Hesse would pick up his usual copy of our subversive rag, as he often called it. We were surprised but not amazed by his reaction.

"I see that the dissident newspaper had something good to say about us," he noted as he came to our work area, cigarette and copy of West Side Stories close together in his hand. I hoped he would not cause the paper to catch fire.

I made a point of clarification which he failed to notice. In theory, the air rescue people were not part of the overall mission of the base. That calling, if one wants to term it as such, was to learn the skills to annihilate all enemies, real or imagined, identified or misjudged. "Yes they did. Nice things about Major Dellafiora's squadron. Deservedly so."

Smith added, "True lifesavers, those air rescue men." His irony also escaped the lieutenant.

"Good thing not all of our militaries is in Southeast Asia," Gianelli noted. "Who knows what tragedy would strike those living in that snow-smothered hell."

Before Schlaeger could add his thoughts, Hesse grunted and returned to his realm down the hall. "Damn, my timing's off," Mike lamented, as he had not made any comment before the lieutenant disappeared.

Later that afternoon, Major Otto ventured into our area. He also had a copy of West Side Stories in hand. He personally checked with each of us on the progress of our assignments, then focused on me with a look suggesting he knew the source of Ed Begay's editorial. "That was quite complimentary of the reservists, that piece with Ed Begay's byline. Whoever he is." His gaze did not leave mine. I could not decide whether to acknowledge in a knowing way or feign ignorance of what the major implied. So I stared back blankly, probably looking like a complete ignoramus. Otto did not press the issue.

The war with the lieutenant entered another pause, not erupting again until almost two weeks later when my three housemates and I encountered Hesse at North Phoenix Mall.

I found it difficult to blend in with others my age who were not in the military but part of the counterculture. After all, they all had long hair. Many of the men had shoulder-length hair and the women's hair was, by and large, at least halfway down their backs. Try as I might blend in, my military haircut sans sideburns defeated my attempts. Tie-dyed tee shirts and bell-bottom pants for whenever I was off duty did not sufficiently offset my hair problems. Yet I had scored a partial victory by ordering a pair of prescription sunglasses with wire rims and octagon-shaped lenses.

"But I need to protect my fragile eyes from the Arizona sun," I had somehow convinced Hesse when he suggested I not wear them on base. "If my eyesight weren't so poor, I'd probably be here for pilot training," I facetiously lamented. "I did…" I emphasized at the time, "…pass the OCS test. But they were only taking men for flight training then. So I had to lower my sights and become an enlisted man."

As usual, the lieutenant had not pressed the issue.

But now, our usual group of housemates were strolling and shopping at North Phoenix Mall. I had on a new pair of, as they were commonly called, Viet Cong sandals, one I had bought at a head shop the previous weekend. Cut away from rubber tires, they completed my off-duty persona. We were just passing the entrance to a record store when the all too familiar voice of Lieutenant Hesse greeted us from the side. The first time we had encountered him outside his fantasy world of Carefree Air Force Base since that time at Black Mountain. He should not have surprised us. It was, after all, a more sparsely populated part of the Phoenix area. Still, it was an unpleasant shock. We greeted him casually, remembering our ranks, although Consuelo merely nodded. Lucky girl.

The lieutenant stared at my feet.

"Showing your support for the VC, Forsbie?" he asked in an accusatory tone as he pointed at my sandals.

We were not in uniform nor on the base, so I decided to do no more acknowledgment of his rank. Besides, he had irked me again with his standard military nickname for me.

"No," I answered indifferently. "I just bought them for their artistic value. The rubber rubs off on my feet in interesting patterns." Which the rubber indeed did. "Plus, I want to be able to blend in with John here," I nodded toward Smith. He caught my sarcasm and added his own comment.

"Say it loud. I'm black, and I'm proud," he grinned. "Taylor and I are brothers. He knows black is beautiful, and he wants to be beautiful."

I felt emboldened by John's support and our being off base. "Besides, I wore a pith helmet during basic training. We all did," I gestured toward Smith and Schlaeger. "I know you've seen all the films and pictures of North Vietnamese soldiers running through the jungle in their pith helmets. I doubt seriously that we were supporting them while learning to become good American fighting men."

Stymied again, Hesse merely grumbled and started to step away. He stopped, and in a tone that seemed threatening, he stated, "See you back on base Monday, Airmen."

Once the lieutenant was beyond earshot, Consuelo growled, "No wonder we call men like him pigs."

None of us replied as we continued on. And Monday came and went without any hint of reprisals from our beloved Lieutenant Hesse, even though he visited our area a couple of times to check on our progress and make certain we weren't loafing or bad-mouthing the war or Nixon.

Chapter 15

The remaining days of the year went smoothly. Neither Hesse nor any of us, including me, found or sought cause to continue the friction. It was as if we had unofficially called a holiday truce. Why not have holiday peace and goodwill toward our fellow men in Arizona while the carnage raged in Southeast Asia?

Of course, not all things went well. I had a hell of a time washing the residue from my VC sandals off my feet but continued to wear them often anyway when off duty. And anytime we mentioned Lieutenant Hesse within Consuelo's earshot, she made certain to refer to him as "pig". I started to find it irritating, since he and I were in our unofficial ceasefire. But then I would remind myself that he was indeed an asshole and so I did not ask Consuelo to cool it. Yes, she had started to get on my nerves at times, but the rent was cheap and the camaraderie with her and our neighbors overall was pleasant. Why ruin a good thing?

Major Dellafiora and some of his crew treated Mike and me to pizza at Salvino's as a way of saying thanks for the articles we had written about their Navajo venture. They were kind enough to suggest our fellow airmen in the office could join us, so everyone did, including the two radio men. We had hardly seen Alan and Allen recently as they found themselves immersed in a project that Major Otto had dreamed up for them. It turned out nice to know that our two broadcast buddies had not changed during our separation.

Major Otto, too, showed holiday spirit by having the whole crew over at his home in base housing for an informal gathering. Everyone, that is, except for the lieutenant. He didn't show and I decided not to ask the major why. But I did wonder if Otto even invited him to anything, knowing his disdain for his co-officer. We had plenty to snack on, but I had a feeling that Mrs. Otto had done all the preparations. I hate to say it, but I figured that was the lot of the typical officer's wife. Do what he wants for when he wants it and put on a false smile. Yet her smiles for us seemed genuine and unforced. Maybe I was letting stereotypes and presumptions rule me more than they should.

New Year's Eve, all the enlisted men gathered at our place and got rip-roaring drunk on hairy buffaloes.

"How can you all drink that shit?" Consuelo grimaced after taking a swig of the concoction. She immediately set her cup on the sink counter then fetched herself a bottle of tequila which she chugged like water for the rest of the time I saw her. How long that was I don't know because I passed out sometime before 1970 rolled in.

I dreamed that the year would start with the appearance of a near-naked Alice Swann, like she had at our last hairy buffalo party. She disappointed me when she came out fully dressed into the living room shortly before noon.

"Too bad, Forsberg," she winked at me. Somehow she knew. Maybe it was my expression of disappointment. "Your memory of that once in a lifetime event will have to suffice."

I nodded a weak and sorrowful acknowledgement. As I did so, I heard Consuelo vomiting in the bathroom.

"Should have stayed with hairy buffaloes, Consuelo," I shouted.

She paused in her discomfort long enough to throw out a reverberating "fuck you, Taylor" at me. I thought I heard her chuckle right after that, but she may have been upchucking. I decided it best to not try to find out.

Shortly afterwards, I threw up. As I upchucked I could hear Consuelo laughing. "I put a curse on you, Forsberg," she crowed. The witch!

Despite my attributing she-devil traits to her at times, and in jest, Consuelo became the source for our adventures early in the new year. For whatever reason, we had spent most of our free weekends either at the house or visiting spots nearby, like Black Mountain and North Phoenix Mall. But a couple of weekends after our hairy buffalo and tequila bacchanal, she suggested, "Let's all go up to Oak Creek Canyon and explore." Without hesitation, she added, "Don't worry guys. I know the way so I'll drive."

None of us were worried about who would sit behind the wheel. John confirmed it by agreeing, "Why would we? We're at your beck and call."

"Yeah. Right," she laughed.

So the next morning, rather than sleep in late, we rose as if it were a workday and after a few breakfast burritos, we clambered into her Econoline and headed north.

The trip up went smoothly, although I felt a pang of regret when we passed the Black Canyon City exit where Angela had left me months before. Her smile and smell stilled lingered with me and I still ached not knowing what had happened to her.

Once in the Sedona area, we spent the day driving wherever we wished. Over red rocks to picnic lunch alongside a barely flowing Oak Creek beneath Cathedral Rock. Afterwards, up a bit of a climb to get a good view of the area stretching off to the southwest. Consuelo wanted to take us to a stunning chapel that had been built into the landscape but my aversion to anything dealing with religion and John's complaint that it would be too touristy vetoed her wish.

On the way back, I became quiet as we passed Black Canyon City again. If the others noticed, they did not press the issue. Other than my melancholy over Angela, the trip went well.

Two weeks later, a journey out to the Wittmann area on the road to Las Vegas became much more interesting.

"What the hell's out there? Anything?" Mike queried when Consuelo suggested that venture.

"You'll just have to come along and see," she teased.

At least we would not pass by the exit for the Mogollon Grill and reignite my thoughts of Angela and all that heartache.

When we finally took a side road a couple of miles on the other side of Wittmann, that bustling metropolis of a few hundred souls who somehow had no better place to live, my hopes sank. I had looked forward to a part of the desert with a fair amount of saguaros. I enjoyed seeing the ones that looked like someone who had just won a championship boxing match, arms off the main trunk raised in triumph. My imagination would try to create human images of some of the others that were not like that. And I marveled at the ones whose main trunk soared twenty feet or more into the cloudless Arizona skies. But the area was disappointingly devoid of saguaros, except for an isolated one here, another there. The area looked even more desolate than the Cowlic Gunnery Range. At least it had bombed and strafed military vehicles and bomb craters. I didn't see anything like that as Consuelo drove us down the dirt road, the tires of her Econoline spewing dust behind us.

"Why the hell did we come here?" I complained after only a couple of miles, just as we passed through a dry wash. "This is as barren as shit."

"I think shit has even more substance," Mike chimed in. I was thankful for his support. John said nothing. Whether it was not to irk his woman or he just couldn't think of anything, I did not know.

"Patience, gringos," Consuelo laughed. "We will get there."

About ten minutes later we got there, or what apparently was the there she had mentioned. A one-story hut, a small building which must have served as a barn at one time, and a trough lacking any water for who knows how long. No vegetation grew within about a hundred feet of the buildings, making the place seem otherworldly and utterly useless.

"If only we had driven another half hour or so. To Wickenburg," I thought to myself. But no!

And now even Consuelo seemed unsure about our visit. "Uh oh!' she muttered, her eyes focused on tire tracks in the sand. Fresh enough to suggest the spot had had visitors recently. "I don't like this." Still, she beckoned for us to follow her inside. With no other choice, we did.

The interior floor told us that someone had indeed been in the house. Boot prints were fresh enough to have not received a cover of dust. They appeared to be from one person and no more. They did not cover much flooring, just from the door to a tattered cloth couch and to some shelves over a wash basin in what served as the kitchen area.

Some canned foods sat on the shelves, but they appeared not to have been touched in some time. The sink held no water.

Staring at the dust-covered cans, I felt compelled to joke. "There's botulism waiting there to devour us." My attempt at humor fell flat. No one laughed.

I looked back towards the main living section, if you could call it that. An area of the couch was cleaner than either side, suggesting that the visitor had sat there for awhile. But there were no other indicators of his presence. No cigarette butts, no wine bottles, nothing to suggest any drug use.

"Why'd you bring us here?" John asked as we stood around gazing at the emptiness.

"Remember me telling you about my Aunt Isabella?" she responded as he nodded in acknowledgement. "She brought me here a couple of times when I was younger. This is where she grew up until they moved to Glendale. She wanted me to see how poor they were when they tried farming here. For whatever reason, she didn't know. But she was proud of how far they had come after this place. I feel close to her here."

"I don't," I blurted out petulantly. "This is about as bleak as it gets."

Consuelo glared at me. "She said it was ten times worse in Mexico. And even though they moved out of this godforsaken place, I feel a part of her remains where she spent some of her childhood."

I could care less about sentimentality. Or exaggeration for that matter. Ten times worse? Give me a break. But I opted not to press the issue. My rent partner, my friend. Why piss her off? I mumbled a soft "I'm sorry" which seemed to please her.

Just then, Mike asked, "We gonna go see what's in the barn?"

Consuelo started to answer but turned her gaze out the glassless window over the sink. Dark clouds hung low some ways off, but they served as a portent.

"We better go," she said. "That looks like a good bit of rain," she nodded toward the gloom not that far distant. "And you know how little it takes out here to flood. We'd better get through that dry wash before the runoff comes. Else we'll be trapped here for awhile. And I don't want to be. I've been in that kind of situation before."

None of us others had been, but we took Consuelo at her word so we returned to the Econoline and clambered in. John sat up front with her and Schlaeger and I occupied the bench seat behind them. She put the van in gear and floored the accelerator, spewing dust as we sped away.

"Wow!" I exclaimed as I straightened back up on my seat. "You trying to give us flight training?" I joked.

"Can't waste time when dealing with a desert flood," she called back, her eyes fixed determinedly on the road. I sensed she had more in mind than the potential for a raging torrent trapping us.

So we sped on. Shortly before we reached the wash, a battered old Ford truck with areas of faded paint came upon us from the opposite direction. As we passed, I looked over and clearly saw a driver I did not want to see. He looked like some actor I had seen in numerous movies and on television, always the bad Mexican. He had narrow eyes and a cigarette dangled from his thin, barely open lips. Those eyes looked at us menacingly as we drove by.

Consuelo did not let up on the gas. In fact, she may have floored the pedal a little more. Within a minute we reached the edge of the wash and as we started across, we could all see the water rushing towards us. We made it across, a bit too close for comfort for me and I let out a huge sigh of relief. John and Mike followed, but Consuelo kept the van racing until we came to the pavement of the main highway. There she screeched to a halt, hard enough to pitch us forward in our seats.

"Whew!" she gasped. "Did you see that hombre? I don't know what else to call him, fellows," she continued. "Looked like quite the bad ass. And there could be only one place out there he could have been heading." She let out a long sigh of relief. "That flood may have saved us a whole shitload of trouble. Don't think he was going sightseeing there."

"Not a relative of yours, then, huh, wanting to visit Aunt Isabella's old haunts?" I quipped. Consuelo responded by staring daggers at me. As for "el hombre", we would not find out if he wanted to come back and off us. Consuelo's dust cloud would have prevented us from seeing if he swerved to come back around. And the torrent came soon enough to keep him on the other side of the wash.

Consuelo turned the Econoline onto the asphalt and headed back to Glendale. We all sat silently for most of the trip. When we did speak, we mentioned something mundane that did not initiate a long conversation. No one spoke of Aunt Isabella or "el hombre." I certainly would not.

I didn't know whether I had truly pissed off Consuelo. Or, if so, how much. I didn't want to learn if I had.

Meanwhile, office uproar had been nonexistent for awhile. Late in the last year, we subversives sometimes made comments about the ongoing My Lai bombshell, but Hesse either chose to ignore them or they went over his head. I prefer to think it was the latter because he never missed an opportunity to unleash a salvo, mundane (our point of view) or pertinent (his), in our cultural war.

Our confusion over law and jurisprudence brought the battle back into open quarreling with the lieutenant in mid-February with the verdict on the Chicago Seven. I have to admit I relished that Hesse decided to open his mouth. Peacetime with him had made me grouchy, something my cohorts continually reminded me of.

"I admit that's a strange verdict," Smith offered as we discussed the trial. "They're innocent of conspiracy charges but five were still guilty of inciting. Seems like they go hand in hand."

Our group nodded in agreement. None of us had any expertise in matters of law, save perhaps for John with his wealth of experience prior to entering the Air Force. So we offered no wisdom to add to the conversation.

But the lieutenant apparently had monitored his unseen listening device (he had to have one, even though we could find no evidence) and sauntered into our area, puffing away as usual on his ever-present Camel. The surgeon general was issuing all kinds of warnings about smoking's harmful health effects, but they apparently hadn't reached Hesse. Gianelli and I immediately started small coughs to indicate the harm he was doing to our health as well, especially me with my ever-present allergies. But they had no effect. Hesse kept on blowing smoke, both literally and figuratively.

"It's quite simple," the lieutenant pontificated. He could be really obnoxious when he felt what he had to say would shoot down our thoughts like we were unarmed Vietnamese villagers. "The prosecution proved one part of its charges against those Commie sympathizers, but couldn't on the other."

I didn't want to continue to display my legal ignorance but I couldn't resist pushing Hesse's ego when I thought he would feel even more self-important. "Howso?" I asked.

"Simple, Forsbie," he replied. Damn it! I had opened the door for him to show his contempt for me by using the nickname I detested. Think I would have learned. "They had the evidence to prove that these radicals went to Chicago to incite all the long-haired hippies to riot. They couldn't show beyond doubt that they had agreed beforehand to do so."

"Didn't think there was a riot, Sir, until the police started clubbing everyone in sight," Schlaeger countered. "Marchers, the press, bystanders, hookers, newspaper vendors, hotel guests, store employees, stray dogs, homeless vagrants."

"The marchers had no right to be there," Hesse replied. "And the others should have known not to be there. The law has to be preserved against these leftists."

"Yep," I retorted. "Protect freedom of speech by bloodying people. And throw in some collateral damage like at My Lai. Right?"

"You guys don't understand war," Hesse shook his head.

"Just like some people don't understand peace," I answered.

"Know your limits, Forsberg!" came a loud command from a few feet away. We hadn't noticed Major Otto entering the area. Who knew how much of the argument he had heard? But he did not press the issue or take sides. Instead, he placed a hand on the lieutenant's shoulder and told him, "Colonel Buell in base ops has something interesting he's proposing to us. I want you to go over and discuss it with him. Find out what you can."

Lieutenant Hesse obliged, dutiful lifer that he was. He put out his cigarette in Gianelli's ash tray, quickly lit up another and then left. The major gave me a look that seemed both stern and yet understanding. He had ended the latest skirmish but apparently left the door open for hostilities to continue. I knew either the lieutenant or I would stoke the fires again. Or maybe Smith or Schlaeger. But someone would.

Even so, Major Otto and I had an exchange that later caused me to wonder if I had lost his blanket approval.

"Your actions are becoming juvenile, Forsberg," he warned.

Maybe I should have backed down, but I didn't. I replied quickly, perhaps too quickly, not giving the major's comments time to register. "But so are the lieutenant's," I countered.

"But he has rank on his side."

"Another reason why I loathe the Air Force, Sir."

Major Otto said nothing more. But I had no doubt what his stern gaze meant. No way I could guess that it might have some understanding in it. Otto turned away and headed back to his office, leaving me to ponder. A lot.

A few days later, all of us house dwellers except for John, were perched in the living room watching the end of the Mod Squad. We didn't think that highly of the series, but Peggy Lipton was good to ogle and Clarence Williams had a great Afro even though it looked too styled for a cool guy of our generation. If it were tailored, we wondered if he could afford it on a policeman's salary. John, who knew a little about Afros, had pointed out this unlikelihood of Clarence's coiffure some weeks back. But he wasn't with us this time.

John came in just as the show's credits were rolling. He had disappeared several nights a week over the last few months. None of us asked why, probably because none of us cared. "Whatever bag he is in doesn't concern me," Consuelo had said for all of us one night the previous week. But as he sat down in the chair next to the table where our obligatory lava lamp perched, he looked around at each of us with a solemn face. He obviously had something important to say but his seriousness caused me to suspect that he was about to announce he had terminal cancer. The faces of the others showed concern, too.

"I've converted to Islam," he announced.

Our levity came instantly.

Consuelo sighed in relief. "I thought you were seeing another chick," she smiled.

"What took you so long?" Schlaeger laughed, noting that such conversions had become commonplace among a large number of Negroes of our generation. "You gonna tell the major and lieutenant?"

In a rare moment of ineptitude for comments, I rejoined with one of the cornier expressions of the time, one that elicited groans from the others and a thrown issue of Time Magazine from Mike. "That'll go over like a screen door in a submarine." I winced at my error just as the Time hit me harmlessly in the right cheek.

Showing some understanding of what John's conversion meant, Mike asked, "So what's your new name?"

"Yusuf Shabazz," Smith, or now Yusuf or Shabazz, whatever he wanted us to call him, replied. "Yusuf means God increases. And Shabazz is a royal falcon or eagle."

I couldn't resist. I hoped that he still had his sense of humor. Converting to a new religion often destroyed ones sense of humor. Especially so soon after the transformation. "Sounds rather militant to me. Isn't Islam supposed to be a religion of peace?" I cracked.

He retorted quickly. "You're an Aries, aren't you? Does that mean you're fired up for pillaging and plunder?"

Smith, or Shabazz, or whatever he wanted us to call him, got me with that zinger. "But what about your name? Will you tell the officers? Will you insist on getting your name tags replaced on your uniforms?"

"Last thing I want is for Hesse to have one more thing to fume about," he reasoned. Then he chuckled. "And you guys can continue to call me by my slave name. Even here. If you don't stay consistent, you'll screw up and call me Yusuf or Shabazz in the office. That would send the lieutenant over the edge."

We all knew well how Hesse would likely respond to John's conversion. Still, the possibility that he would pontificate, perhaps clenched teeth and all, presented an opportunity we could not resist. It came with a suggestion from Mike, reliable fellow that he was.

"Maybe somehow, we can bring up Muhammad Ali in one of our office conversations," he proposed. "With the lieutenant's uncanny ears, he'll be among us in a minute. And he'll say plenty."

So of course, the next day Lieutenant Hesse did not disappoint us. Such a reliable guy.

Schlaeger started the discussion innocently enough by bringing up Joe Namath. "His flamboyant lifestyle pisses a lot of people off."

Each of us white fellows brought up some other names before John interrupted with feigned belligerence.

"Shee-it!" he mocked, going into his persona that he used his first day as our 'token Negro'. "Those guys are mild. They ain't nuthin' lak Jim Brown, brothers Tommy Smith and John Carlos. And don't forget Muhammad Ali."

Suddenly, the ever eavesdropping lieutenant was in our midst, exhaling a long column of smoke before he spoke. He frowned directly at Smith and with a condescending tone, suggested with the authority of his rank, "You mean Cassius Clay, don't you, Airman." It was not a question.

John stared back at Hesse coldly, saying nothing.

If the lieutenant noted the contempt Smith directed his way, he did not show it. Instead, he began preaching about the "ungrateful Negroes of America". As he railed, I noticed how calm our Islamic warrior stayed in his chair. He certainly showed the peaceful side of his new religion.

"After all this country has done for Smith and Carlos, they should have been stripped of their medals and forced to hitchhike back to the States," Hesse continued. "And Clay! My God! He renounced his God-given name and heritage to embrace a bunch of nonsense. He should be jailed for life for his refusal to serve this great country."

I wanted to add "in its insanely stupid war', but I sat marveling at John/Yusuf. My friend sat in his chair stoically, undoubtedly holding back the emotions broiling inside him.

Hesse grumbled a few more words, puffing more smoke our way before returning down the hall. None of us said much about anything the rest of the day in the office, staying diligent in whatever work we had or invented. Nor did we three say much as we drove back home.

Things erupted after dinner. As we lounged in the living room, the television still off, Smith/Shabazz unleashed a torrent of pent up anger. Although not as pissed as he was, Mike and I spewed some venom of our own.

For her part, Consuelo did not want our exasperation to end there. "There must be a somewhat innocent way to get back at that pig," she offered. "Something to piss him off or scare him, but without him knowing you guys are involved."

We sat there musing within ourselves for several minutes. No one suggested anything although I could tell from the intensity in her eyes that Consuelo wanted to come up with an idea. Then she turned to Mike.

"Didn't you mention once that that asshole does that competitive walking thing?" she asked. "You know, where they have to have their feet hit the ground different than when running? Sort of like a half-paralyzed and awkward chicken?"

Mike nodded.

"Do you know if he practices his stumbling anywhere off the base? We can't risk what I have in mind on it."

Mike thought for a moment, then replied, "Yeah. I remember shortly after joining the office coming across an old Combat Crew Courier with an article about him and his hobby. I seem to recall it said that he did his workouts week nights and weekend mornings out at Black Mountain."

"Did it say what times, like sunset or sunrise?"

"No, but I would guess those times."

She turned to Smith/Shabazz. "Good. You and I will go on a recon Saturday morning to Black Mountain." Then she turned to Schlaeger and me. "You guys can't go. Too many of us might give away what I have in mind."

Neither I nor Mike expressed hurt at the snub. We both would rather sleep in on weekends. Whatever she was planning would probably meet with our approval. As if it mattered. If Consuelo wanted to do it, we couldn't stop her.

That Saturday she and John/Yusuf left before sunrise, long before either I or Schlaeger would awaken. They returned with us both still asleep, so we did not hear whether they succeeded until after I stumbled into the kitchen shortly before lunch. Mike moseyed in a few minutes later.

"I nearly ruined it early on," Consuelo laughed. "Why anyone would walk like that, even to win a race, is beyond me. I burst out laughing when I saw the man doing that walk. He looked like a drunken chicken with a rod up its ass."

"Fortunately, we were parked far enough away that he didn't hear us," Smith/Shabazz interrupted. "I don't think he recognized the Econoline, either."

"He stayed on one of the mostly flat trails for his walk," Consuelo continued. "Nice thing is there are lots of areas of heavy brush and large rocks along most of the route. I'll get three or four of the guys in the neighborhood to go with me tomorrow morning to scare the shit out of that pig."

"I'm going…" John/Yusuf started, but Consuelo cut him short. He didn't object, especially after she gave her reason.

"No you're not. I want to make sure he never suspects any connection to you guys. I'll get Eddie and Manuel and a couple of others to go with me this afternoon to figure out the best way they can scare him. And tomorrow, I'll drop them off and then park at that Seven-Eleven just down the road from the entrance. We'll get it done."

The three of us went to bed that night wishing that somehow we could join her and her fellow hombres. But Consuelo was right about the risk. I had trouble falling asleep, feasting in my thoughts about what a grand story she would tell us the next day.

She and her friends left Sunday morning well before sunup, Eddie letting her drive his car because of the slim possibility that somehow Hesse would make a connection to her van if he happened to see it.

Especially if he stopped at the Seven-Eleven to relieve himself if indeed they scared the shit out of him.

All the participants in the escapade complied. Consuelo dropped her four companions off in the Black Mountain parking lot well before sunup, the conspirators going over who would hide where and who would harass Hesse with what on his walk. They had already decided that they would try to wait to start menacing him until he was on the last leg of his journey. The path formed a loop so they fanned out to their hiding places on what they hoped would be the lieutenant's return stage.

Fortunately, Hesse complied.

He arrived even before the sun started creeping up over the eastern horizon. Later, I would wonder why anyone would go out for a walk at Black Mountain before sunrise, what with the possibility of rattlesnakes slithering about. But that was ignorant or brave Hesse for you. Take your pick. I had the same thoughts about the timing of the guys who would menace him, except I did not question their intelligence. Strange what a difference in attitude on people will allow.

The first threat came just as the sun peered over the skyline.

"Hey, Gringo. You walk like a chicken. You should be afraid," one of the four shouted from behind a stand of boulders. The shout startled Hesse, who looked about on all sides but neither saw anyone nor quickened his pace.

A few hundred yards later, Eddie shouted from behind a stand of desert brush, "Quieres morir, pendejo?" Hesse did not understand Spanish, probably not even words he would commonly hear in

Arizona, words like "amigo" and "adios". But Eddie's snarl menaced the lieutenant that he did not bother to look around. He did, however, bother to quicken his pace.

That acceleration caused his stride to become even more ridiculous for the final two jeerers who could barely hold back their laughter. Both shouted almost identical versions of "we banditos love to attack gringos who are out alone so early." The last menace caused Hesse to break into a run. "Forget the damned race walking. I gotta get out of here," he probably thought as he dashed the final few hundred yards to his car. He jumped in, laid rubber and sped off. At least we guessed that because Eddie told us when they returned that fresh tire marks and the scent of burnt rubber graced the parking lot.

We celebrated by getting royally drunk on hairy buffaloes, each of us passing out sometime early in the evening. Fortunately, none of us had a hangover the next morning and drove to work, innocent airmen, one and all three of us.

Chapter 16

An angry Lieutenant Hesse greeted us all as the staff gathered in the main office to begin our day and week. If Consuelo's combatants had frightened him the previous morning, he showed no signs of it now. But I felt safe for the three of us co-conspirators. No way could he know or even suspect our involvement. But he was raging like a mad bull.

"I swear, Major," the lieutenant continued a rant as we entered, "those wetbacks thought they could scare me. But they didn't."

I wanted to blurt out what Eddie had told us about tire tracks and the smell of burning rubber but thought better of it.

Ever enlightened, Otto asked him, "How do you know they were Mexicans?" I thought the major phrased his question for our benefit. As if we needed any reminders of Hesse's many prejudices.

"Because some of the threats they hurled at me were in Spanish," Hesse seethed.

I sensed a slight glint in the major's eyes. Was he toying with the lieutenant as he commented? "A lot of people around here speak Spanish. Not just the Mexicans. Maybe they were frat boys from ASU on an all-night binge."

Exasperated, Hesse answered, "Okay. Well, the accents were definitely Mexican." His next line suggested he had become perturbed by Otto's reactions. "I've been around here long enough to know them when I hear them."

"I know you have, Lieutenant," the major replied as he took his seat behind his desk. "But we have today's work and the week's assignments to consider. So we will now get on with our meeting."

That ended Hesse's tirade and got us into a general rundown of our parts in the Carefree mission for the week. When the major dismissed us, I hesitated as the others, including Hesse, left. I turned back towards Major Otto.

"You have something in mind, Airman Forsberg?" he asked.

Again I paused, wondering if I would be stepping out of bounds. But the major had been up front with me before so I decided to take the risk "Why didn't you admonish him about his name-calling?

Now, Major Otto hesitated. Perhaps I had gone too far.

"He's a lifer. So am I. I would never chastise him in front of you enlisted men, especially since I think all of you are here because of the draft and not for your love of military service," he replied. "I'm not going to damage his ego or his career unless he does something harmful."

I spoke without thinking, trying to make light of the issue. "He's harming my psyche."

"That's quite enough, Forsberg," the major replied, his visage leaving no doubt I had overstepped the boundaries. "Remember. I control your leash."

I got the message. "Yessir. Sorry, Sir!" It still paid to be polite to the major. He had, indeed, allowed me to roam most freely in my anti-Hesse, anti-Air Force attitude.

As it was, whether Major Otto's doing or not, Lieutenant Hesse received TDY orders shortly afterwards for the American air base in Panama.

"He ought to love the wetbacks down there especially well," John/Yusuf chuckled as we drove home that afternoon after we had heard of Hesse's assignment. He had wanted to say something as soon as we heard back at the office, but wisdom told him to wait until neither the major nor lieutenant could hear.

"Serves him right," I replied. I paused before continuing. "I have to bet Major Otto had something to do with it."

"I would, too," Mike chimed in. "Seems like old Otto doesn't have any fondness for Hesse either. Wonder if he's also spinning wheels to get him transferred." Whether the major had that kind of pull or not, we would find out in a few weeks that we would lose the warmth and charm of the lieutenant. But more animosity would transpire before that happened.

"Learn any Spanish while in Panama, Lieutenant?" Gianelli asked when Hesse made his first appearance in our work area upon his return. He seemed to be puffing more deeply and frequently on his cigarettes than before he left. I secretly hoped he had suffered from threats by eager Latinos who could read his attitude. Not that the lieutenant had to work at showing his disdain.

"Hell no," Hesse replied. "I don't want anything to do with that language. It's bad enough when I have to live in a place like Panama. Damned wetbacks everywhere."

I had not thought of it before, but I now surmised that Hesse conducted all his bank, grocery, gasoline, and other transactions on base. Few Latinos worked at Carefree, save for the Nicaraguan contingent. So that would keep him in his pure white haven as much as possible even with a few Negroes roaming the base. I did not want to pursue his prejudices against the Latinos directly but I felt obliged to continue the dig. I turned towards John/Yusuf.

"Hey John," I called, grabbing his attention from some article he was editing. "I see Congress lowered the voting age to eighteen."

I knew I could count on John/Yusuf's ability to take a hint and carry on with it. "Yes, indeed I do," he smiled. "That means more brothers, more Mexicans, more youths who think like we do to help this country." He did not have to say to get us out of Vietnam. He did not have to look towards Hesse. I didn't either. We didn't need to. The lieutenant's loud grunt of disgust told us we had struck a nerve. I didn't even know he had left our work area until Mike announced, "He's gone."

A somewhat calm environment remained in the office until early April, when Mike ignited a new flame, commenting about old flames, so to speak. The lieutenant was nearby, speaking with Gianelli about an assignment of his. Looking at an article in the morning Republic, Schlaeger casually began speaking to no one in particular but looking in my direction. It became apparent that he wanted Hesse to overhear.

"I see Nixon signed into law a bill requiring a stronger health warning on cigarette packages," he observed just as the lieutenant took a deep drag on his Camel. "And the poor cancer stick makers won't be able to advertise on radio or tv anymore. What are the nicotine addicts to do?"

Hesse left his spot beside Gianelli and strode defiantly over to Mike, stopping in front of his desk, trying to tower over Mike while he remained seated. "I'm not addicted, Schlaeger," he fumed while crushing his cigarette in Schlaeger's ash tray, apparently trying to make his point.

"Oh, I would never insinuate that you're addicted, Sir," Mike responded, trying his best to sound respectful and not contemptuous of Hesse. "But a lot of people are. You see them puffing away all day, one fag after another," he commented. Chain smoking definitely described the lieutenant, but he did not catch the irony.

"You had better not," Hesse growled, turning away and forgetting his discussion with Joe. As he headed back down the hall, he reached into his pocket, pulled out another cigarette, and lit it. Mike and I merely shook our heads while Joe and John/Yusuf both chuckled slightly.

I had received an assignment to do a story on some members of the Officers Wives Club who were stitching a quilt, so I decided to go to their meeting room and interview those who happened to be working on it that day.

When I returned through the office door, I noted a woman with short dark hair talking to Schlaeger. She seemed familiar, and rightfully so.

"Here's Taylor now," Mike announced, nodding in my direction.

The woman turned to look. It was Angela, looking every bit the stereotypical middle-class female, what with the haircut and matching navy blue blouse and skirt. Whatever happened to the hot, sultry hippie woman I once knew? She started towards me but stopped when I held back.

"Aren't you glad to see me, Taylor?" she asked, a slightly hurt expression crossing her lips.

Talk about conflicting moods. She still looked great, despite her apparent sellout to the establishment. After all, how could I complain about that, me standing there in my fashionable Air Force summer tans? But I felt anger boiling in me as well, and the two emotions came out in my reply.

"Well, yeah," I stammered, far from convincingly. "But seeing as the last time I saw or heard from you came, what, a year and a half ago? There you were, at a distance, trudging up the ramp to the interstate at Black Canyon City. A weak goodbye was scribbled on paper. Not a word since then."

"I can explain," she said. She started to expand her reply, but I cut her short. Perhaps too short, but at that point, I didn't give a damn. A year-and-a-half with no word on whether she had lived or died or been raped and murdered and left in the desert for scavengers influenced my coldness. Plus, dealing with the likes of Air Force life in general and Lieutenant Hesse, in particular, had soured me.

"I'm not going to go over Days of Our Lives in front of my buddies," I spoke haltingly, alluding to one of the many insipid soap operas permeating daytime television. As I said it, I noticed Mike and Joe with slightly sympathetic smiles looking at Angela. John/Yusuf had buried his gaze into an article he had probably already edited twice. At least Hesse had not appeared to muck things up.

Angela held up her hands in mild surrender. "I understand," she tried convincing me, but my mood told me not to buy it. Then she reached down, picking up an ever-durable government pen from Mike's desk, set down a sheet of typewriter paper, and proceeded to write. When she finished, she handed the paper to me. "Here's my address and phone. When you feel like talking, you can reach me."

Grudgingly, I took the sheet from her. Both of us remained expressionless as she walked out the door.

"Asshole!" Mike growled at me. I turned toward him, startled, but the glare from his eyes told me he meant every word. All one of it.

"You got some serious thinking to do, brother," John/Yusuf notified me, looking up from his editing. His serene and sincere expression told me that this advice came from the peace-loving Muslim he now claimed to be.

I replied to neither of them. What the fuck did they know about our relationship, especially the sweet sorrow of our parting back at the Mogollon Grill? We spent the rest of the day trying to concentrate on our tasks. I know I had trouble doing so. I don't know how the others did. Even lunch was subdued as Joe and I sat quietly, forcing ourselves to eat the usual bland fare in the chow hall. We all could not leave the office at the same time; someone had to cover at lunchtime. But Mike and John/Yusuf came up with lame excuses not to join us anyway.

Our trip home was even more silent than a morgue, if that's possible. Once back, I remained quiet until Consuelo came up to me after she and John/Yusuf had had some time together. "You need to hear from me," she said, standing firmly over me, her arms folded against her breasts. "And you won't dare say no." I decided that her glare meant or else, so I relented. She could be so damned headstrong.

We went outside and stood on the Bermuda lawn, staring at the distant Estrella Mountains and not at each other as we spoke.

Consuelo basically echoed Mike's "asshole" statement from earlier in the day as she berated me. I tried defending myself, but my meager attempts failed me. Besides, Consuelo was on a roll and barely gave me any chance to talk. It's hard talking to an irate woman, and she added to her fury by threatening to raise my rent and cut off feeding me. "You can drive to fucking Jack-In-The-Box every night for all I care," she admonished me.

I did enjoy Bonus Jacks somewhat, but a daily diet of them turned me off. "All right," I relented. "I'll call Angela and go see her tomorrow. If that'll make you happy."

"It isn't about me, dipshit," Consuelo replied. She could stay so charming when angered. "It's about you. As much as you've pined for her since I've known you, and undoubtedly before, it might actually make you happy, moron."

I actually couldn't find a way to dispute her. Maybe she was right. I had seen and heard enough wisdom from her before. "You have a way about you," I admitted.

"Better fuckin' believe it, gringo," she smiled. To my relief.

So the next afternoon, after returning to the house, I called Angela and, with Consuelo's insistence, asked when would be a good time for me to go over. "Unless I call you back, make it around 7:30. I think I can get my roommates to go shopping or something."

Apparently, she succeeded because I did not hear back from her. When I knocked at her door, she greeted me in cutoff shorts and a tee shirt. Damn, she looked fetching! She still stirred an urge in me, and I started to melt right there, even as a crucial part of me stiffened. Even before she closed the door behind us.

334

"Do we need to talk first?" she asked with that sly grin of hers. "Or do we make love first?"

I was hopeless. "When do you expect your roomies back?" My penis was starting to react in an even more forceful way.

"Sooner than I'd like," she teased, removing her tee shirt. Then she came up to me and unzipped my pants, pulling my cock out and squeezing it before I could catch my breath. Thankfully, she hadn't lost her touch.

We fell to the floor in an instant and made love, me climaxing much too quickly. "Sorry," I apologized. "It's been much too long."

She looked surprised but pleased. "Have you been celibate all this time?"

"Not if you count my hand," I laughed.

"I bet it wasn't as good as mine. Or that other part of me you just had your way with," she smiled fetchingly. "I've been celibate, too."

That pronouncement thrilled me, and we learned quickly that I needed little time to perform again. Much to our mutual satisfaction. We lay embraced on the floor for a few minutes before Angela rose and reached for her clothes. "Well, guess it's time for us to catch up on more mundane matters," she announced, slipping her underwear back on. "You sure haven't lost your touch, babe."

Had Angela deserted me at Black Canyon City? Well over a year ago? How could I think that? "Nor have you," I smiled, kissing her deep in the mouth while trying to retrieve my pants. After a few more deep kisses, we managed to get fully dressed. Good thing, too. In the door came her roommates.

"Oh, sorry," one of them said with a knowing glance. "Maybe we should—"

Angela interrupted her. "Don't worry. I think we're going out for a couple of drinks together. We've already done what matters," a coy smile came to her lips as she squeezed my arm. Good thing she didn't squeeze my member in front of her roommates. Who knows what I might have ended up doing before an audience?

Who was I to refuse such a great idea? "Let's get something to eat, too," I suggested. "But not at Jack In The Box," I explained that reference as we drove to a nearby restaurant, her hand resting on my thigh.

The place was nice enough, but as I perused the menu, I worried that I did not have enough cash. Angela sensed my concern.

"Don't fret," she smiled. "We can go Dutch."

"You may have to pay for it all," I tried to joke. My contribution would have to be cash. One-stripe airmen were not prime candidates for credit cards. I reached for my billfold and opened it. To my relief, I had more money than I thought. Certainly enough to cover the bill. "You won't have to save me from the embarrassment," I sighed.

We then began to catch up after we ordered. Angela immediately assuaged my fears that she had suffered some terrible indignity when she struck out on her own that day.

"Fortunately, two girls picked me up almost immediately," she began. "They had been in Phoenix for a family emergency for one of them and were headed back to Northern Arizona."

"The university in Flagstaff?"

"Yep," she smiled. "Both were students there. We got to talking. They weren't pushy or anything, but by the time we reached Flagstaff, they had convinced me without even trying that I should finish my degree. They invited me to move in with them, and in all my confusion and turmoil after just leaving you, I agreed. It all worked out fine."

"Much to my relief now," I sighed as the waitress brought our salads.

"Forgive me?" Angela pleaded.

"I'm here, aren't I?" I paused. "Yes. I thought our romp back at your apartment proved that."

"Maybe we were just horny as hell," she laughed. An elderly couple in a nearby booth frowned in disapproval. I guess their sex life had lain dormant for awhile.

Angela told me that she had switched to elementary education and had finished her studies in December. She then moved to Glendale with her current roommates, friends she had made at Northern Arizona. "I'm subbing pretty regularly. And I have a contract to begin full-time in the Fall. I also will be working in a school program during the summer, so I'm getting paid consistently."

When I asked how much, even for her part-time work, I moaned at her answer. "That's worse than my slave wages."

She raised her water glass and I did mine in tribute. "I'll be rich come September. Relatively speaking."

When she told me her starting salary, I burst out laughing. "That's so little. But—"

"But what?"

"It looks like a Rockefeller income compared to mine."

"Straighten out and start earning some stripes." It sounded like an order, but she did smile.

"It'll still be a pittance," I groaned as she nodded in agreement.

For the rest of our dinner, we engaged in the customary chit chat. She told me more about her experiences in Flagstaff ("I learned to ski, too") and how much she enjoyed the small bit of substituting she had done thus far. "I'm looking so forward to full time teaching come Fall," she beamed and I knew her sincerity.

I told her about the guys in the office, even going back so far as to tell her about George Long and Chuck Mitchell. She shook her head in disbelief at the saga of Long and Air Force bureaucracy. She winced in disgust when I told about some of my dealings with Lieutenant Hesse. Then I told her about Consuelo and her persuasion.

"Can't wait to meet her. I like her already," Angela replied.

"We both owe her a lot," I agreed.

I took Angela back to her apartment and lingered there awhile before going back to the house. I had hardly entered through the door before Consuelo accosted me, a glint in her eye. "How'd it go, Forsberg?" she asked, although I knew she already knew. I couldn't help but fire back in jest.

"You know how it went. Look how long I was gone," I smiled.

"Ah, yes," Consuelo replied, then reached out and gave me a huge hug and a kiss on the cheek. "You're not as dumb as I thought," she joked. Her eyes fell to my crotch. "And I bet a certain part of you rose from the ashes of celibacy," she grinned that knowing smile of hers.

"I couldn't bear the thought of an endless diet of Bonus Jacks," I countered to our mutual laughter. "And you know we made up for lost time," I cracked.

Always eager to get in the last word, Consuelo countered, "Not totally yet. But it won't take long, lover boy," she taunted as she planted another platonic kiss on my cheek.

The day had ended so well. I went to sleep that night more relaxed than I had been in some time. No doubt love making with Angela had much to do with it, but merely mending fences with her had improved my outlook. Little did I know that it would get an even greater boost the next day.

Oddly, the lift came from the mouth of the lieutenant. Not so strange, it came in his normal manner, parading down the hall to our work area, puffing away at his Camel. He stopped by my desk, a calculated move.

"I know at least some of you will jump for joy at this," he announced, looking at no one in particular but the words coming out of the side of his mouth closest to me. "I've received orders for Germany."

I wanted to do as Hesse suggested, namely jump for joy, but thought better of it. Instead, I sat expressionless at my desk. No need to show my exhilaration.

"What, Forsbie?" He seemed perplexed at my passivity. "You're not thrilled?"

"Just goes with being a career man, Sir. But I thought you would have volunteered for Southeast Asia. Where the action is."

"Oh, there will be plenty of action over there," he assured me. Or maybe himself. "We've got Brezhnev and his nukes to deal with."

I wanted to say something like "I bet ole Leonid will shake in his boots when he hears you're coming" but decided not to. Perhaps it was time to de-escalate my own cold war with the lieutenant. Angela's mild suggestion the night before that I not be such a splinter in the butt of the Air Force had had some effect on me.

None of the other men said anything, no congratulations, no well-wishing. So Hesse picked up the ash tray from Joe's desk, put out his Camel, set the ash tray on my desk, then turned and walked away. I immediately emptied it into a waste basket then placed it back on Gianelli's desk. "I know you missed this while it was gone," I cracked. Joe let out a soft laugh.

As the days passed, I actually felt a sense of relief. Major Otto bolstered that for me one day when he pulled me aside.

"Once the lieutenant is gone, I'll be doing the airman proficiency reports at least until his replacement arrives," he smiled. "I'll write a positive one on you so that maybe you'll finally get that second stripe."

Just a few days back, that would have convinced me that I had sold my soul to the devil but change indeed hung in the air. I now felt more desire for extra income. Having the woman you love back in your life and talking of a future together can do that to a man. I knew I would keep writing for West Side Stories. Mike, John/Yusuf, Consuelo and others would all disown me if I stopped. And what were the chances that the new assistant officer would be as big an asshole as Hesse? Slim or none, I felt. And the major had always treated me respectfully. Like Huck Finn, I thought I would turn over a new leaf.

Like his, mine didn't last long. Damned fate has to punch you in the gut sometimes.

Leave it to Hesse's hero Nixon to screw things up. On the last day of April, he announced that he had broadened the land war into Cambodia. It was enough to make me want to celebrate May Day. My regular companions leaned the same way, especially the ever-reliable revolutionary Consuelo.

"You're a fucking pig!" she screamed at the television when Nixon made the announcement. Fortunately, John/Yusuf grabbed her arm before she could fling her plate of goulash and break the screen.

We grumbled about the madman in the White House for much of the rest of the evening.

I decided to add the whole month of April to our rage. "April is the shits," I moaned. "I had my first draft physical in April. Martin Luther King gets assassinated in April. Now Nixon invades Cambodia in April," I complained.

"You were born in April," Mike reminded me. "And Angela came back."

"What's any of that got to do with it?" I countered, not in the mood to change my mind.

So I went to bed doubting myself over my decision to cool my war with the establishment in general and the Air Force and Lieutenant Hesse more specifically.

341

Even so, I held back at the office the next day. We all did. Perhaps it helped that the lieutenant was only a couple of weeks away from his reassignment to combat Brezhnev in Europe. Consequently, Hesse spent most of that day outside the office doing whatever he needed or wanted to do and didn't hang around to stir the pot like he had so often in the past.

Several of us decided "what the hell" and planned a trip for Saturday, the girls suggesting a visit to a place a little more than an hour north of Glendale where some visionary named Solarium or something like that lived. I didn't care what his name was. He was trying to create some sort of commune or something. My mind couldn't stay focused on our trip, and I became even more bummed when we arrived there and found the place with an overabundance of wind chimes. Christ, wind chimes were about as normal as one could get. And thanks to Cambodia, I wasn't feeling that Middle American at the moment. Nevertheless, I stayed subdued, not wanting to ruin the day for the women as they gushed over various chimes. Angela even bought one. I complimented her on her choice, but only half-heartedly. She noticed but let it slide.

Sunday, our same group decided to hike in the White Tank Mountains west of Glendale. But by late morning, we deemed it too hot to continue and headed back to the house. We picked up lunch at a Jack in the Box near home. Several days had passed since I had had my last Bonus Jack, so mine tasted good. And I thought the fries were better than usual.

But then came Monday when everything went to hell. And then some.

Chapter 17

Despite my anger about Nixon expanding the war, I held back on shirking my duties when the day began. We had done most of our talking and fuming over the weekend. Even in our Monday meeting in Otto's office and afterwards, Lieutenant Hesse did not stoke any fires to raise hostilities and erase the truce in place for weeks now.

No. National Guardsmen two thousand miles away would take care of that.

Towards mid-afternoon, I had gone to the headquarters of the avionics maintenance squadron to interview a master sergeant there who had built quite a reputation as a pitcher for the base softball team. Turns out he was a braggart who I took an immediate dislike to. He claimed he could outpitch Eddie Feigner. Feigner was the king in the King and his Court, a group of four softballers who barnstormed the country playing against local yokels in every town, village, and hamlet willing to shell out some bucks to his team to help raise some money for charities. I had seen Feigner pitch more than a decade ago, had not seen this self-centered trumpeter in action, but I felt certain Feigner could hurl circles around this buffoon.

"Ever pitch against him?" I asked, trying to keep my tone from insinuating that this lifer was a first-class turd.

"No," he admitted, but without hesitation added, "but I'd whip his butt."

The old me, the journalist, would have run with a story based on this display. But I had made the decision to sell my soul and become a public relations hack. So I knew when I wrote the story, I would focus on the master sergeant's diamond achievements for Good Ole' Carefree AFB and just casually mention that he would love a shot at King Feigner.

Those thoughts never made it to my typewriter.

When I returned to the office, Alan Cline was making a rare appearance outside his broadcast booth. He and my fellow writers stood together, solemn-faced, talking with one another. Hearing my approach, he turned to me.

"Bad news, Forsberg," he barely mouthed. I dreaded that something like the cancellation of Hesse's orders had come through.

The news was far worse.

Cline didn't wait for me to ask. His expression grew even more solemn. "National Guardsmen shot some students at your alma mater," he continued.

I stopped cold, unable and perhaps unwilling to digest what Alan had just told me. Finally, all I could utter was, "What?"

Alan hesitated, apparently uncertain of whether to tell me more, although obviously, I would hear more somewhere, somehow. Finally, he repeated, "Student protesters were shot at Kent State."

My mind tried to clarify for me the depth of his statement. What? Suitcase State? Apathy State? My school, where the most profound anti-anything message I had seen or heard of while there was the walkout on Vice President Humphrey a couple of years ago? I finally walked over to my chair and sat down glumly. I stared down for a moment at my Swedish map and flag. My ancestral homeland suddenly had new meaning for me as a welcome place for Americans opposed to the war, especially deserters, who opted for a home away from being pawns in the establishment's worthless war.

"What do you know?" I asked.

"Not sure we know anything for certain yet," he answered. "You know how first reports from news like this lack accuracy? But it seems certain some students were killed."

I silently told myself, "Fuck it!" But things would get worse.

For close to an hour, Cline would go back to the radio booth where Klein was following news updates. As much as the rest of us wanted to go there, prudence told us to stay at our desks and work on whatever assignments lay before us. Alan would come back with whatever news he thought we should know.

I could not concentrate on my work. Although I had graduated from Kent more than two years before, I knew some of the students still there. I wondered if any of them were victims. So much had happened since I left Kent and the faint rumblings of discontent at Apathy State. Now campuses overflowed with radicalization that I knew even my alma mater could not be totaling immune. Chicago with the Democratic convention and the Days of Rage last year. Asshole Nixon's still-to-be-revealed so-called secret plan to end the war. Last week's expansion into Cambodia undoubtedly sparked rage at Kent, causing the shootings. And when Cline told us that they had taken place outside Taylor Hall, I grew even more concerned. Taylor served as the home of the journalism school, and I feared the worst for some of my acquaintances. Just knowing that hell broke loose near Taylor Hall caused me to wonder if I would have been a victim had it happened when I attended the school. I could merely have been in the proverbial wrong place at the wrong time.

Then the peace and serenity of the past several days in our office came crashing down, compliments of Lieutenant Hesse. He came strutting into our work area for what he probably thought would be his parting shot before shipping out a few days later. He had no suspicion of the severity of my reaction once he opened his mouth. Nor did I until he spoke.

The lieutenant stopped and lurked over my desk as I kept my face buried in the assignment I wasn't reading. Then the words came out of his mouth.

"Well, Forsbie," he crowed. "Looks like some of your buddies back at your alma mater got what they deserved today. That'll teach…"

He got no further as I raged up from my chair. "You goddamn fuckin' son of a bitch!" I screamed as I lunged at him. I hadn't sprung at a target that quickly since I pulled off Angela's panties two nights ago. But here I was, making war, not love.

I thrust my fist into his face, wanting to break his nose and knock out every one of his teeth. The force of my impact smashed him against a partition, causing it to crumple and knocking us both to the floor.

I did not get the chance to hurt him further. All four of the guys in our area were grabbing me, pulling me away from Hesse.

"Don't man!" John/Yusuf screamed as they separated us. "Shit, Taylor!" the others echoed, almost in unison.

Trying to rise from the floor and clutching his nose, the lieutenant growled, "You're gonna love the brig, Forsbie."

Like, I gave a shit.

Hesse immediately went to my phone and dialed security police to report me. Major Otto, hearing the commotion from all the way down in his office, came running in. Seeing the fury in my eyes and the damage I had done to the lieutenant, he looked at me with a cold stare.

"I won't help you here, Airman. You've crossed the line," he informed me.

Like, I gave a shit.

Three security policemen arrived shortly and hauled me away, Hesse promising to come down and press charges in a while. Still full of rage, I didn't even think to say goodbye to my friends or ask them to tell Angela. They probably did, but justice acted so swiftly that I didn't know for sure.

Maybe it was political. Maybe Major Otto did put in a good word for me. Maybe the Air Force didn't want to burden American taxpayers with the cost of my incarceration, what with them already encumbered by the war in Southeast Asia. But justice came swiftly.

They hastened me before a three-man panel of my so-called peers. All of them ranked major or above. Certainly, no one-stripe airman joined in the proceedings. I had a chance to testify in my own defense, even though I really had none. A lowly airman striking an officer? Yeah, right. My state of mind over what had happened at Kent State would have no effect on those three lifers. So I declined. Let Hesse have his revenge.

Like, I gave a shit.

The panel sentenced me to a dishonorable discharge, busting me to airman basic, and ordering all forfeiture of pay. But the rest of my sentence surprised me. They were going to see that the Air Force discharged me as quickly as possible. In the meantime, the service would transport me to a military prison near Tonopah, Nevada, to await my separation. The site occupied desert land even more desolate than the Cowlic Gunnery Range. Not exactly a country club, one of my guards told me.

Like, I gave a shit.

I could only hope that the bureaucracy would speed me through faster than it had George Long. I gave a shit about that, too.

I spent my final night at Carefree with a cot behind bars, given a meal of the usual mess hall crap. A cohort, most likely Schlaeger, was allowed to bring a few uniforms, underwear, and one set of my civilian clothes in a duffel bag. One of my guards, probably a graduate of some sadist school, smiled like a B movie villain as he tore my single stripes off my 1505 shirts. I didn't do it to his face, but I got my revenge when I grinned at the civvies Mike had included; tie-dyed shirt, bell bottoms, and boots.

At least I would not make that long bus journey alone. Two other misfits would join me. I never found out what their crimes were. Our two guards prevented us from talking to one another. I don't know if it was Air Force policy or if they were pissed at being assigned to ride in a prison bus with three malcontents through the southwestern desert for hours. Plus, the bus had to come back to Carefree, so they would probably have to return by the same means, only without the three hardened criminals they had to prevent from escaping into a landscape of sidewinders, scrub brush, and sand. I smiled at the thought.

"Wipe that grin off your face, asshole," one of the SP's snarled at me.

Damn! It was going to be a long day's drive to Tonopah with nothing but silence, barren scenery, and only two pit stops at isolated gasoline stations where our escorts allowed us to use the filthy facilities and grab something to eat from the limited variety of goodies available. They didn't even give us a stopover in Las Vegas. I had no money for the tables anyway.

Our guards and the driver, meanwhile, lunched on sandwiches and Dr. Peppers they had packed like they were on a picnic. I couldn't begrudge them for trying to make the best of a horseshit situation. But the bastards could have let us get something decent to eat from one of the few roadside diners we passed. I wondered if I had just cause to complain or sue for cruel and unusual punishment. But I doubted that was available in the military justice system.

The drawn-out journey gave me time to reflect. So I did. The Tonopah trek was worse than having my life pass before my eyes, but still…

I had plenty to be royally pissed about, but for a while, I could not shake images of Bless-Ed back in Ohio struggling with his demons that the government seemed to ignore. Or had he fired a bullet through his brain, ending his misery? At least my status as a pariah would end soon. Granted, not as soon as I would like, but soon. Better than Bless-Ed's fate, no doubt.

My thoughts didn't move from those about Bless-Ed soon enough, so I lost interest and drifted off to sleep, such as it was. Usually, the bouncing of the bus or the jostling of one of the guards would awaken me any time shortly after I drifted off. I couldn't dislike an inanimate object like the bus, but I started feeling a genuine hatred for my guard the second time he shook my shoulder. Even passing through two sister garden spots like Santa Claus and Grasshopper Junction could not elicit any humorous thoughts about what sorry-ass places they were. Who the hell would want to live in such spots? It's not like they didn't have somewhere else where they could live meaningful lives.

Once we neared Las Vegas, something triggered my mind to return to reflection. I wondered about Sheena, the dancer in the leopard bikini I had so insolently lambasted at the enlisted men's club months ago. Had she taken my so-called suggestion and moved to Sin City to learn how to be an improper showgirl? Or even a decent one, for that matter.

As we continued on through the desolate landscape beyond Vegas and neared Alamo Air Force Base, I pondered whether Lieutenant Karen Howe still rejected advances from hopeful horny lowly airmen. Or had she found a career officer to wed, with all the joys and baggage that would come with such a marriage? And why did I even care?

I worried if Angela would still be waiting for me when I returned to Glendale from my imprisonment in this desert wasteland, short as my sentence might be. Considering she had come looking for me at Carefree after all those months of separation, I assured myself that she would. Maybe she would go with me to Iowa to visit Mitchell and his outhouse once I left prison. Maybe even venture with me to Maine, just so long as she would promise not to stare at the dent in George Long's skull. But who knew for sure? And I wanted to ask him if the Air Force had billed him for their painting over his farewell message at the barracks. Would those visits be part of Angela and me going off in search of America like Simon and Garfunkel? But that would take something we didn't have. Money. Still . . .

I thought about how my parents had reacted when or if they heard of my discharge. I felt certain I knew the answer. Mothers never give up on their children. That's left to the fathers.

I even wondered if Hesse would somehow find a way to get into a fistfight with Brezhnev and become a champion of the Cold War. I felt like I might have let Otto down after all he had done for me. But he was, after all, a career man, so he probably felt I got what I deserved.

Finally, we came upon the high barbed wire fences of the military prison where I would spend the rest of my association with the Air Force. Our driver pulled up outside a one-storey building marked by a "Processing" sign. Our visit there with a surly, overweight senior master sergeant took little time before he called for a couple of guards to take us three malcontents to a barracks.

When we entered, an all-too-familiar face greeted us. I didn't want to show my concern, but I feared that if I looked around, those demons Evers and Brophy would appear from my past. Why? Because none other than Joey Messina, the bane who had initiated my life of discontent, stood before us. The five stripes of a tech sergeant now adorned his uniform sleeves. But why should I worry? He had shown no recognition of me when our paths had crossed in basic training at Lackland.

Messina accepted our papers and perused them, then turned to my two fellow travelers. "You two go out to the parade ground across the street and wait." Then he looked at me, expressionless. "You stay here."

Once the two were gone, Messina approached me, not stopping until his wide-brimmed DI's hat almost touched my chin. A contemptuous look crossed his face as he stared up at me. I sensed what was coming, and he didn't disappoint me.

"You wanna go outside about it tonight, Forsberg? You wanna go outside about it? Eh?"

#

Epilogue

Intrigued

I stood on the periphery

Of the primeval swamp

Two thousand light years from home.

The chaos, a tsunami of change

Freedom and imprisonment

The Lizard King and the White Rabbit.

But I disappeared into the same ancient

Yesterday.

> Taylor Forsberg
>
> Tonopah Military Prison, Nevada
>
> Memorial Day 1970

CPSIA information can be obtained
at www.ICGtesting.com
Printed in the USA
LVHW010848120623
749514LV00006B/288